*Eisenhower Center Studies on War and Peace*

# TRANSMISSION IMPOSSIBLE

# TRANSMISSION IMPOSSIBLE

## American Journalism as Cultural Diplomacy in Postwar Germany 1945–1955

JESSICA C. E. GIENOW-HECHT

LOUISIANA STATE UNIVERSITY PRESS Baton Rouge

Manufactured in the United States of America
First printing
08 07 06 05 04 03 02 01 00 99 5 4 3 2 1

Designer: Glynnis Weston
Typeface: Weiss
Typesetter: Coghill Composition
Printer and binder: Edwards Brothers, Inc.

Library of Congress Cataloging-in-Publication Data

Gienow-Hecht, Jessica C. E., 1964–
Transmission impossible : American journalism as cultural diplomacy in postwar Germany, 1945–1955 / Jessica C.E. Gienow-Hecht.
p. cm. — (Eisenhower Center studies on war and peace)
Includes bibliographical references and index.
ISBN 0-8071-2310-2 (alk. paper) ISBN 0-8071-2409-5 (pbk.: alk. paper)
1. Neue Zeitung (Munich, Germany) 2. Germany—History—Allied occupation, 1945. 3. United States—Relations—Germany. 4. Germany—Relations—United States. I. Title. II. Series.
PN5219.M793N484 1999
071′.3′0943364—dc21 98-50189
CIP

The author is grateful to the editors and publishers of the following publications for permission to use material from her previously published articles: "When Spengler Saw Jefferson: The U.S. Army Newspaper *Neue Zeitung* and the Image of America in Postwar Germany, 1945–1947," in *Faces in the Mirror: American and European Reciprocal National Invention,* ed. Stephen Fender (Keele, U.K.: Keele University Press, 1996); "Trial by Fire: Newspaper Coverage of the Nuremberg Trial, 1945–46," in *Studies in Periodical and Newspaper History 1995 Annual,* ed. Michael Harris and Tom O'Malley (Westport, Conn.: Greenwood Press, 1997); "Anti-Communism and Other Enemy Images in the U.S. Occupation of Germany, 1947–48," in *Enemy Images in American History,* ed. Ragnhild Fiebigvon Hase and Ursula Lehmkuhl (Providence, R.I.: Berghahn Books, 1997); and "Art Is Democracy and Democracy Is Art: Culture, Propaganda, and the *Neue Zeitung* in Germany, 1944–1947," *Diplomatic History* 23 (Winter 1999): 21–43.

The paper in this book meets the guidelines for permanence and durability of the Committee on Production Guidelines for Book Longevity of the Council on Library Resources. ♾

*To my parents,*
HERBERT *and* IMINA GIENOW,
*who instilled in me*
*a love of history*

# CONTENTS

# ILLUSTRATIONS

# TEXTUAL NOTE

ON AN EDITORIAL NOTE, I HAVE RETAINED A NUMBER OF GERMAN WORDS IN the original spelling, among them *Kultur, Volk, Abendland*, and *Feuilleton.* While I have tried to explain their meanings as fully as possible in the context, it is my impression that these words ultimately are not translatable. *Kultur* and *Volk*, for example, bear very different meanings than culture and folk (or people). *Abendland* (often vaguely translated as "occident" or "West") has no exact counterpart in English prose. The term *Feuilleton* (a derivation from the French *feuille*, leaf, dating back to the nineteenth century), describes a highbrow politicized cultural section in a newspaper and is unknown in the Anglo-American vocabulary. *Feuilletons* typically served as a means to voice hidden satirical criticism of social and political events.

A number of my quotations reflect a form of Germanized English that may sound rather awkward. European émigrés and German natives working in military government often did not master the English language as fully as their superiors. For the sake of authenticity, I have refrained from correcting their spelling and grammar. All interviews cited have been conducted by myself if not specified otherwise. I quote my interviews fully (including date and place) only in the very first reference. After that, I simply mention the name of the interviewee. In cases where I interviewed people more than once, the reference will give the date, and, if the second interview took place in a different city, also the location.

# ACKNOWLEDGMENTS

THIS STUDY IS THE UNEXPECTED RESULT OF MY EXTENSIVE CONVERSATIONS with Horst Rademacher, a journalist based on the Pacific Coast, about the development of the German postwar press and the difficulties of writing for a foreign audience. In the summer of 1990 I took an internship in the foreign office of the *Frankfurter Allgemeine Zeitung* in San Francisco. In the depths of the Castro and the Mission districts, at the California sea coast and in the desert of the San Joaquin Valley, Horst introduced me to the art of writing transcultural articles.

A seminar under the direction of Richard Holub at the University of California at Berkeley during the same summer, provided me with the opportunity to produce my first essay on this new research interest. Hermann-Josef Rupieper, then a fellow at the Woodrow Wilson Institute, was the first to provide the encouragement needed so desperately by every beginning researcher who is haunted by self-doubts.

At the University of Virginia, Joseph Kett not only helped me to grapple with intricacies of culture and *Kultur* but also granted me great latitude in pursuing my topic and extended his friendship. Melvyn Leffler's hard questions challenged me to rethink and rewrite this entire manuscript at least twice. Stephen Schuker provided advice that went far beyond the call of duty. And Alice Cooper turned out to be a most valuable teacher and friend when my enthusiasm was flagging.

Interviews with contemporary witnesses acquainted me with a multitude of characters who opened their homes, hearts, and minds to share their personal recollections with me, thus contributing additional information and human interest for this book. My special thanks go to Max Kraus, who took me by the hand and introduced me to the circus of *Neue Zeitung* protagonists still living on both sides of the Atlantic Ocean; to W. Phillips Davison, who was always ready to compose long epistles loaded with information whenever I seemed to be at the end of my wits; to Peter Wyden, whose hilarious imitations of former colleagues in his living room in snowed-in Connecticut helped me to almost see long-deceased protagonists of this study in action; to Ernst Cramer, for welcoming me more than once to his office in the Axel Springer tower in Berlin, for making the treasures of the archives of the Ullstein Aktiengesellschaft accessible to me, and for putting in a good word for me when I applied for funding; to Egon Bahr, for sparing an hour of his precious time during an SPD convention in Bonn; to Jack Fleischer, for taking me out to lunch and dinner in Little Rock, Arkansas, while unfolding his memoirs of the years 1947–1948; to Henry Kellermann, for critically reviewing my thesis; to Hans-Joachim Netzer, Carl Hermann Ebbinghaus, Jack Stuart, Walter and Isolde Kolbenhoff, Hans Lehmann, Olaf Meitzner, Inge Ungewitter, Eva Fischer and Konrad Kellen for inviting me into their respective homes located somewhere between Berlin and Pacific Palisades in California; to Peter Bönisch, Robert Lochner, Ernest Wynder, Karl Löwenstein, and William Konecky, for taking time from their strenuous jobs to dive with me into the past; and to Anita Naef and Harold Hurwitz, for letting me peek into their private archives.

I also wish to acknowledge the efforts of the many archivists I confronted with my often confusing questions and *Bestellzettel*. Particularly I wish to thank Frau Meyer at the Institut für Zeitgeschichte and Herr Dr. Saupe in the Bayerisches Hauptstaatsarchiv, who helped me find my way through countless catalogs and collections. David Pfeiffer, Wilbert Mahoney, and Al Taylor in the National Archives drew my attention to otherwise neglected resources. Thanks also to Herr Dr. Bülow at the Deutsche Literaturarchiv in Marbach and to Dennis Bilger at the Harry S. Truman Library.

Virginia Mosser spent many hours trying to correct my sometimes faltering prose; I will never forget her eternal patience nor the steamy summer days she and I spent working on the manuscript. Lisa Szefel read parts of this manuscript and helped me enhance my sense for the art of metaphors, while Stephen Glaros extended editorial advice that proved equally helpful. Thanks also to Larry Maloney and Larry Arend, who made time in their busy schedules to read final versions of this manuscript. Otto Bergmann opened his home and his refrigerator to me during the many months when I plodded through Record Groups 226, 165, 59, and others in the National Archives in Washington, D.C.

I consider myself very fortunate to publish this book with the Louisiana State University Press at a time when the publishing process has become especially difficult for young scholars at the beginning of their careers. My editors at the Press, including Sylvia Frank, John Easterly, and Donna Perreault, were exceptionally understanding and helpful. Special thanks also go to my copy editor, Sabine Seiler, whose bicultural background greatly benefited this book. Her eagle eyes detected faults I would never have found, and her advice was always right on target.

Generous support from the German Marshall Fund and the Axel Springer Foundation provided the means for extensive research stints in the United States. A travel grant from the Truman Library allowed me to do research in a most pleasant setting in Independence, Missouri. The Goldsmith Award from the John F. Kennedy School of Government at Harvard University, a grant from the Quadrille Ball Committee of the Germanistic Society of America, and a fellowship from the American Jewish Archives in Cincinnati, Ohio, enabled me to continue the research and writing process. Dean Robert Husky from the Graduate School of Arts and Sciences at the University of Virginia always lent an ear when my budget ebbed during my final years in graduate school. I also wish to commend my former colleagues in the Graduiertenkolleg Gruppen, Schichten und Eliten at the Universität Bielefeld, where I completed a postdoctoral fellowship in 1995–1996. They created a most inspiring and amicable environment that provided me with the time and input I needed to revise and complete this book.

I dedicate this book to my parents, Herbert and Imina Gienow, who not only instilled in me a love for history but inspired me to study American history in the United States. I apologize to them for having extended a planned one semester abroad into seven years of graduate school and research. Without their constant encouragement and support, I'd probably still be composing ads for newspapers back in the Ruhrgebiet, where I was born.

Finally, *tausend Dank* to my husband, Heiko, my intellectual interlocutor, whom I met when I embarked on this project. He watched this book grow and saved me from insanity when the drudgery of archival research, critical reviews, and serious computer viruses seemed to dictate the premature end of my work. Though dedicated to a completely different academic field, he offered thoughtful questions and suggestions that did much to shape my central argument.

# ABBREVIATIONS

## ARCHIVES, LIBRARIES, REPOSITORIES

| | |
|---|---|
| **AJA** | American Jewish Archives, Cincinnati, Ohio |
| **BArch** | Bundesarchiv, Koblenz |
| **BHStA** | Bayerisches Hauptstaatsarchiv, Munich |
| **BPIA** | Bundespresse- und Informationsamt, Bonn |
| **DDEL** | Dwight D. Eisenhower Library, Abilene, Kans. |
| **DLS** | Schiller-Nationalmuseum, Deutsches Literaturarchiv, Marbach |
| **FES** | Friedrich Ebert Stiftung, Bonn |
| **HRHRC** | Harry Ransom Humanities Research Center, University of Texas at Austin |
| **HSTL** | Harry S. Truman Library, Independence, Miss. |
| **IfZ** | Institut für Zeitgeschichte, Munich |
| **LAB** | Landesarchiv Berlin |
| **MBU** | Mugar Memorial Library, Boston University |
| **NARA** | National Archives, Washington, D.C. |
| **PRO** | Public Record Office, Kew/Richmond |
| **RASZ** | Redaktionsarchiv Süddeutsche Zeitung |
| **RG** | Record Group |
| **SHGB** | Stiftung Haus der Geschichte der Bundesrepublik Deutschland, Bonn |
| **SUL** | Syracuse University Library |
| **UAAB** | Ullstein Aktiengesellschaft Archiv, Berlin |
| **WNRC** | Washington National Research Center |

## GOVERNMENT AND MILITARY AGENCIES AND ORGANIZATIONS

| | |
|---|---|
| **ACA** | Allied Control Authority |
| **ACC** | Allied Control Council |
| **AG** | Army Group |
| **BE** | British Element |
| **CAD** | Civil Affairs Division |
| **CIA** | Central Intelligence Agency |
| **CIC** | Counter Intelligence Corps |
| **Civ.** | Civilian |
| **DISCC** | District Information Services Control Command |

| | |
|---|---|
| **FO** | Foreign Office |
| **HICOG** | Office of the High Commissioner in Germany |
| **HUAC** | House Un-American Activities Committee |
| **ICD** | Information Control Division |
| **JCS** | Joint Chiefs of Staff |
| **MOI** | Ministry of Information |
| **OMGBS** | Office of Military Government, Berlin Sector |
| **OMGB (OMGBY)** | Office of Military Government in Bavaria |
| **OMGUS** | Office of Military Government (U.S.) in Germany |
| **OSS** | Office of Strategic Services |
| **OWI** | Office of War Information |
| **PID** | Political Intelligence Department |
| **POLAD** | Political Adviser |
| **POB** | Publishing Operations Branch |
| **POS** | Publishing Operations Section |
| **P & PW** | Publicity and Psychological Warfare Detachment |
| **PR/ISC** | Public Relations/Information Services Control (British) |
| **PWD** | Psychological Warfare Division |
| **PWE** | Political Warfare Executive |
| **SHAEF** | Supreme Headquarters of the Allied Expeditionary Forces |
| **SMAD/SMA** | Sowjetische Militäradministration/Soviet Military Administration |
| **USFET** | United States Forces, European Theater |
| **USIA** | United States Information Agency |

## GERMAN POLITICAL PARTIES AND GROUPINGS

| | |
|---|---|
| **CDU** | Christlich-Demokratische Union |
| **F.D.P.** | Freie Demokratische Partei |
| **HJ** | Hitler-Jugend |
| **KPD** | Kommunistische Partei Deutschlands |
| **NSDAP** | National-Sozialistische Deutsche Arbeiterpartei |
| **PDS** | Partei des Demokratischen Sozialismus |
| **SED** | Sozialistische Einheitspartei Deutschlands |
| **SPD** | Sozialdemokratische Partei Deutschlands |

## MEDIA

| | |
|---|---|
| **BBC** | British Broadcasting Corporation |
| **CBS** | Columbia Broadcasting System |
| **DANA** | Deutsche Allgemeine Nachrichten-Agentur |
| **DENA** | Deutsche Nachrichten-Agentur |
| **RIAS** | Radio in the American Sector (Berlin) |

# TRANSMISSION IMPOSSIBLE

# INTRODUCTION

*It was the best of times, it was the worst of times, it was the age of wisdom, it was the age of foolishness, it was the epoch of belief, it was the epoch of incredulity, it was the season of Light, it was the season of Darkness, it was the spring of hope, it was the winter of despair, we had everything before us, we had nothing before us, we were all going direct to Heaven, we were all going direct the other way. . . .*

—Charles Dickens, *A Tale of Two Cities*

SO MANY BOOKS, PICTURES, AND FILMS IN VARIOUS TONGUES HAVE TOLD THE story of World War II, so many writers have tried to grasp its horror. So many charts and numbers have analyzed the drama, so many studies have endeavored to rationalize the end. None of those has numbed human perception; the pain one feels at the sight of bombed-out Dresden and Coventry has never vanished. Europe in the fall of 1945 lay in ruins. The war had leveled centuries of civilization, ancient cities and cathedrals, hallowed beliefs and ideas. Holocaust survivors roaming the streets bore witness to one of the most gruesome crimes against humanity. Somber groups of policy makers, military officials, and civilians from different countries discussed how to relieve shortages of food, coal, housing, and other basic necessities.

An additional concern beset Germany: how to instill values that would ensure peace? Few in the U.S. Office of Military Government in Germany (OMGUS) knew how to facilitate this task. In the fall of 1945, OMGUS launched one of its most successful information campaigns when it founded a newspaper, *Die Neue Zeitung*, in downtown Munich. The paper existed until January 1955. Its purpose was to foster the democratic "reeducation" of German society; to inform locals of U.S. foreign policy, viewpoints, and the American way of life; and to present them "with a model of U.S. journalistic practice." The *Neue Zeitung* became an extremely influential instrument of public opinion. Many observers in the military government, however, believed it was a political disaster and wished it had never been established.

This is the story of the *Neue Zeitung*.[1] It elucidates the transmission of

1. For eyewitness accounts and preliminary analyses of the *Neue Zeitung*, see Hans-Joachim Netzer, "Die *Neue Zeitung*," *Gazette: Internationale Zeitschrift für Zeitungswissen-*

cultural values between the United States and Germany after World War II. Paradoxically, none of the top policy makers intended the *Neue Zeitung* to be a prime tool of U.S. diplomacy in Germany. Yet it turned out to be a successful transmitter of American core values. A unique group of editors, consisting of both German-speaking émigrés and German journalists, was responsible for this success. These men and women had a singular understanding of how to present U.S. values to a German audience because they themselves were deeply immersed in German culture; they were friends, foes, and reeducators at the same time. They were the ideal agents for cultural transmission in the postwar period. Their story refutes the theory of "cultural imperialism" that argues that postwar U.S. policy makers made a conscious effort to export pure American culture in order to gain access to new markets for their consumer products. Instead, it highlights the importance of self-conscious transmitters as interpreters in the process of cultural diplomacy.

Scholars of American foreign policy in the postwar period are split on the issue of control. In this context, "cultural imperialism" and "reeducation" have figured prominently in the historical discussion. Cultural imperialism refers to the assumption that one nation deliberately attempts to impose its culture, ideology, goods, and way of life on another country. In the United States, critics of cultural transmission as an instrument of diplomacy investigate if, why, and how much American culture reached and influenced foreign nations under governmental and private auspices. Early postwar scholars such as Peter Grothe or Thomas Sorensen have lamented the absence of

---

*schaft*, 2, no. 1 (Leiden, 1956): 13–26; Hans Habe, *Im Jahre Null: Ein Beitrag zur Geschichte der deutschen Presse* (Munich: Verlag Kurt Desch, 1966); Dominique Herbet, *Die Neue Zeitung: Un journal américaine pour la population allemande, 1945–1949* (Villeneuve-d'Aseq: Presses Universitaires du Septentrion, 1997); Kyong-Kun Kim, "Die *Neue Zeitung* im Dienste der Reeducation für die deutsche Bevölkerung, 1945–1946" (Ph.D. dissertation, Ludwig-Maximilians-Universität, Munich, 1974); Susanne Bittorf, "Die *Neue Zeitung* im Spiegel Münchener Gesellschaft und Kultur: Eine Fallstudie zur amerikanischen Umerziehungs- und Demokratisierungspolitik in Deutschland, 1945–1949" (Master's thesis, Ludwig-Maximilians-Universität, Munich, 1982); Sabine Rollberg, "Von der Wiederauferstehung des deutschen Geistes: Eine Analyse des Feuilletons der *Neuen Zeitung*, 1945–1949" (Ph.D. dissertation, Albert-Ludwig-Universität, Freiburg, 1981); Wolfgang Burkhardt, "Die Feuilleton- und Kunstbeilage der *Neuen Zeitung*: Ein Beitrag zur Geschichte der Nachkriegspresse in Deutschland" (Master's thesis, Freie Universität Berlin, 1969); Jens Wehner, "Zur politischen Kultur im Nachkriegsdeutschland: Die *Neue Zeitung* in den Jahren 1945–1949 (unter besonderer Berücksichtigung des Feuilletons unter der Leitung Erich Kästners)" (Staatsexamensarbeit für das Lehramt an Gymnasien, n. p., 1981); Bettina Wegwitz, "Erich Kästner als Redakteur: Journalist der Nachkriegszeit für die *Neue Zeitung* und den *Pinguin*" (Master's thesis, Ludwig-Maximilians-Universität, Munich, 1989). Presently, there is one more study underway: by Alexa Esselbach, a graduate student of English and history at the University of Munich.

an aggressive cultural foreign policy.[2] The critics of cultural imperialism, conversely, portray hegemonic U.S. forces manipulating political bodies overseas. Historians and political scientists such as Akira Iriye and Samuel Huntington have linked the expansion of American political influence to the export of American culture.[3] In a number of studies, communication scientist Herbert Schiller has identified a strong link between the domestic business, military, and governmental power structure on one hand, and on the other, the "mind managers," i.e., the leaders of U.S. communications who joined forces to manipulate consumers at home and abroad. Carrying this line of thought even further, scholars writing in the 1980s, such as Ralph Willett and Emily Rosenberg, claimed that in the twentieth century U.S. foreign policy makers purposely began to "spread" American culture, information, and the concept of a free and open economy in order to expand the national market. According to these historians, U.S. officials were interested in foreign markets but not in an international cultural and ideological dialogue.[4]

2. Peter Grothe, *To Win the Minds of Men: The Story of the Communist Propaganda War in East Germany* (Palo Alto, Calif.: Pacific Books, 1958), 191–241; Thomas C. Sorensen, *The Word War: The Story of American Propaganda* (New York: Harper & Row, 1968). For a critical appraisal of the American image abroad, see Franz M. Joseph and Raymond Aron, eds., *As Others See Us: The United States Through Foreign Eyes* (Princeton, N.J.: Princeton University Press, 1959); William J. Lederer and Eugene Burdick, *The Ugly American* (New York: Norton, 1958); R. B. J. Walker, "The Developing Role of Cultural Diplomacy in Asia," in *Issues and Conflicts: Studies in Twentieth Century American Diplomacy,* ed. George L. Anderson (Lawrence, Kans.: University of Kansas Press, 1959), 45; John Boardman Whitton, ed., *Propaganda and the Cold War: A Princeton University Symposium* (Washington, D.C.: Public Affairs Press, 1963).

3. Morrell Heald and Lawrence S. Kaplan, *Culture and Diplomacy: The American Experience* (Westport, Conn.: Greenwood Press, 1977); Samuel Huntington, *American Politics: The Promise of Disharmony* (Cambridge, Mass.: Belknap Press, 1981), 239–245; Akira Iriye, "Culture and Power: International Relations and Intercultural Relations," *Diplomatic History* 10 (spring 1979): 115–128; Iriye, *Power and Culture: The Japanese-American War, 1941–1945* (Cambridge, Mass.: Harvard University Press, 1981), viif.; Hugh De Santis, *The Diplomacy of Silence: The American Foreign Service, the Soviet Union, and the Cold War, 1933–1947* (Chicago: University of Chicago Press, 1980); James C. Thomson, Jr., Peter W. Stanley, and John Curtis Perry, *Sentimental Imperialists: The American Experience in East Asia* (New York: Harper & Row, 1981); Michael Hunt, *American Foreign Policy and American Values* (Chicago: Peacock Publishers, 1988); Frank Ninkovich, "The Currents of Cultural Diplomacy: Art and the State Department," *Diplomatic History* 1 (Summer 1977): 215–37.

4. Herbert I. Schiller, *Culture Inc.: The Corporate Takeover of Public Expression* (New York: Oxford University Press, 1989); Schiller, *Communication and Cultural Domination* (White Plains, N.Y.: International Arts and Sciences Press, 1976), 1; Schiller, *Mass Communications and American Empire* (New York: Augustus M. Kelley, 1969), 14; Schiller, *The Mind Managers* (Boston: Beacon Press, 1973); Emily S. Rosenberg, *Spreading the American Dream: American Economic and Cultural Expansion, 1890–1945* (New York: Hill and Wang, 1982);

Regarding the second historiographical trend mentioned above, the term *reeducation* stems from the effort of the United States to reeducate Germany (and Japan) after World War II along the lines of a Western, democratically oriented model. The historical scholarship on reeducation has focused on various aspects of the program, the effort, or lack of effort, on the part of the reeducators, and the question of whether or not these programs were a "success." Scholars writing in the 1950s and 1960s, such as Harold Zink and John Gimbel, deemed reeducation and the democratization of Germany a political success because the country became a parliamentary democracy within the Western orbit.[5] Revisionists of U.S. reconstruction and reeducation efforts in Germany, such as Carolyn Eisenberg, Lutz Niethammer, and Ernst-Ulrich Hulster, claim Washington decision makers did not exert enough persuasion; foreign nationals accepted financial and structural assistance without needing to conform, comply, or in any way conciliate.[6] The United States, then, is viewed as either a grand movie director controlling the behavior of shallow actors or as a duped show producer overwhelmed by an irreverent set of stage performers.

My profile of the *Neue Zeitung* has a less sweeping scope than the analyses cited above. It focuses on one case study of "cultural diplomacy." Using the example of this information tool, it investigates the core values that U.S. officials transmitted to the German population in postwar Germany and portrays how these values changed over time. It also describes the reaction of the German public to the *Neue Zeitung* and it examines the emerging

Pavel Gurevich, *Dialogue of Culture or Cultural Expansion?* (Moscow: Progress Publishers, 1990); Frank Ninkovich, *The Diplomacy of Ideas: U.S. Foreign Policy and Cultural Relations, 1938–1950* (Cambridge, Mass.: Cambridge University Press, 1981), 4, 6, 74f., 165ff., 181–83; Ralph Willett, *The Americanization of Germany, 1945–1949* (London: Routledge, 1989), 21–27.

5. Edward Litchfield et al., eds., *Governing Postwar Germany* (Ithaca, N.Y.: Cornell University Press, 1953), 467; Arnold Brecht, "Re-establishing German Government," *Annals* 267 (1950): 28–42; Harold Zink, *The United States in Germany, 1945–1955* (Princeton, N.J.: Van Nostrand, 1957), John Gimbel, *The American Occupation of Germany: Politics and the Military, 1945–1949* (Stanford, Calif.: Stanford University Press, 1968).

6. Lutz Niethammer, *Entnazifizierung in Bayern: Säuberung und Rehabilitierung unter amerikanischer Besatzung* (Frankfurt: Fischer, 1972); Ernst-Ulrich Huster et al., eds., *Determinanten der westdeutschen Restauration, 1945–1949* (Frankfurt: Suhrkamp, 1972); Karl-Ernst Bungenstab, *Umerziehung zur Demokratie? Re-Edukation-Politik im Bildungswesen der U.S. Zone, 1945–49* (Düsseldorf: Bertelsmann Universitätsverlag, 1970); Carolyn Eisenberg, "U.S. Policy in Post-War Germany: The Conservative Restoration," *Science & Society* 46 (Spring 1982): 24–38; Paul W. Gulgowski, *The American Military Government of United States Occupied Zones of Post World War II Germany in Relation to Policies Expressed by Its Civilian Governmental Authorities at Home, During the Course of 1944/45 Through 1949* (Frankfurt: Haag + Herchen Verlag, 1983), 217–82, 363, 364, 371, 372, 380, 398, 399.

conflicts among U.S. officials, editors, and German readers regarding the newspaper's message. The project's generating questions are: Were U.S. policy makers and their representatives in Germany as dominant and aggressive as the scholars of cultural imperialism would lead us to believe? Or were they as blind and ridden by anticommunism as the revisionists of U.S. occupation policy have claimed? Did Americans in Germany display arrogance or ignorance?

From the beginning, a specter haunted the American occupation program in Germany. U.S. officials wished to inculcate democratic values in the German population without using methods that resembled totalitarian ones. Both fascist and communist leaders employed egregious indoctrination techniques. The promotion of democracy had to be conducted according to standards of free speech and objectivity. The evolving, increasingly inflammatory, political and social contours of the Cold War complicated this task.

U.S. officials were reluctant propagandists. Their behavior is not congruent with the model of cultural imperialism. Throughout the occupation period, U.S. planners at home and abroad never completely agreed on the issue of cultural foreign policy. They could not decide whether the forceful promotion of American values abroad was appropriate at all. Even though they may have intended to spread American ideas, culture, and ways of life in Germany, they were uncertain about how to do it. Furthermore, although individual policy makers aspired to indoctrinate the Germans,[7] the political and military infrastructure never gave them the opportunity to fully realize such ambitions. No matter what cultural vision top officials in the State Department may have had, precious little of it trickled down to the level of those on the scene. Moreover, OMGUS officials paid scant attention to Washington concerns. For the most part, the editors of the *Neue Zeitung* developed and realized their own policy. Directives from Washington were usually discarded and sometimes ridiculed. Even at the height of the Berlin blockade, there was no coherent policy for the newspaper.

This dilemma thrust a set of inexperienced German-born émigrés into the spotlight, lending them power and influence beyond their wildest dreams. They were merely third-rank soldiers, yet they formed the core of what became a crucial tool for shaping public opinion. In downtown Munich, they established the *Neue Zeitung* to disseminate democratic ideas in Germany. While high-ranking American officials suggested a straightforward explica-

7. See, for example, Arthur Whittier McMahon, *Memorandum on the Postwar International Information Program of the United States* (Washington, D.C.: Department of State Publication 2438, U.S. Government Printing Office, 1945); Benjamin Floyd Pittenger, *Indoctrination for American Democracy* (New York: Macmillan, 1941).

tion of the tenets of democracy, the privates-turned-editors elaborated a strategy that would more appropriately suit their audience. They draped democratic notions in traditional German clothing designed to suit the taste of the German *Bildungsbürgertum* (the educated middle class), which had been most apprehensive about modernity, mass consumption, and democracy.

The men and women involved in daily operations who had to contend with pedestrian concerns often dictated the course of policy. They had to field muddled, often conflicting, orders regarding the conveyance of American core values from Information Control authorities. The proliferation of contending opinions meant that no clearly defined lines of responsibility existed. These considerations combined with the fact that philosophical quandaries were not covered by standard military operations granted the editors great latitude in determining the paper's composition.

Their actions as mediators between no-nonsense occupation authorities and a skeptical reading public offer a glimpse into the transfer of cultural values. In the 1930s, most of the *Neue Zeitung* editors had emigrated to the United States fleeing Hitler's discriminatory laws. They had undergone an immersion into American culture that unwittingly prepared them for their postwar work of spreading new ideas. But unlike their American colleagues, these émigrés did not feel alienated or even compelled to adapt in order to convert natives. They were natives themselves, born and raised in German culture. This bicultural experience resulted in a well-tempered mission.

An examination of the profiles and prosaic concerns of ground-level workers reveals the transformation that grand strategies sometimes undergo. In the case of the *Neue Zeitung* a discrepancy existed between those who claimed to govern policy and those who actually held the reins of power. The maneuvers of the newspaper editors within the military bureaucracy in a war-torn country reveal the major role minor individuals can play in the making of policy and the transmission of cultural values.

Some revisionists of occupation historiography such as Edward Peterson have argued that OMGUS failed at reeducation because policy makers in Washington did not create well-defined strategies.[8] The story of the *Neue Zeitung* underscores this failure but reveals a different cause. Those documents explaining initial plans and intentions regarding Germany's democratization reflected more how U.S. officials wanted to see themselves rather

8. Edward Peterson, *The Many Faces of Defeat: The German People's Experience in 1945* (New York: Peter Lang, 1990), 55f.; Gulgowski, *American Military Government*, 217–82, 363f.; Rüdiger Liedtke, *Die verschenkte Presse: Die Geschichte der Lizensierung von Zeitungen nach 1945* (Berlin: Verlag für Ausbildung und Studien in der Elefanten Press, 1982).

than viable reeducational plans and actions in Europe. American policy makers refrained from developing a clear-cut program and from overt pro-democratic propaganda for a variety of reasons. From the beginning, there was a great deal of confusion within the military government: responsibility was not clearly assigned, there was rapid and constant changing of personnel, and no one viewpoint regarding democratization ever became dominant. More importantly, U.S. policy makers did not want to be associated with totalitarian indoctrination. As a result, throughout the occupation period, the *Neue Zeitung* was able to display great diversity.

Revisionists and cultural imperialists are correct in stating that the development of reeducation and cultural transmission in postwar Germany between 1945 and 1949 must be considered in the context of both anticommunism and antifascism. Most students of the American occupation in Germany identify a shift in the U.S. reeducation program in 1947–48. They agree that in the end reeducation was shaped by, if not sacrificed for, the Cold War when the German audience turned from evil Nazis into wooed partners needed to strengthen the Western camp.[9]

Yet these scholars fail to pay due attention to the importance of German public opinion in the grander scheme of events of that time. Anticommunism had been one of the foremost features of National Socialist ideology. Untiringly, the Nazi propaganda minister Joseph Goebbels had warned the German audience of a "Jewish-Bolshevik" conspiracy. If U.S. officials preached anticommunism to postwar Germans, they might be seen as duplicating Nazi propaganda.

Instead, reeducation continued as a fundamentally antifascist campaign. According to the editors of the *Neue Zeitung*, not the Soviets but the East German communists were the foremost threat to Germany's reconstruction. They not only displayed the same totalitarian propaganda and methods as Hitler but even recruited Nazis among their own ranks. They were driving a wedge between the Allies in order to create another dictatorship. In other words, antifascism was not abandoned within the concept of reeducation but reinforced. Only the link between the Nazis and the East German communists made it possible to win West German sympathies for the cause of the Cold War.

Again, the men and women who initiated this concept of reeducation

9. Hansjörg Gehring, *Amerikanische Literaturpolitik in Deutschland, 1945–1953: Ein Aspekt des Reeducationsprogramms* (Stuttgart: Deutsche Verlags-Anstalt, 1976), 78, 108; Hans Borchers and Klaus W. Vowe, *Die zarte Pflanze Demokratie: Amerikanische Re-education in Deutschland im Spiegel ausgewählter politischer und literarischer Zeitschriften, 1945–1949* (Tübingen: Narr, 1979), 65; Peterson, *The Many Faces of Defeat*, 55f.

were not top policy makers. In 1946–47, top policy makers were still much too afraid of publicly treading on diplomatic mine fields and risking Allied cooperation. Despite the inter-Allied disputes over reparations, economic reconstruction, and administrative jurisdiction in Germany, U.S. officials were careful not to let these conflicts escalate. Instead, the initiators in the reeducation effort were the foot soldiers, like the journalists of the *Neue Zeitung*, who could afford to confront communism much earlier. Their function seemed to be so marginal on first sight, yet they ended up as key actors in the political development of the following years.

Since the early 1990s, scholars have begun to pay more attention to individual case studies of German/European-American social and cultural interaction. In this context, the adaptation of American values—notably popular culture and mass consumption—by non-American people, frequently referred to as "Americanization," has played a prominent role. Hermann-Josef Rupieper has stressed the interaction between U.S. officials abroad and local citizens in the realm of sociopolitical affairs. Kaspar Maase, Richard Pells, and others have examined the impact of American consumer culture, music, and symbols on Germany. Diverse as these studies are, they concede that cultural transfer existed, but locals often resisted, modified, and even corrupted it.[10]

10. C. W. E. Bigsby, "Europe, America and the Cultural Debate," in *Superculture: American Popular Culture and Europe*, ed. C. W. E. Bigsby (Bowling Green, Ohio: Bowling Green University Popular Press, 1975), 1–27; Kaspar Maase, *Bravo America: Erkundigungen zur Jugendkultur der Bundesrepublik in den fünfziger Jahren* (Hamburg: Junius Verlag, 1992); Axel Schildt, *Moderne Zeiten: Freizeit, Massenmedien, und "Zeitgeist" in der Bundesrepublik der 50er Jahre* (Hamburg: Christians, 1995), 398–423; Uta G. Poiger, "Rock'n Roll, Kalter Krieg und deutsche Identität," in *Amerikanisierung und Sowjetisierung in Deutschland, 1945–1970*, ed. Konrad H. Jarausch and Hannes Siegrist (Frankfurt: Campus, 1996), 275–89; Hermann-Josef Rupieper, *Die Wurzeln der westdeutschen Nachkriegsdemokratie: Der amerikanische Beitrag, 1945–1952* (Opladen: Westdeutscher Verlag, 1993); Richard F. Kuisel, *Seducing the French: The Dilemma of Americanization* (Berkeley, Calif.: University of California Press, 1993); Reinhold Wagnleitner, *Coca-Colanization and the Cold War: The Cultural Mission of the United States in Austria after the Second World War*, trans. Diana M. Wolf (Chapel Hill, N.C.: University of North Carolina, 1994); Wagnleitner, "The Irony of American Culture Abroad: Austria and the Cold War," in *Recasting America: Culture and Politics in the Age of Cold War*, ed. Lary May (Chicago: University of Chicago Press, 1989), 285–301; Richard Pells, "American Culture Abroad: The European Experience since 1945," in Rob Kroes, Robert W. Rydell, and Doeko F. J. Bosscher, eds., *Cultural Transmissions and Receptions: American Mass Culture in Europe* (Amsterdam: VU University Press, 1993), 67–83; Pells, *Not Like Us: How Europeans Have Loved, Hated, and Transformed American Culture Since World War II* (New York: Basic Books, 1997); Peter Breit, "Culture and Authority: American and German Transactions," in *The American Impact on Postwar Germany*, ed. Reiner Pommerin (Providence, R.I.: Berghahn Books, 1995), 125–48; Peter Duignan, *The Rebirth of the West: The Americanization of the Democratic World* (Lanham, Md.: Rowman & Littlefield, 1996); Rob Kroes, *If*

The story of the *Neue Zeitung* confirms these findings but it alters the emphasis. As in the area of politics and economics,[11] the Germans picked those U.S. offerings that fit their own needs. The reason for their choices lay not merely in the appeal of these values but in the engagement of the agents who transformed them.

The following chapters retrace the history of the paper, the editors' conflicts with the War Department, and the *Neue Zeitung*'s political and philosophical development over the course of a decade. This study focuses on the occupation period of 1945 to 1949. During these years the *Neue Zeitung* made its most noteworthy contribution in the field of cultural transmission. Under the High Commission in Germany (1949–1955), the civilian successor of the U.S. military government, the paper split into three completely different editions, making an overall analysis impossible.

The first chapter outlines the larger context of occupation policy and psychological warfare, including the interplay between reeducation and cultural interaction and the emerging role of the *Neue Zeitung*. Chapter 2 provides a biographical analysis of the staff and its critics. Chapter 3 examines the paper's content between 1945 and 1947. The fourth chapter depicts the response to the paper by the German public and by American officials.

The second half of this study examines the significance of the *Neue Zeitung* in the unfolding Cold War. Chapter 5 portrays the growing Soviet resentment of this newspaper. The sixth chapter describes the attempted shift of the *Neue Zeitung* from an information medium to a propaganda instrument in 1947–1948 under an American-born editor in chief. It also examines the public and official reactions to this change of editorial policy. The last chapter illuminates the final effort of U.S. officials to turn the newspaper into a mouthpiece of the U.S. military government in Germany. An epilogue sketches the final years of the paper between 1949 and 1950 and the

---

*You've Seen One, You've Seen the Mall: European and American Mass Culture* (Urbana, Ill.: University of Illinois Press, 1996), 162–78; Roger Rolin, ed., *The Americanization of the Global Village: Essays in Comparative Popular Culture* (Bowling Green, Ohio: Bowling Green State University Popular Press, 1989), 1–10; Lothar Bredella, ed., *Mediating a Foreign Culture: The United States and Germany* (Tübingen: Narr, 1991), 7–14. See also John Tomlinson, *Cultural Imperialism: A Critical Introduction* (Baltimore: Johns Hopkins University Press, 1991), 8, 140–69, 174ff.

11. Geir Lundestad, *The American "Empire" and Other Studies of U.S. Foreign Policy in a Comparative Perspective* (Oslo: Norwegian University Press, 1990); Klaus Schwabe, "German Policy Responses to the Marshall Plan," in *The Marshall Plan and Germany: West German Development within the Framework of the European Recovery Program*, ed. Charles S. Maier and Günther Bischof (New York: Berg, 1991), 228; Alan S. Milward, *The Reconstruction of Western Europe, 1945–51* (London: Methuen, 1984), 493f.

subsequent careers of former staffers. It attempts, additionally, to measure the *Neue Zeitung*'s long-term influence in postwar Germany.

My account endeavors to delineate the significant role played by *Kultur* in the German response to U.S. initiatives. Over the past two hundred years this term has acquired varying definitions, and it is a hopeless endeavor to define it authoritatively. Until the late nineteenth century, culture meant primarily "high culture," comprising masterpieces of art, music, and literature. According to German and American elites, self-cultivation was the duty of an individual and related to *Bildung* (knowledge, education).[12]

In the early twentieth century, American culture—similar to U.S. citizenship—came to be regarded as a shared system of beliefs and customs that is open to anybody. Until the advent of postmodernism, to be American did not mean to be ethnically delimited.[13] German *Kultur*, in contrast, has much more clearly identifiable historical and Germanic roots. Until the late 1960s, the term referred exclusively to high culture, which represented a distinct part of a country's national heritage that could be attained only by an educated elite. There existed, of course, competitors to German highbrow culture such as trivial literature, entertainment music, melodrama, films, and folk culture expressed through songs, fairy tales, music, and art—but those did not count as *Kultur*.[14]

My study utilizes on the distinction between culture and *Kultur*. U.S. officials in Germany tended to equate culture with the American way of life. This concept included high and popular culture but was not historically

12. Matthew Arnold, *Culture and Anarchy: An Essay in Political Social Criticism* (London: Smith, Elder, 1869); John Storey, *Introductory Guide to Cultural Theory and Popular Culture* (New York: Harvester/Wheatsheaf, 1993), 21–27; Lawrence W. Levin, *Highbrow/Lowbrow: The Emergence of Cultural Hierarchy in America* (Cambridge, Mass.: Harvard University Press, 1988); Todd Curtis Kontje, *The German Bildungsroman: History of a National Genre* (Columbia, S.C.: Camden House, 1993); Gert Selle, *Kultur der Sinne und ästhetische Erziehung: Alltag, Sozialisation, Kunstunterricht in Deutschland vom Kaiserreich zur Bundesrepublik* (Cologne: Dumont, 1981).

13. Thomas C. Molnar, *The Emerging American Culture* (New Brunswick: Transaction Publishers, 1994); Raymond Williams, *Culture and Society, 1780–1950* (New York: Columbia University Press, 1958); Herbert J. Gans, *Popular Culture and High Culture: An Analysis and Evaluation of Taste* (New York: Basic Books, 1974).

14. For further study on the correlation between *Bildung* and *Kultur* see Georg Bollenbeck, *Bildung und Kultur: Glanz und Elend eines deutschen Deutungsmusters* (Frankfurt: Insel Verlag, 1994); Franz Rauhut, "Die Herkunft der Worte und Begriffe 'Kultur,' 'Civilisation,' und 'Bildung,'" *Germanisch-Romanische Monatsschrift* 3 (April 1953): 81–91; Georg Jäger, *Schule und literarische Kultur* (Stuttgart: J. B. Metzlersche Verlagsbuchhandlung, 1981); Eric J. Hobsbawm, "Kultur als Ghetto," in *"Kultur-Zerstörung"? Zehnte Römerberggespräche in Frankfurt a. M.*, ed. Hilmar Hoffman (Königstein/Ts.: Athenäum, 1983), 60–69; Kontje, *The German Bildungsroman*, 110.

grounded or ethnically defined. Foreigners could appreciate and participate in it. American culture was what the world would want if the world only knew about it: Babe Ruth and Ernest Hemingway, Glenn Miller and Ginger Rogers.

American-born officers who attempted to transmit American values, culture, and ideas to the German people did not realize that Germans would never accept American culture as *Kultur* simply because it did not reflect their own cultural traditions and their own history. For the average German citizen, who may have also valued trivial cultural productions, *Kultur* exclusively embraced high culture; it represented a distinctive component of the country's heritage. In the United States, Mickey Mouse was part of culture, while in Germany only artists on the level of Johann Wolfgang von Goethe or Wolfgang Mozart would be thus considered. Middle-class Germans refused to accept as comparable an American culture that included such popular elements as baseball, jazz, and Hollywood because *Kultur* was not a way of life but a superior value.

Such subtle distinctions, while invisible to the foreign eye, did not escape the attention of the German émigrés who ran the *Neue Zeitung*. They realized that the challenge for U.S. officials in Germany was not to familiarize educated Germans with American culture but to encourage them to expand their closed concept of *Kultur* and accept other concepts and ideas. Their expertise underscores the credo that guides the marketing of any product: its success depends to a large degree on the salesperson. In the "sale" of American culture in postwar Germany, the agents determined yield.

# 1

# BETWEEN THE CRACKS: BIRTH OF AN ENTERPRISE, 1944–1945

THERE WAS LITTLE ACTIVITY IN THE STREETS OF MUNICH ON THE NIGHT OF 17 October 1945. Curfew orders in the American zone forbade German citizens to leave their homes after dark. An American soldier riding his bike to see his girlfriend or a military jeep dashing back to its headquarters were the only signs of life. That night, in a basement among the ruins of Schellingstraße in Munich's central district, the presses of Joseph Goebbels's former Nazi paper, *Völkischer Beobachter*, began to turn their wheels, to stamp, to squeak. Copy after copy, the machines spat out reams of printed paper, watermarked with the emblem of the Nazi swastika. Bold black letters on top of each copy read *Die Neue Zeitung*. Upstairs there were cheers and drinks for everyone. Colonel Clifford A. Powell, deputy chief of the operations branch in the Information Control Division (ICD) of the U.S. military government in Germany, wished several other American officers good luck with their mission.[1]

But what was the *Neue Zeitung*? Where did it spring from? What was its purpose? Two developments were crucial in the history and purpose of this newspaper: the goals of the ambiguous Allied plans to "reeducate" Germany and the Psychological Warfare Division (PWD), which was instrumental in the plan to "reform" the German mind.

At the Potsdam Conference, in July/August 1945, representatives of Great Britain, the Soviet Union, and the United States mapped out the economic and political future of Germany. According to the stipulations, Germany would be treated as an economic unit while being cut temporarily into three (later four) occupation zones, each governed by an Allied military governor. An Allied Control Council located in Berlin would decide on measures concerning all of Germany. Leaders at the conference placed the area comprising today's Bavaria, Baden-Württemberg, Hesse, Bremen, and the south of Berlin under the authority of the American military government,

1. Neue Zeitung, 18 October 1945, Bibliotheksarchiv, Ludwig-Maximilians-Universität, Munich, p. 1; Stefan Heym, *Nachruf* (Munich: Bertelsmann Verlag, 1988), 384.

"Everybody's work matters!"

*This cartoon by D. Low was published in the first issue of the* Neue Zeitung, *18 October 1945.*

which was named the "Office of Military Government (U.S.) for Germany" (OMGUS). General Lucius D. Clay, until 1947 deputy military governor and then military governor, led the occupation bureaucracy until his resignation in 1949.[2]

At Potsdam, the Western Allied governments grappled with Germany's industrial and cultural reconstruction. Political and economic experts agreed that cooperation with the Germans was necessary. However, in order to destroy the influence of the National Socialist cadre, the Germans had to undergo *reeducation.*[3] Stemming from the vocabulary of psychiatry, *reedu-*

2. Wolfgang Benz, *Potsdam 1945: Besatzungsherrschaft und Neuaufbau im Vier-Zonen-Deutschland* (Munich: Deutscher Taschenbuch Verlag, 1986; 2d ed. 1992), 110; Wolfgang Krieger, *General Lucius D. Clay und die amerikanische Deutschlandpolitik, 1945–1949* (Stuttgart: Klett-Cotta, 1987); John H. Backer, *Winds of History: The German Years of Lucius DuBignon Clay* (New York: Van Nostrand Reinhold, 1983).

3. Helmuth Mosberg, *Reeducation: Umerziehung und Lizenzpresse im Nachkriegsdeutschland* (Munich: Universitas, 1991), 40; James P. Warburg, *Germany: Bridge or Battleground* (London: Heinemann, 1947), 181–253; James F. Tent, *Mission on the Rhine: Reeduca-*

*cation* has become one of the more perplexing terms in twentieth-century history. In the early 1940s, American social scientists, such as Margaret Mead, associate curator of anthropology in the American Museum of Natural History, and Theodore Abel, professor of sociology at Columbia University in New York, advocated thorough psychological reorientation as the only way to prevent the resurrection of fascism in Central Europe. At a joint conference in New York in 1944, anthropologists, psychiatrists, psychologists, and sociologists stated that "to make an enduring peace with Germany will require more than merely militar[y], political or economic measures, or any combination of these. It will require a change in the Germans themselves."[4]

The scientists believed a spiritual change in Germany needed to take place in the public arena as well as in every citizen's mind. Germans were to be subjected to a thorough process of reeducation that would familiarize them with the values, rules, and institutions of a modern democracy similar to the American model: discussion, individualism, mutual adjustment, cooperation among equals, a constitution, universal suffrage, a representative government, and a system of checks and balances. The broad goals discussed by the social scientists were eventually incorporated into the Joint Chiefs of Staff (JCS) directive 1067, often labeled the four "Ds": denazification, democratization, demilitarization, and decentralization. *Denazification* referred to the effort to remove all Nazis from leading positions in German society. *Democratization* (later reeducation and still later reorientation) meant the attempt to turn every individual German into a responsible citizen who would have an independent political and critical opinion while subscribing to the principal pillars of a democracy. A middle-of-the-road system would include every stratum of society in all relevant processes of decision making.

At the end of the war, American troops flooded into Germany with no coherent overall national policy for the occupation, let alone for Germany's reeducation. President Franklin D. Roosevelt's reluctance to create a definitive blueprint significantly contributed to the proliferation of opinions. As Rebecca Boehling has recently shown, the War Department and the State Department favored a "soft peace"; the Treasury Department harbored a more interventionist design geared toward the pastoralization of Germany;

*tion and Denazification in American-Occupied Germany* (Chicago: University of Chicago Press, 1982), 13.

4. "Report of a Conference on Germany after the War," called by the Joint Committee on Post-War Planning, April, May, June, 1944, reprinted in Mosberg, *Reeducation*, 171–81; Richard Brickner, "Is Germany Incurable?" *Atlantic Monthly* 171 (1943): 84–93.

and the Office of Strategic Services continuously advocated the potential of the "Other Germany" that could form a new democratic postwar society. This confusion, never resolved, was carried into the occupation of Germany.[5]

In the end, the occupation became the army's job for more than four years. This development exacted its price. The rather abstract and idealistic definition of reeducation endorsed by scientists, policy makers, and intellectuals proved useless to U.S. military officials. Trained as soldiers, they expected clear orders rather than philosophical concepts. "I had no policy given to me as to what kind of democracy we wanted," Clay recalled many decades later. "I did not have very much experience in the field myself, never having voted myself."[6]

The key agency for the reeducation of the German mind became the Psychological Warfare Division (PWD), a subdivision of the War Department. PWD was a brainchild of the Office of Strategic Services (OSS), forerunner of the CIA, which was in charge of secret service operations abroad. At the same time, the Office of War Information (OWI), Washington's mouthpiece during the war, functioned as the PWD's resource for facts, news, and publication material.

Psychological warfare comprised the use of propaganda to break the enemy's resistance, demoralize its army, and boost the morale of one's own troops.[7] But beyond that, as the historian Fitzhugh Green has argued, American planners in Washington had many different notions of what they hoped psychological warfare would achieve. The only strategy everyone in the OSS and the OWI agreed on was that Western propaganda should never resemble fascist or communist techniques and should remain as truthful as possible.

OSS and OWI had little influence in the field. After the invasion of Normandy, PWD propagandists operated as part of the Supreme Headquarters of the Allied Expeditionary Forces (SHAEF) in Europe. They employed various devices such as loudspeakers and leaflets as well as regular radio programs. Those media addressed *Wehrmacht* soldiers in the German language in an attempt to convince them of their hopeless strategic situation. Promis-

5. Rebecca Boehling, *A Question of Priorities: Democratic Reform and Economic Recovery in Postwar Germany* (Providence, R.I.: Berghahn Books, 1996), 15–40; Tent, *Mission on the Rhine*, 13–14.

6. Lucius D. Clay, "Proconsuls of a People, by Another People, for Both People," in *Americans as Proconsuls: United States Military Government in Germany and Japan, 1944–1952*, ed. Robert D. Wolfe (Carbondale, Ill.: Southern Illinois University Press, 1984), 105f.

7. William E. Daugherty, *A Psychological Warfare Casebook*, 4th ed., (Baltimore: Johns Hopkins University Press, 1968), 2.

ing good treatment, security, warm shelter, and better food in Allied POW camps, U.S. propagandists tried to encourage German soldiers to surrender before they were killed in action.[8]

The PWD soon took control of the presses and radio stations in the occupied areas, using them to prepare the ground for a new democratic postwar media system—central in the reeducation strategy. Its three-step plan sketched the application of the German press as an essential component of reeducation—one of the very few points upon which all four Allies agreed. First, the entire Nazi press and propaganda system was to be completely dismantled. Each power would then distribute press licenses to German anti-Nazis. When German editors seemed to be "democratic enough" the press market would finally be opened to free competition.[9]

For this purpose, the PWD divided its responsibilities among two detachments subordinated to the chief office in Paris with a civilian, Luther Conant, at its head. One group, the press office, prepared for the establishment of a permanent press and served as part of the long-term denazification and reeducation program of the U.S. Military Government in Germany. The other group, the Publicity and Psychological Warfare Detachment (P & PW), headed by an Hungarian-born émigré named Hans Habe, maintained headquarters in Luxembourg. It produced *Mitteilungsblätter*, information flyers, and broadcast messages designed to provide German soldiers and civilians in the frontier villages with news.[10] This group, a medley of German-related émigrés trained in psychological warfare and information control, would later form the core of the staff of the *Neue Zeitung*.

From the beginning, the Psychological Warfare Division self-consciously remained aloof, cooperating only loosely with the rest of the army and with the OWI in Washington. Although the OWI released detailed plans concerning the reconstruction of the German information media, not a single one of these documents ever reached the division in Europe; the PWD therefore had to plan its actions by itself.[11] Meanwhile, in the field, combat soldiers

8. Daniel Lerner, *Psychological Warfare Against Nazi-Germany: The Sykewar Campaign, D-Day to VE-Day*, 2d ed. (Cambridge, Mass.: M.I.T. Press, 1971), 46–60; Fitzhugh Green, *American Propaganda Abroad* (New York: Hippocrene Books, 1988), xiif., 20; Daugherty, *Psychological Warfare Casebook*, 130–35.

9. Harold J. Hurwitz, *Die Stunde Null der deutschen Presse: Die amerikanische Pressepolitik in Deutschland*, 1945–1949 (Cologne: Verlag Wissenschaft und Politik, 1972), 36, 41, passim; Michael Balfour, "Reforming the German Press, 1945–49," *Journal of European Studies* 3 (1973): 268–75.

10. Hurwitz, *Stunde Null*, 49.

11. Ibid., 24, 29, 32, 45; Peter Mallwitz, "Nachbemerkung" in Stefan Heym, *Reden an den Feind*, ed. Peter Mallwitz (Munich: Bertelsmann, 1986), 350–51.

## ALLIED PSYCHOLOGICAL WARFARE CHAIN OF COMMAND, 1944–1945

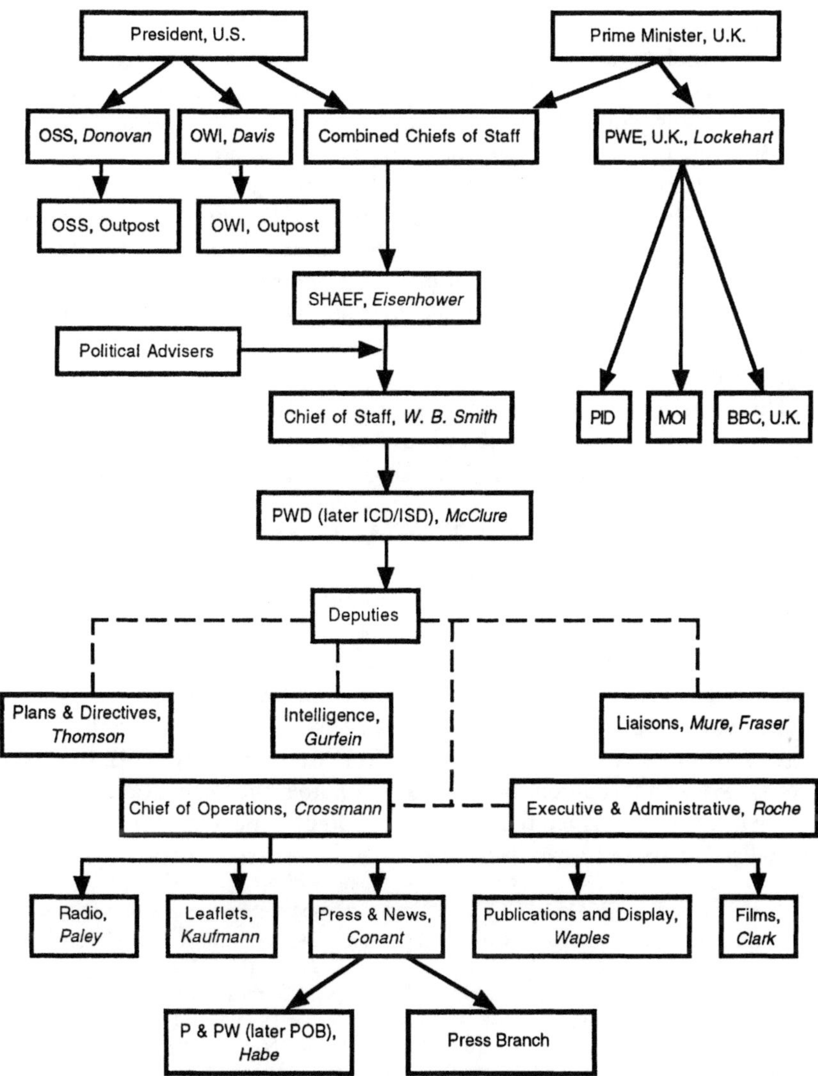


Solid lines indicate lines of authority; dotted lines indicate direct affiliations on the same administrative level.

Chart based on Lerner, *Psychological Warfare Against Nazi-Germany*, 47–59.

ridiculed the psychological warfare propagandists as "using trumpets to blow down the walls of Jericho." The idea of employing intellectual techniques on the battlefields of Europe seemed ludicrous because none of the propagandists had experienced combat firsthand. "We were little outsiders [*sic*]," recalls Konrad Kellen, an interrogator in the Second Mobile Radio Broadcasting Company. "People did not like that. Not so much because we were supposedly cowards as because of our privileged positions."[12]

Moreover, factionalism split the PWD because the division consisted of mavericks. Employment in psychological warfare required researchers and intellectuals familiar with information media, human psychology, and, above all, the German language, mind, and culture. As a result, the PWD by 1944 had attracted a conglomeration largely composed of German-speaking schoolmasters, university dons, literary agents, advertising experts, stockbrokers, psychologists, journalists, authors, farmers, and barristers. Many of these individuals were political and Jewish émigrés who had fled the Third Reich in the 1930s and subsequently entered the U.S. military service. They had received training in leaflet writing, broadcasting, persuasion tactics, and technical matters at Maryland's Camp Sharpe. While intellectually gifted, these men tended to sneer at professional soldiers and disdained military orders and hierarchy.[13] Many American-born officers within the PWD in turn resented the assignment of former German émigrés because of their European liberal or socialist backgrounds. Others were concerned that the émigrés were either too soft on German war crimes or too anti-German.[14] Such disputes were understandable: they merely reflected the frequent mutual suspicion between highbrows and lowbrows.

The War Department hired hundreds of foreign-born nationals despite protests from individual investigators. In a study in early 1942 on János Békessy, who had adopted the name Hans Habe, the Foreign Nationalities Branch of the OSS warned that he was the son of "one of the worst 'revolver journalists' that [*sic*] have lived in Europe in the past thirty years."[15] His

12. Konrad Kellen, interview, Los Angeles, 27 July 1993.

13. Daugherty, *Psychological Warfare Casebook*, 126, 131, 157ff.; Daniel Lerner, ed., *Propaganda in War and Crisis: Materials for American Policy* (New York: George Stewart, 1951), 278ff.; Lerner, *Psychological Warfare Against Nazi-Germany*, 350–64; Peter Wyden, "Die bunte Truppe von Camp Shapiro," *Rheinischer Merkur* 18 (5 May 1995): 37.

14. Habe, *Im Jahre Null*, 10–13, 103; Hurwitz, *Stunde Null*, 24; Lerner, *Psychological Warfare Against Nazi-Germany*, 72; Boehling, *A Question of Priorities*, 123–25, 269.

15. "The Bekessy's [*sic*], Washington D.C.," n. d. ("Received" on 16 September 1942), RG 226, Office of Strategic Services, Foreign Nationalities Branch Files 1942–1945, Int-15Hu-522, National Archives, Washington, D.C. (hereafter cited as NARA); "Report on Hans Habe," March 1942, ibid.; Hans Habe, *Ich stelle mich* (Vienna: Verlag Kurt Desch, 1955), 233–35; Bruce F. Pauley, *Hahnenschwanz und Hakenkreuz: Der Steirische Heimatschutz und der öster-*

father's Budapest magazine, *Ost-Kurier*, had worshiped alternately the communists and the fascists, before helping to lay the groundwork for Hitler's takeover in Hungary. At age nineteen, Habe had joined the Austrian Fascist movement, *Heimwehr*, of Prince Ernst Rüdiger von Starhemberg, where he was supposedly attached to Major Emil Fey, leader of the Vienna *Heimwehr* and later Austrian vice chancellor. In his autobiography, Habe mentions his employment as an editor for Starhemberg's three dailies, emphasizing that he never became a formal party member of the *Heimwehr*. Yet there is no doubt that he exposed himself as a classical Central European survivor—a *Mitläufer*—who adapted to the winds of history and held a high ethos only about what constituted good journalism.

Even worse, the report continued, the Békessys had always been ashamed of their Jewishness, a fact confirmed in Habe's autobiography. When on trial in Vienna in 1924, his father, Imre Békessy, declared himself to be "a protestant of Augsburgian confession," and even denied being Hungarian. The investigator woefully concluded that Habe's political attitude "is reactionary and everything else but democratic."

The investigation of PWD member Stefan Heym exposed similar doubts. Heym, alias Helmut Flieg, had emigrated via Prague to the United States. Already by the age of twenty-four, he had become editor in chief of a communist weekly in Manhattan, the *Deutsches Volksecho* (German People's Echo). Despite the fact that one observer explicitly labeled him as "inappropriate" for a leading position in the Military Intelligence Service, Heym received U.S. citizenship and joined Habe's Psychological Warfare School at Camp Sharpe.[16]

Although some accusations were pure hyperbole, they should have caused doubts about the émigrés' reliability as propagandists for the American cause. Two factors predominated over these concerns. First, no key person ever read these reports. OSS members such as Henry Kellermann still recall that these reports were a "mid-level" affair, based on deficient research, written by badly trained personnel, and often distorted by internal rivalries among OSS staff members. Second, the U.S. army did not have available an adequate number of American-born soldiers with the requisite

---

*reichische Nationalsozialismus, 1918–1934,* trans. Peter Aschner (Vienna: Europaverlag, 1972), 47–86; Pauley, *Eine Geschichte des österreichischen Antisemitismus: Von der Ausgrenzung zur Auslöschung*, trans. Helga Zoglmann (Vienna: Kremayr & Scheriau, 1993), 224–28; Pauley, *Hitler and the Forgotten Nazis: A History of Austrian National Socialism* (Chapel Hill, N.C.: University of North Carolina Press, 1981), 73–75, 124–25.

16. "Report from a Czechoslovak program held at Town Hall in New York City on February 15, 1943," n. d., RG 226, OSS, Foreign Nationalities Branch, Entry 100, INT-9CZ-265, MF C0002, NARA; Heym, *Nachruf*, 77, 114, 129, 151, 175, 240–4, 252, 262, 265, 362.

cultural and linguistic abilities to address the German audience persuasively. Thus the army had no choice but to employ the exiles.[17]

Émigrés working in the P & PW developed a particularly independent position. Theoretically subject to the press section, Habe's group operated under General Omar Bradley's Twelfth Army Group as "combat personnel," and remained autonomous in relation to the press office. Members of the PWD's press office consequently perceived Habe's publishing activity as a threat to their operation because both groups competed for local readers and prestige. The PWD prepared the ground for the postwar press and the P & PW published its leaflets.[18] This rivalry marked the beginning of an ongoing struggle between the press officers on the one hand and the outsider Habe and his newspaper on the other.

Hans Habe would become a key personality in the postwar reconstruction of the German press. One of the most colorful personalities in the history of the American occupation in Germany, he was born in 1911 in Budapest, as the only son of a wealthy Jewish-Hungarian publisher. After the family moved to Austria, his father earned renown as publisher of a Viennese sensational daily. Rumor had it that Imre Békessy made more money with articles he did not print (because people who feared scandal silenced him with substantial bribes) than with those that actually appeared. After having studied law, literature, and German, Hans Habe at the age of twenty-one became Europe's youngest editor in chief while working for the Viennese paper *Der Morgen*. In 1935 he rose to international prominence when he discovered that the family name of Germany's *Führer* was not Hitler but, in fact, Schicklgruber, a revelation that, Habe later boasted, had delayed the *Anschluß* by several years.[19]

Following the fall of France in 1940, Habe left his voluntary French army post and emigrated to the United States. With his worldly manner, noble air, personal charm, and vanity—he dyed his hair red, changed his shirt several times a day, and had his hands manicured—he quickly gained entry to the elite political circles in Washington and New York. Among many others, he befriended Eleanor Roosevelt and Joseph Davies, former U.S. ambassador to the Soviet Union. Shortly thereafter, Habe, whose reputation reportedly surpassed that of Casanova, Aly Khan, and Rubirosa combined, married Davies' stepdaughter Eleanor. Eleanor's grandfather was Charles W. Post

17. Henry Kellermann, interview, Chevy Chase, Md., 16 May 1994; Kellen, interview; Daugherty, *Psychological Warfare Casebook*, 126, 131, 157ff.; Lerner, *Psychological Warfare Against Nazi-Germany*, 72, 350–364; Lerner, ed., *Propaganda in War and Crisis*, 278ff.

18. Hurwitz, *Stunde Null*, 50.

19. Habe, *Ich stelle mich*, 100–23, 143–59, 212–30.

(1854–1914), owner of General Foods and originator of the prepared food industry, including *Postum Coffee* and *Grape Nuts*, in the United States.[20]

The success of Habe's professional career matched his social conquests. His first novel, *A Thousand Shall Fall*, an autobiographical account of the desperate situation of the French army at the Western front, made him an overnight sensation. He won a position as temporary lecturer at West Point. In 1942 Habe was drafted and assigned to the Military Intelligence Training Center at Camp Ritchie, Maryland. The following year, he was promoted to organizing a top secret camp at nearby Camp Sharpe designed to train foreign émigrés for psychological warfare. In 1944 his division was sent to Normandy.[21]

Habe never fit into the army. Fellow soldiers described him as a ridiculously overdressed and extremely extroverted person who, even during the muddy battles in the winter of 1944, wore a freshly ironed uniform every day. Some soldiers admired his nonconformity. "It was like perpetually being at a show, at a circus just to see this guy perform," sergeant Peter Weidenreich marveled fifty years later. "I would have paid money for it!" Many others saw this iconoclasm as unalloyed arrogance. Numerous American press control officers were parochial journalists from small towns who chafed at the consciously self-styled cosmopolitan who, as W. Phillips Davison, later on chief of the Plans and Directives Section, observed, loved to write and had his own ideas about everything."[22]

Once the war was over, U.S. officials quickly realized that the idea of an inter-Allied concept for the reconstruction of the new German press would probably never work as envisioned. The four occupation governments could not agree on a clear definition of a "free and independent press." Soviet press officers issued licenses only to political parties and unions while the Western Allies certified individual persons. British press officers showed more tolerance of former Nazi journalists than did their French and American colleagues.[23]

20. Habe, *Ich stelle mich*, 381–413; Cholly Knickerbocker, "The Smart Set" (newspaper column, n. d., n. p.), Hans Habe Collection, box 12, Department of Special Collections, Mugar Memorial Library, Boston University (hereafter cited as MBU); *Who's Who in America*, vol. 1 (Chicago: Marquis, 1968), 985.

21. Hans Habe, *A Thousand Shall Fall* (New York: Harcourt, Brace, 1941); Habe, *Ich stelle mich*, 389f.

22. Peter Wyden (former Weidenreich), interview, Ridgefield, Conn., 20 March 1993; W. Phillips Davison, Princeton, N.J., letter to the author, 17 January 1992; Daugherty, *Psychological Warfare Casebook*, 165.

23. Norbert Frei, "Die Presse," in *Die Bundesrepublik Deutschland: Geschichte in drei Bänden*, ed. Wolfgang Benz (Frankfurt: Fischer Taschenbuch Verlag, 1983), 3: 280–291.

As a peacetime successor of the PWD, the Information Control Division (ICD) was supposed to conduct media efforts in the U.S. zone under the guidance of Robert A. McClure, formerly head of the PWD. The task of the ICD was the control of cultural affairs including literature, theater, music, film, radio, and all printed media, as well as the research of political information for OMGUS. Two so-called District Information Services Control Commands (DISCC), created in February 1945, were responsible for the practical implementation of the plans in the "western military district" (DISCC 6870, located in Stuttgart) and the "eastern military district" (DISCC 6871, located in Munich). Press affairs were assigned to the Press Branch, which issued licenses and monitored German editors for the new press, and the Publishing Operations Branch (POB), which the successor of Hans Habe's P & PW and distributed official OMGUS publications.[24]

More than the other occupation powers, U.S. press officers opposed the revival of German local newspapers (*Heimatzeitungen*), party publications, and sensational journalism. No one who had published in Germany after 1932 was to be granted permission to write for a democratic daily. Each newspaper had to keep two licensees, an editor and a publisher, in order to guarantee the separation of news and opinion. Through scrutiny and censorship, exchange programs, and journalistic schools, the ICD hoped to control the democratic reform of the German press.[25]

During the months following VE-Day, Habe's unit, the Publishing Operations Branch, and part of the ICD developed into a powerful newspaper trust. Habe's men supervised the publication of thirteen army group newspapers for the German population with up to 4,632,000 copies per issue.[26]

24. The Information Control Division was created on 12 May 1945, before the PWD ceased to exist on 13 July 1945. According to Clay, the ICD was formally made part of OMGUS on 11 December 1945, while Frei mentions 10 December 1945, and Gehring—basing his information on Edward Breitenkamp—15 February 1946. Gehring, *Literaturpolitik*, 25–27; Norbert Frei, *Amerikanische Lizenzpolitik und deutsche Pressetradition: Die Geschichte der Nachkriegszeitung* Südost-Kurier (Munich: Oldenbourg, 1986), 25; Lucius D. Clay, *Decision in Germany* (Garden City, N.Y.: Doubleday, 1950), 60; Edward Breitenkamp, *The U.S. Information Control Division and Its Effects on German Publishers and Writers, 1945–1949* (Grand Forks, N.D.: University Station, 1953), 7; Frei, *Lizenpolitik*, 23–25.

25. Norbert Frei and Johannes Schmitz, *Journalismus im Dritten Reich* (Munich: Becksche Reihe, 1989), 186, 280–291; Heinz-Dietrich Fischer, *Parteien und Presse in Deutschland seit 1945* (Mainz: Schünemann Universitätsverlag, 1971), 49–51; Frei, "Die Presse," 276; Kenneth-Raymond Nelson, "United States Occupation Policy and the Establishment of a Democratic Newspaper Press in Bavaria, 1945–1949," (Ph.D. dissertation, University of Virginia, Charlottesville, 1966).

26. "The Fifth Mobile Radio Station," brochure produced in the field by the Fifth Mobile Printing Section, Bad Nauheim, Germany, October 1945, courtesy of Max W. Kraus; Hurwitz, *Stunde Null*, 80–81; Habe, *Im Jahre Null*, 483.

They knew that this newspaper empire would not last forever. American press officers would soon start licensing German newspaper men whose papers were designed to replace Habe's temporary publications. Captain Habe, however, had plans of his own.

Originally, the activity of Habe's unit was meant to be temporary. But as the war came to its end, the papers of the P & PW developed into Allied newspapers for the German population. Following the publication of information flyers, Habe's unit began to publish army group papers in twelve different German cities with a total circulation of 400,000 copies on average per issue.[27] The bulk of the papers was produced in Bad Nauheim, Hesse, a small idyllic spa near Frankfurt, where the PWD moved in April 1945.

Habe's sophisticated publications aroused the ire of many American press officers. In charge of licensing German newspapers, they resented Habe's deliberate competition with their efforts, depriving them not only of potential readers for the newly founded German papers but also of talented men whom they would have liked to employ in their own section.[28]

The latent conflict between the P & PW and the licensing branch over the reconstitution of the German press escalated after Germany's surrender. The DISCCs, in charge of the practical implementation of the PWD plans, wanted to establish as soon as possible a licensed press run by German editors and controlled by U.S. press officers. DISCC officials calculated that such a venture would enjoy popular support and relieve the military of an active participation in press matters.[29] Habe, conversely, felt that his division, the P & PW, could do a better job providing German readers with quality newspapers than could inexperienced German non-Nazi editors whom the PWD was supposed to license. For this reason, his division opposed the licensing of German newspapers and continued to publish the army group papers as long as possible.

Hans Habe did not oppose U.S. reeducation in Germany. He supported the political goals of Mead and Abel. He believed the Allies should implement a Western-style democracy in Germany in order to integrate the country into the world community. In the early stages of the war, Habe had

27. Habe, *Im Jahre Null*, 70; Elisabeth Matz, *Die Zeitungen der US-Armee für die deutsche Bevölkerung, 1944–1946* (Münster: Verlag Fahle, 1969); Hurwitz, *Stunde Null*, 80.

28. Habe, *Ich stelle mich*, 483; Hurwitz, *Stunde Null*, 78, 85; Wyden, interview.

29. N. D. Kehm, Headquarters Ninth U.S. Army, Office of the Army Chief of Staff, G-2 to General Robert A. McClure, Chief, PWD/SHAEF, 21 May 1945, RG 260, OMGUS, Information Service Division (ISD), 5/268–1/18, Institut für Zeitgeschichte, Munich (hereafter cited as IfZ). The term *licensed press* described the pool of German democratic editors who, after careful screening, were "licensed" to publish local newspapers. Nonetheless, the ICD press branch still controlled and sometimes censored these publications.

toured the United States for many months at the invitation of the War Department, calling for an "American Educational Expeditionary Force" in postwar Europe, an army consisting of 100,000 professors "to teach European people, and not only the Germans, to appreciate freedom and peace."[30]

Despite this promotional activity, he often disapproved of U.S. strategies. In his opinion, the Allies had to make democracy appealing by presenting it like a movie, not a lecture, to the German audience. Like moviegoers, the Germans would view the reeducation program with both curiosity and skepticism, always considering if they should continue watching or leave the theater. In order to make the audience "stay," as in a theater, the political reformation had to catch the Germans' attention, stir their natural curiosity, cater to their historical experience, and woo their taste in matters of *Kultur.* And as with a good movie, the program had to include famous actors, a dynamic plot, and many dramatic scenes.

According to Habe, the Germans should not only reeducate themselves, as Clay had stated, but had to convert to democratic principles with flying colors, filled with enthusiasm and the realization that it was the one best system in the world. But they would only do so if they felt they had a choice—like moviegoers. Habe was convinced that reeducation could be brought about only through a dialogue between victors and vanquished, based on tolerance and mutual understanding informed by a shared interest in each other's ideology and culture.[31] In philosophy and in practice, Habe began to emerge as one of the first postwar cultural ambassadors.

On 23 June 1945 Habe began pouring out proposals to the ICD regarding "a single overt newspaper for the U.S. zone"—the *Neue Zeitung*. In his outlines, he refused to turn over the task of reeducation to the licensed press. Reeducation, he argued, would be a failure if his newspaper trust was removed. "It will take many years before we have out of the mental bewilderness of Germany, created an aristocracy which than can really lead Ger-

30. Fenton Roskelley, "Concentration Camp Menu Not Much, Says Hans Habe," in *Spokane Daily Chronicle*, 6 May 1941; David W. Hazzen, "Teacher Hope for Europe: 100,000 American Need[ed], Says Author," *The Oregonian*, 22 May 1942; Mary Sterne, "America Sole Hope of World—Habe," *The Anniston Star*, 14 July 1942; Anne Meredith, "American-Controlled Europe Solution to War, Says Writer," *The New Orleans*, 18 July 1942. All of the above articles in Hans Habe collection, MBU; Habe, *Ich stelle mich*, 483, 496; Matz, *Zeitungen der US-Armee*, 78f.

31. Captain Hans Habe, Headquarters, ICD/USFET, "Verlagshaus Amerika," 20 August 45; and "Air-Strip Plan," 4 September 1945, to Commanding General ICD/USFET, RG 260, OMGUS 5/266–1/17, Bundesarchiv Koblenz (hereafter cited as BArch); Hans Habe, interview by Harold J. Hurwitz, Munich, 23 January 1950, RG 260, OMGUS 3/429–2/39, IfZ; Hans Habe, "Amerikas Niederlage in Deutschland," *Aufbau*, 21 March 1947, p. 1.

many into the family of free people," Habe claimed in his trademark pidgin English.[32] German underground forces were currently preparing for World War III, he warned, and it would be a sign of American weakness not to block their dangerous influence on the German audience.

Habe proposed that a model paper could attract readers by following an extremely high literary standard that would induce "the best liberal minds among the living German writers to contribute regularly 'think' pieces." The emphasis on an appealing cultural section alluded to the tradition of a *Feuilleton* in German newspaper history, dating back to the early nineteenth century. The ultimate goal of drafting the best authors from inside and outside the country was to lead Germany toward "internationalism." By showing Germans enticing examples of other free societies, this newspaper would render democracy more appealing.

Finally, Habe flatly proposed that each section should be led by an American (i.e., émigré) chief working with an entirely German staff. This was risky; the current non-fraternization order forbade U.S. soldiers to communicate and cooperate socially with German citizens.[33]

Habe's proposal evoked strong criticism. An ICD memorandum ridiculed his inappropriate "enthusiasm to do an outstanding job" and his intention to give considerable space to literature. Technical questions worried the chief of the Plans and Directives Section, C. A. Thompson, who denounced Habe's initial estimates for a proposed circulation of two million copies per issue as a wild fantasy. The debate over publication numbers generated the most controversy. While officials such as William Paley argued that the U.S. army paper should not come out more often than those of the German licensees (twice per week), Habe demanded a minimum of at least four runs. "The Germans," he said, "are psychologically difficult cases—they are to be compared with a man who is intelligent but hard of hearing. Only a constant hammering of certain ideas will penetrate into the German mind."[34]

32. Interoffice Memorandum from Guy della Cioppa for Colonel Paley to Captain Hans Habe, 14 July 1945, RG 260, OMGUS, 5/270–1/28, IfZ; Memorandum 20 August 1945, RG 260, OMGUS/ICD 5/266–1/17, BArch; Habe, interview by Harold J. Hurwitz, Munich, 23 January 1950, RG 260, OMGUS 3/429–2/39, IfZ; Habe, *Im Jahre Null*, 82; Habe, *Ich stelle mich*, 484.

33. Captain Hans Habe, Headquarters, ICD/USFET, "Verlagshaus Amerika," and "Air-Strip Plan," BArch; Habe, *Im Jahre Null*, 95.

34. Colonel William Paley, USFET/ICD, to Lieutenant Colonel Murphy, 23 August 1945, RG 260, OMGUS 5/266–1/17, BArch; Memorandum, Lt. Colonel C. A. Thompson, Office of the Chief, Plans and Directives, PWD/SHAEF, 17 July 1945, quoted in Hurwitz, *Stunde Null*, 101; Hans Habe to Commanding General, ICD, USFET, 4 September 1945, RG 260, OMGUS 5/266–1/17, BArch.

Open criticism of the project persisted. After the first issue of the *Neue Zeitung* appeared, chiefs of the DISCCs, the Intelligence Section, and a number of press control officers charged that the newspaper contradicted official regulations, that it would overpower its licensed counterparts, that it undermined the ICD's mission, that it would discredit U.S. intentions to restore a free press in Germany, and that no official communication had reached their respective divisions outlining the reasons for the venture.[35]

Habe had already secured official approval from his bosses three weeks before the first issue appeared. In September 1945, the headquarters of the United States Forces European Theater (USFET), the predecessor of OMGUS, defined the mission of the *Neue Zeitung*: it would be a model of a democratic newspaper and "a reminder that the occupying authorities retain the machinery to replace the system of licensing newspapers in the event it becomes necessary." It would provide a voice of the military government and, above all, "a means of projecting American viewpoints into Germany." The proclamation confidently stressed the "reeducational" character of the zonal newspaper. It would not attempt to compete economically with the licensed German papers nor carry advertisements.[36] Even Robert Murphy, the political adviser of the State Department in Germany, argued that the circulation of the paper would increase the department's influence in the U.S. zone.[37]

Habe procured approval for most of the stipulations he requested, including a vague consent to the operation's cultural mission. Occupation authorities cautioned that the paper must be the military governor's mouthpiece and remain, above all, the voice of America in Germany. Instead of two million copies per issue, as projected by Habe, the ICD approved a distribution plan allowing for merely 363,600 copies in eighty-seven towns and cities in the American zone, each receiving between 1,500 and 65,000 copies per issue. Officials from the Plans and Directives Section expected the paper would reach one potential reader in fifteen or twenty.[38]

35. Lt. Col. James G. Chesnutt, Chief Press Section, DISCC, 13 October 1945, to his Commanding Officer, RG 260, OMGUS/ICD 5/241–1/7, BArch. OMGUS officials used the terms *branch* and *section* interchangeably for the lower echelons of military government divisions (W. Phillips Davison, electronic mail to author, 19 May 1998).

36. Headquarters United States Forces European Theater to Commanding Generals, September 1945, FO 1056/56, Public Record Office, Kew/Richmond, Great Britain (hereafter cited as PRO); Memorandum from Lt. Colonel William H. Kinard, ICD, USFET, to Colonel C. R. Powell, 21 September 1945, RG 260, OMGUS, ISD 5/241–1/7, BArch; Hurwitz, *Stunde Null*, 112–13.

37. Albert Norman, *Our German Policy: Propaganda and Culture* (New York: Vantage Press, 1951), 36; Hurwitz, *Stunde Null*, 113.

38. Headquarters USFET, "Circulation Figures for Zonal Newspaper, *Die Neue Zeitung,*

Once the ICD had accepted the establishment of the *Neue Zeitung*, it demanded the paper be published in Frankfurt, close to the division's headquarters and the American sponsored newswire service, DANA (*Deutsche Allgemeine Nachrichtenagentur*). Habe, conversely, wanted to locate his project in the printing plant of Joseph Goebbels's foremost Nazi paper, the *Völkischer Beobachter*, in Munich's artistic district of Schwabing. The argument that the site offered the only "sufficiently large facilities to take care of any information control printing requirements" proved irrefutable. The plant even had enough paper in storage.[39]

The move south offered another advantage to Habe. Decentralization efforts within the military government beginning in the late summer meant that the *Neue Zeitung* and the POB would fall under the jurisdiction of the Office of Military Government for Bavaria. The position between the zone-wide and the regional administration would permit the editorial staff a degree of independence that otherwise would not have been allowed.[40] Habe secretly nurtured one more goal for his endeavor: he wanted to revive the camaraderie and team spirit that had prevailed in his multinational operation during the previous two years. He had reveled in organizing a propaganda machine in Camp Sharpe and guiding this operation from the beaches of Normandy to the ICD center in Bad Nauheim. The *Neue Zeitung* would be his monument to himself and his boys in the P & PW and carry on the old *esprit de corps*. "I do feel," Habe wrote on 11 October 1945, "that the old team spirit has not vanished, which against many odds . . . we [the émigrés] have maintained throughout war and peace."[41]

---

Munich," 11 October 1945, RG 260, OMGUS 2/541–1/7, IfZ; E. N. Reinsel, Headquarters ICD/USFET, to Captain Hans Habe, "Proposed Distribution for Zonal Newspaper," 5 October 1945, RG 260, OMGUS/ISD 5/241–1/7, BArch; Lt. Colonel William H. Kinard, Chief, Plans and Directives Section, ICD/USFET, memorandum to Colonel C. R. Powell, "Zonal U.S. Newspaper," 21 September 1945, RG 260, OMGUS/ISD 5/241–1/7, BArch; "Activities of the Media Sections," approximately August/September 1945, Secret Report from British Observer, FO 1056/57, PRO.

39. Lt. Colonel J. L. Lazonby to Lt. Colonel Unger, "Use of *Völkischer Beobachter* Plant in Munich," 8 August 1945, RG 260, OMGUS/ISD 5/241–1/7, BArch; Colonel B. B. McMahon, Infantry to Press Section, ICD/USFET, 19 September 1945, RG 260, OMGUS 10/116–3/5, Bayerisches Hauptstaatsarchiv, Munich (hereafter cited as BHStA); Oron J. Hale, *The Captive Press in the Third Reich* (Princeton, N.J.: Princeton University Press, 1964), 17–38; Heym, *Nachruf*, 384; Habe, *Ich stelle mich*, 492.

40. Hurwitz, *Stunde Null*, 63, 87, 112, 337; Matz, *US-Zeitungen*, 152–4, 168; Habe, *Im Jahre Null*, 87, 130; Carl Hermann Ebbinghaus, interview, Hinterzarten, 25 October 1992; Joy Darlene Winkie, "A Study of the United States Information and Propaganda Activities in the Federal Republic of Germany" (Master's thesis, University of Minnesota, Minneapolis, Minn., 1958), 11.

41. Memorandum by Hans Habe, ICD/USFET, 11 Oct. 1945, RG 260, OMGUS/ICD 5/266–1/17, BArch; Peter Wyden, *Stella* (New York: Simon and Schuster, 1992), 240.

Habe envisioned a largely autonomous enterprise. General Dwight D. Eisenhower, now military governor in Germany, harbored more interventionist designs. He resented the Germans because their resistance had forced him and his soldiers to destroy large parts of Central Europe, killing innumerable civilians.[42] No bureaucrat at heart, he also felt misplaced in the occupation administration. Ike's stint as military governor proved an anticlimax to his wartime experience. Disliking the jurisdictional and political disputes in occupied Germany, he happily left the country in late 1945 to become the army's chief of staff. He was outraged at the Germans' wartime behavior and as military governor of the U.S. zone, he enthusiastically enforced denazification, including JCS 1067. "The German is a beast," he wrote to his wife in 1944. And in another context: "God, I hate the Germans." It would take years to alter this attitude.[43]

Eisenhower reserved a column on the front page of the premier issue of the *Neue Zeitung* to express his intentions clearly. "The *Neue Zeitung*, although it is published in the German language, in no way attempts to be a 'German' newspaper," he wrote on 18 October 1945. "Militaristic ideas must be erased from the German mind. For all civilized nations on this earth, aggresion [*sic*] is immoral; the Germans, however, have to be educated to this self-evident truth."[44] By no means would the paper be a tool of intercultural communication, as Habe had envisioned it.

The statement reflected an unflinching attitude. Habe reacted strongly when General Eisenhower dictated this declaration to him in his office in the Frankfurt IG-Farben building. In response to Habe's question about Germany's future, Ike related: "The Germans don't have to worry about politics. They have to make sure that they have enough to eat, for we are not going to feed them forever." Eisenhower, more concerned with the organization of material supplies and administrative hassles in the U.S. zone, ignored the émigrés' distinction between "good" and "bad" Germans. Instead, the general continued, "you have to tell the Germans. That's the language they un-

42. Günter Bischof and Stephen E. Ambrose, eds., *Eisenhower and the German POWs: Facts against Falsehood* (Baton Rouge, La.: Louisiana State University Press, 1992), 25, 31.

43. Stephen E. Ambrose, "Eisenhower and the Germans," in Bischof and Ambrose, *Eisenhower and the German POWs*, 29–38. See also Robert Murphy, *Diplomat Among Warriors* (Garden City, N.Y.: Doubleday, 1964), 296; Stephen E. Ambrose, *Eisenhower*, vol. 1, *Soldier, General of the Army, President Elect, 1890–1952* (New York: Simon and Schuster, 1983), 415–32; Eisenhower to Edward Everett Hazlett, Jr., 27 November 1945, reprinted in Dwight D. Eisenhower, *The Papers of Dwight David Eisenhower*, ed. Alfred D. Chandler, Jr., and Louis Galambos (Baltimore: Johns Hopkins University Press, 1978), 6:552–57.

44. "General Eisenhower an die *Neue Zeitung*: Opening Words—Zum Geleit," *Neue Zeitung*, 18 September 1945, p. 1.

derstand." Habe disagreed. Merely "telling the people" would not elicit acceptance. "This is not a popularity contest," the general replied abruptly.[45]

To Eisenhower the relation between Germans and Americans was invariably a monologue with Americans talking and Germans obediently listening. Habe strove to give locals a voice and to initiate a cultural dialogue between the two peoples. These two different goals lay at the heart of a conflict that would affect the paper for the next decade: How could one communicate with one's former enemies?

Captain Hans Habe's proposal in 1945 to create a U.S. newspaper in German for the vanquished people reflected a binational concept of mutual communication and understanding. In sharp contrast to the U.S. government's policy of austerity that accused all Germans of "collective guilt," Habe and many of his fellow émigrés maintained a more nuanced view. They had a foot each in German and U.S. culture and an interest in making German civilians and U.S. soldiers interact. Habe believed that an overemphasis on Americana would alienate his readers and deepen their skepticism about the occupation army. He proposed a carrot-and-stick approach: reeducation wrapped in the context of German culture. The public response would prove the success of this concept.

The Information Control Division welcomed the idea of having a voice in the American occupation zone but did not view it as a necessity. Although the *Neue Zeitung* would be regarded as "the overt organ of the U.S. Military Government," it was, in fact, a rather accidental enterprise. It had sprung from the mind of a European émigré with journalistic expertise who happened to be in the U.S. Army. The emerging conflicts would lead to an ongoing tug-of-war over the nature of both the newspaper and the entire reeducation program.

45. Hans Habe, *Our Love Affair with Germany* (New York: Putnam's, 1953), 105ff.; Habe, *Im Jahre Null*, 85ff.; Habe, *Ich stelle mich*, 490ff.; Ambrose, *Eisenhower*, 421.

2

# WHAT IS AN AMERICAN? PROFILES OF THE ACTORS

*We do not benefit from the poets who are now writing voluminous war novels. Those books will be printed and read in two years—presuming there will be any paper. And until then, good heavens, until then the whole globe including Europe, in the midst of which, of course, lies Germany, may have exploded and turned into minced meat.*

—Erich Kästner, "Der tägliche Kram" (1946)

WHAT MUST IT HAVE BEEN LIKE TO BEGIN PUBLISHING A NEWSPAPER, USUALLY a minor and routine endeavor, among the ruins of postwar Munich? Both the returning émigrés and their German colleagues experienced profound torment, devotion, enthusiasm, and perseverance. Staffers in Schellingstraße 39 as well as their critics shared a belief that they were shaping the postwar world. But each faction nurtured different strategies for accomplishing this goal. The following paragraphs introduce the men and women Hans Habe recruited for the *Neue Zeitung* as well as his supporters and his opponents.

No clear statistics exist detailing the editorial staff. Initially, it consisted of some fifty members, but there is no consensus about the ratio of Germans to Americans. Sources range from "half Germans, half Americans" to only 20 percent German and 80 percent American members on the staff.[1] Collective memories, however, converge on two points. As a group, the émigrés were accepted by the German staff as legitimate functionaries of a conquering army; despite their German heritage, the émigrés spoke English, wore uniforms, formulated policy, managed daily operations, and decided on articles in closed-door sessions. However, as individuals they were received more hesitantly and generally not easily accepted as Americans.

1. Selective list of German editors, Hans-Joachim Netzer collection, ED 352, IfZ; Netzer, "Die *Neue Zeitung*," 15; Hans Wallenberg, "Dank an die Mitarbeiter," *Neue Zeitung*, 21 October 1946, p. 11; Matz, *Zeitungen der US-Armee*, 77; Kurt Koszyk, *Pressepolitik für Deutsche, 1945–1949* (Berlin: Colloquium Verlag, 1986), 45; Habe, *Im Jahre Null*, 89.

For example, the German reporters always felt that the émigré Hans Wallenberg "wanted to make clear that he was not an American." Son of an old Jewish journalist family from Berlin, Wallenberg had received his training in the prestigious Ullstein publishing house after completing his studies in philosophy and law. Under the worst financial strains, he emigrated to the United States in 1938, where he eventually joined a printing shop in downtown New York and received U.S. citizenship. But Wallenberg never became an American at heart. A heavy Berlin accent made his English difficult to understand. The thirty-eight-year-old was arrested several times by the U.S. military police while driving a German Mercedes that supposedly had belonged to the *Führer.* "Where are you from?" a military policeman harshly asked him on one occasion. "From New York," the editor replied with his thick Berlin accent. "What are the subway stops between 125th Street and Borough Hall on the IRT?" queried the MP, using a common trick to test the integrity of dubious individuals in uniform. Without hesitation, Wallenberg listed them, and added in driving off: "I can also tell you all the stops from Berlin to Potsdam."

Wallenberg also voiced his sympathy for Germans who had fallen prey to Hitler's rhetoric. One night he confessed to Ernst Lemmer, vice chairman of the Christian Democrats in the Soviet zone, that "I cannot rule out the possibility that if I had stayed in Germany, I would have become a member of the NSDAP."[2]

The European-born émigrés conducted their operations relatively free from interference. The only genuine American staff member of influence was the military and technical supervisor, twenty-seven-year-old Captain William S. Konecky, a New York printer, who was the highest-ranking officer among the staffers and thus, militarily, in charge of the entire plant. Yet the young man spoke no German and "didn't care" about the philosophy of the paper. Konecky was "very fond" of Captain Habe. So fond that even

2. Jack M. Stuart, interview, New York, 12 July 1993; Hans-Joachim Netzer, interview, Munich, 13 December 1991; and Carl Hermann Ebbinghaus, interview; "Profilierter Publizist und rühriger Organisator: Gespräch mit Hans Wallenberg," *Allgemeine unabhängige jüdische Wochenzeitung*, 24 December 1971, p. 11; Hans Wallenberg, interview by Alfred Fischer; Herbert A. Strauss and Werner Röder, *International Biographical Dictionary of Central European Emigrés, 1933–1945* (Munich: K. G. Saur, 1980–1983), 1: 790–91; Wyden, *Stella*, 115; Axel Springer, "Zum 65. Geburtstag von Hans Wallenberg: 'In Berlin wird der Kampf um die Freiheit gewonnen,' " *Die Welt*, 27 November 1972, p. 4; questionnaire filled out by Hans Wallenberg, MA 1500/62, IfZ; W. P. Davison, "Building a Democratic Press," address delivered before the Nassau Club, Princeton, N.J., 8 January 1947, manuscript, RG 260, OMGUS/ISD 5/238–3/11, IfZ; Peter Bönisch, interview, Munich, 22 September 1992; Egon Bahr, interview by author, Bonn, 16 November 1992; Egon Bahr, *Zu meiner Zeit* (Munich: Blessing, 1996), 30.

though Habe and his boys had once had the villa they inhabited full of German women, he hesitated to court-martial them for violating the nonfraternization ban and instead fined them two-thirds of a month's pay. Thus like most U.S. soldiers in postwar Germany, they enjoyed a luxurious life in a world of plenty amid hunger and deprivation. They lived in villas that had formerly belonged to the local elite, often on a far better scale than they had ever enjoyed at home. They were young, at an age when men are flexible and open to changes, challenges, and adventures. They had German girlfriends who adored them because they had an air of victory, wealth, and worldliness. And they were rich because their pay was high and the exchange rate—ten occupation marks to the dollar—was low. Some of them participated in a flourishing black market in which U.S. cigarettes, at ten marks each, formed the currency.[3]

With himself head of the publication branch, Habe appointed Captain Hans Wallenberg as chief editor of the paper. Lieutenant Stefan Heym, from Chemnitz, a best-selling author with a home in New York, led the political and literary section. Twenty-three-year-old Sergeant Peter Weidenreich, born in Berlin and, in civilian life, a reporter for the *Daily Metal Worker* in New York, took charge of the Berlin bureau. Sergeant Ernest Wynder from Westphalia, an aspiring medical student, directed the Monitoring Services while Sergeant Erich Winters, a former business student, led the World News section. Karl Löwenstein from New York, born in Westphalia, tended to technical matters. Sergeants Jules Bond and Arthur Steiner, Habe's cohorts from earlier days in Vienna, joined the editorial board.[4]

Most surprisingly, despite the editors' Jewishness, their often painful exile, and their experiences in German concentration camps, they often came to feel concern rather than hatred for the local population. "When I came to [Germany] . . . I had, of course, a strange feeling," Karl Löwenstein remembers today. "But when I saw the first children, little children on the

3. William S. Konecky, interview, New York, 23 March 1993; manuscript by James Warburg, n. p., n. d. (1946?), Dean Acheson papers, box 27, "Assistant Secretary and Undersecretary of State, 1941–1948," folder "State Department—Under Secretary—correspondence, 1945–47," Harry S. Truman Library, Independence, Miss. (hereafter cited as HSTL); Peter Wyden, interview.

4. Captain Hans Habe, Headquarters, ICD/USFET, "Verlagshaus Amerika," and "Air-Strip Plan," BArch; Max W. Kraus, interviews, Washington, D.C., 6 and 13 August 1991; Ernest Wynder, interview, New York, 19 March 1993; Peter Wyden, interview; Karl Löwenstein, interview, New York, 22 March 1993; and William Konecky, interview; Stefan Heym, Berlin, letter to the author, 6 January 1993; Andrew Gregoriades, Geneva, letter to the author, 6 December 1992; Strauss and Röder, *International Biographical Dictionary*, vol. 2, pt. 2, p. 1115; U.S. Department of State, *The Register of the U.S. Department of State,* No. 15 (Washington, D.C.: Government Printing Office, 1950), 52, 114, 287, 525.

street, begging for whatever, my whole attitude changed. How could I possibly hate children?" Their concern was often coupled with a sense of culpability. Ever since Ernst Cramer learned that his family had been killed by the Nazis, he had been blaming himself for not leaving Germany in time to help his parents flee the country: "I did not recognize early enough that the Nazis were serious when they talked about the 'extinction of the Jewish race.' When we began to realize the horrible truth, it was too late."[5]

The interrelationships among the people involved with the paper are crucial to understanding the atmosphere and mission characterizing the venture. Both the émigrés and the Germans were divided by sharp generational differences shaping their understanding of the job and Germany. The lines between the editorial staffers at the *Neue Zeitung* did not run vertically, that is between Germans and Americans, but horizontally, between the younger and the older generations.

Those who had been older than twenty at the time of their emigration clearly reflected upon their feelings for the Germans and the purpose of their mission. As journalists or writers in the 1930s, they had been persecuted for racial and political reasons. They had emigrated not only physically but also intellectually. Returning to Germany proved to be much more evocative for them than it did for the younger generation. One exiled writer explained the many sources of poignant resonance: "I cannot forget the first word that I learned, the first landscape that I saw, the first friendliness, the first pain, the first enthusiasm. Those were German . . . and they will remain part of my nature."[6]

Ernst Cramer, for example, vehemently rejected the notion of being a true American. At the age of twenty-five, this son of a German-Jewish cigar store owner in Augsburg had left the country following his release from the Buchenwald concentration camp in 1939. Shortly after the Japanese attack on Pearl Harbor, Cramer volunteered for the U.S. army because, as an expelled German, he felt this was "his" war. "These people had kicked me out," he recalls today. "And now all kinds of other people . . . fought for reconstructing democracy in this country. It's just as simple as that, I told myself. . . . This war, I have to be in it."[7]

Hans Habe, two years Cramer's senior, was even more outspoken about

5. Karl Löwenstein, interview; typewritten manuscript, "Dankrede von Ernst Cramer aus Anlaß der Verleihung der Ehrendoktorwürde der Bar-Ilan Universität," speech given on 30 October 1994, in the Centrum Judaicum Berlin, courtesy of Ernst Cramer.

6. Martin Gumpert, "Berlin: Ein Nekrolog," *Neue Zeitung*, 22 February 1946, *Feuilleton*.

7. Cramer counted among Habe's "psycho boys" in Camp Sharpe and joined the *Neue Zeitung* as deputy editor in chief in 1948. Ernst Cramer, interviews, Berlin, 16 December 1991 and 6 January 1993; Wyden, *Stella*, 72f.

his intentions in Germany. "In order to serve a country, it is sufficient to believe in her institutions, her principles, and in her righteousness. My emotional affection, however, belongs to Europe." Like a missionary spreading the gospel among the savages, Habe thought he would spread new democratic ideas and faith among the ignorant Germans, preaching a catechism of tolerance, individualism, self-sufficiency, public discussion, optimism, and the pursuit of happiness.[8]

Sergeant Stefan Heym, born in 1913 in the Saxonian town of Chemnitz, felt a similar missionary fervor. Fellow soldiers secretly called him "*Dichterfürst*," the Prince of Poets. Heym was the author of *Hostages*, a best-selling novel about the Nazi occupation in Prague, that had recently been turned into a movie starring Hollywood actress Luise Rainer. For Heym, this war was not an army job, as it was for the younger émigrés. It represented the climax of all wars, "a mortal clash of ideologies in which we were privileged to make our typewriters sing."[9]

The younger of the "Habe boys," who had gone to the United States as children or teenagers, conversely, viewed the *Neue Zeitung* merely as a military job. Most of them had emigrated along with their parents and had received an American education. Filled with gratitude to the United States, they saw themselves as Americans who coincidentally mastered German.[10] Sergeant Peter Weidenreich, barely twenty-two years old, regarded himself as a Berliner by accident of birth, but the city, now essentially a burned-out mass of rubble, had ceased being his home long ago: "Home was on East Twentieth Street in Manhattan." Nothing had been left of his parents' former house on Kantstrasse 128 except a crumbling facade that was soon to be razed to make room for a parking lot. "It was like going back to my *kinderzimmer* [nursery]. Kind of interesting but not that big a deal." His privileged status—he earned $7,500 a year as the chief of the Berlin bureau of the *Neue Zeitung* and wore tailor-made suits—did not outweigh his disgust. "I wanted out. I hungered for the real world, for the comforts of the conventional, for life consistent with my age and status as an American, not some hybrid in Berlin."[11]

Consequently, the young émigrés gave little thought to their jobs in psy-

8. Habe, *Ich stelle mich*, 430, 440; "Don Juan oder Cäsar," *Sonntagsjournal*, no. 28, 9 July 1972, p. 10–16; Habe, *Ich stelle mich*, 483, 496; Matz, *Zeitungen der US-Armee*, 78f.

9. Heym, *Nachruf*, 362; quote in Peter Wyden, *Wall: The Untold Story of Divided Berlin* (New York: Simon & Schuster, 1989), 522.

10. Kurt Wittler, interview, San Francisco, 22 July 1993; Kurt Wittler, Pasadena, Calif., letter to the author, 18 August 1993.

11. Wyden, *Stella*, 237–38, 243f.; Wyden, *Wall*, 179; Peter Wyden, interview; Wyden, "Die bunte Truppe von Camp Shapiro."

chological warfare. "In those days, [I] did not specifically reflect on what Germany under Hitler had done to my family," remembers Ernest Wynder who had gone to the United States in 1938 at the age of sixteen. Dark-haired, with bushy eyebrows and almost piercing eyes, the aspiring physician had finished his education in New York in 1943 before joining the Mobile Radio Broadcasting Group in Gettysburg. His fellow sergeant, Max Kraus, then a twenty-five-year-old sergeant with a Harvard degree, concurs: "I never really tried to put this into a philosophical concept. We all were much too busy to do what we were supposed to do . . . for that to sit back and say 'Why am I doing this and what am I trying to achieve?' "[12]

Accounts from the young exiles offer a consistent, composite résumé. They had no serious girlfriends, no complete education, no career, and no network of associates in Germany before their emigration. All they wanted was to return home to America and lead a normal life. Some even went to court to anglicize their names legally because, as Weidenreich described it, "it kept getting mangled and seemed too much of a load to carry around."[13]

The age of the individual émigré at the time of his departure acted as a more crucial influence on his or her views about life, war, and propaganda than any other factor. Those who were seventeen or younger when they left Germany had fully assimilated into American life. They perceived themselves as Americans, attempted to lose their German accents, and most of them married American women. Those who were twenty or older at the time of their departure, and who had perhaps even spent some time in another refugee country, developed a much more complex view of Germany and their mission in the war. Their primary education had been European. Their first love had been a Czech, an Austrian, or a Hungarian girl. Many eventually married women of European descent. And they always retained a strong German accent, as most people cannot master the accent of another language with native fluency if they start to learn that language after puberty. The turning point seems to be the age of seventeen, between Max Kraus, born in 1920, and Stefan Heym, born in 1913.

This differentiation is crucial for two reasons. It points to a distinctive group of soldiers who shared certain ties to the country they were supposed to reeducate. Only generational differences split them. The older émigrés had greater power and bore more responsibility in the printing plant.

12. Ernest Wynder, Memorial Center for Cancer and Allied Diseases, New York, letter to Hans Habe, Munich, 5 May 1954, Hans Habe Collection, Landesarchiv Berlin (hereafter cited as LAB); Wynder, letter to the author, 27 July 1993; Ernest L. Wynder, interview, and Max Kraus, interviews, Washington, D.C., 6 and 13 July 1991.

13. Wyden, *Stella*, 34.

Though both groups had roots in Germany and in the United States, those who exerted the most influence in the plant had the least cultural attachment to America.

German *Kultur* had formed the émigrés' *Bildung* (knowledge, education). Since the nineteenth century, *Bildung*, a key value of the German bourgeoisie, had been an important factor contributing to Jewish identity in Germany. As Abraham Peck and others have shown, *Bildung* included "character formation, moral education, the primacy of culture and a belief in the potential of humanity." Before the war, it offered a bridge for Jewish intellectuals to communicate with their non-Jewish German counterparts when all other avenues of professional and social contacts were closed off.[14] And as was to be expected, in 1945 the émigrés picked up the reins where they had laid them down before their escape from Germany.

What is surprising is the absence of any separate Jewish identity; in fact the editors' Jewishness was a very peripheral feature of their identity. In their private lives as well as later in the pages of the *Neue Zeitung*, the émigrés always defined themselves by their German heritage, never by their Jewish descent. Even when commenting on the foundation of the Jewish state and the rise of anti-Semitism in postwar Germany, they declined to hint at their background. Freelance contributor Alfred Kantorowicz, for example, had been an editor for the renowned *Vossische Zeitung*. In 1931, the thirty-two-year-old had joined the KPD, and two years later he went underground and eventually into exile. In one of his essays in the *Neue Zeitung*, he condemned the burning of German literature by the Nazis, but he did not mention the burning of Jewish synagogues by so much as a word. Most of the non-Jewish staffers at the *Neue Zeitung* could never tell if an émigré had left the country because of political or ethnic reasons. Hans Wallenberg, as Isolde Kolbenhoff remembers, "was for us a typical Berlin journalist. Only many years later did I hear that he was a Jew."[15] It was their Central Euro-

14. Abraham J. Peck, ed., *The German-Jewish Legacy in America, 1938–1988: From Bildung to the Bill of Rights* (Detroit: Wayne State University Press, 1989), 5; George L. Mosse, "The End Is Not Yet: A Personal Memoir of the German-Jewish Legacy in America," in Peck, *The German-Jewish Legacy*, 1–15; David J. Sorkin, *The Transformation of German Jewry, 1780–1840* (New York: Oxford University Press, 1987); George L. Mosse, *German Jews Beyond Judaism,* (Bloomington, Ind.: Indiana University Press, 1985); Jessica C. E. Gienow-Hecht, "Art Is Democracy and Democracy Is Art: Culture, Propaganda, and the *Neue Zeitung* in Germany, 1944–1947," *Diplomatic History*, 23 (Winter 1999): 21–43.

15. Alfred Kantorowicz, "Erinnerung an den 10. Mai 1933," *Neue Zeitung,* 13 May 1946, *Feuilleton*; Strauss and Röder, *International Biographical Dictionary,* 2: 593; Alfred Kantorowicz, autobiographical summary, manuscript, John Lehmann collection, Harry Ransom Humanities Research Center, University of Texas, Austin (hereafter cited as HRHRC); letter from John Lehmann, Piccadilly, Wisconsin, to Alfred Kantorowicz, New York City, 14 November

peanness and the fact that they were, culturally speaking, mainstream Germans that connected the émigrés with the German staff.

Profiles of the German women and men hired by the *Neue Zeitung* reveal the same generational split as the émigré portraits. While most of the older staff members nourished a political agenda, the younger reporters regarded the plant as a training ground.[16] Habe listed two main criteria in selecting employees: newspaper experience and untainted politics. "If you cannot find people with newspaper experience," he told Max Kraus, "then find politically clean people who strike you as intelligent and can be trained as journalists." Those instructions ignored two military government orders. First, the screening center of the Counter Intelligence Corps (CIC) had to clear prospective journalists before they could start working, and second, the nonfraternization order forbade U.S. soldiers to communicate privately with German citizens. But Habe, impatient, felt the nonfraternization order reflected "satanic nonsense" in the first place.[17]

Habe believed securing German names with high recognition would open the way to the newspaper's success. Stars from the pre-Nazi past would lend an air of both glory and familiarity to his "movie" called democratization. Erich Kästner, one of the most renowned novelists in Weimar Germany, became the chief of the cultural section. Kästner's fabulous tales, such as the criminal story *Emil und die Detektive*, fascinated children. The dark-haired author, whose bushy black eyebrows gave him a stern appearance, had refused to leave the country, despite the fact that Nazi orders forced him to publish under a pseudonym.[18]

---

1940, ibid.; Hans Habe, "Nicht jener brutale Antisemitismus," *Neue Zeitung*, 16 August 1946, p. 5; "Der Sprung in die fremde Sprache," *Neue Zeitung*, 8 November 1946, *Feuilleton*; "Der jüdische Staat," *Neue Zeitung*, 12 December 1947, p. 4; "Steigender Antisemitismus," *Neue Zeitung*, 5 May 1947, p. 2; Isolde Kolbenhoff, wife of Walter Kolbenhoff, telephone interview, Germering, 15 April 1997.

16. Wyden, *Stella*, 243; Beatrice del Bondio-Reventlow, letter to the author, 21 February 1993; Bittorf, "Die *Neue Zeitung* im Spiegel Münchener Gesellschaft und Kultur," 15; Wolfgang Burkhardt, "Die Feuilleton- und Kunstbeilage der *Neuen Zeitung*," 13; Netzer, "Die *Neue Zeitung*," 16.

17. Max W. Kraus, interview, 6 July 1991; "Major O'Hara hat ein Geheimnis," handwritten manuscript for a novel, Hans Habe Collection, MBU; Habe, *Im Jahre Null*, 117; Hurwitz, *Stunde Null*, 83, 106f., 124, 148.

18. Reference card Erich Kästner (Berthold Bürger), Documents of the Prussian Department of the Interior, ref. 4709/71, Fb 223, IfZ; Max W. Kraus, interview, 6 July 1991; Wehner, "Zur politischen Kultur im Nachkriegsdeutschland," 25–26; Luiselotte Enderle, *Erich Kästner* (Munich: Rowohlt, 1966), 50–92; Kästner, *Der tägliche Kram: Chansons und Prosa, 1945–*

Since most of those with clean records were too young to draw on a writer's background, the *Neue Zeitung* hired many "green" reporters. Twenty-four-year-old Hildegard Brücher, later Hamm-Brücher, a chemistry student from the Ruhr area, became the correspondent for natural science articles. Twenty-three-year-old Egon Bahr from Thuringia had worked for the Soviet-licensed paper *Berliner Zeitung*. His boss had not been very happy with his individualistic reporting that lacked "the viewpoint of the class struggle." When Bahr insisted on attending meetings of the East Berlin City Council, the deputy mayor Karl Maron urged the young man's dismissal. In the fall of 1945 Bahr enlisted in the Berlin bureau of the *Neue Zeitung*.[19]

Young Olaf Meitzner had worked on an assembly line in the Messerschmidt arms factory in Augsburg until Germany's surrender. After the war, Meitzner worked as an interpreter in the local military government before Max Kraus decided to try his research abilities: "Find out if the mayor of Augsburg [Wilhelm Ott] is a Nazi," Kraus told Meitzner. When he returned with a negative answer, he received a slap on the shoulder and a job contract as a reporter.[20]

Inge Ungewitter had spent the war in South America before she returned to Munich in 1945. A beautiful girl in her twenties, she had an expressive face and slim figure, both of which constantly caught the American GIs' attention. One day, as she waited in a *Neue Zeitung* office for her date, editor Egon Jameson yelled at her: "Why the heck are you standing around here? Do something useful!" The next day the paper hired Ungewitter as a cartoonist.[21]

According to Directive No. 4 of the military government, only people who had openly opposed the Hitler regime were to be employed in the postwar press. Journalistic abilities did not constitute a qualification. Former

---

*1948* (Zurich: Atrium, 1949), 1–7; Erich Kästner, *Notabene 45: Ein Tagebuch von Erich Kästner* (Berlin: Cecilia Dressler Verlag, 1961), 191–95; Klaus Kordon, *Die Zeit ist kaputt: Die Lebensgeschichte des Erich Kästner* (Weinheim: Beltz & Gelberg Verlag, 1995), 159–74; Bettina Wegwitz, "Erich Kästner als Redakteur: Journalist der Nachkriegszeit für die *Neue Zeitung* und den *Pinguin*," (Master's thesis, Ludwig-Maximilians-Universität, Munich, 1989).

19. Ursula Salentin, *Hildegard Hamm-Brücher: Der Lebensweg einer eigenwilligen Demokratin* (Freiburg i. Br.: Herderbücherei, 1987), 22–36; "Wer ist Frau Hamm-Brücher? Das 'unbequeme Weibsbild' der FDP" in *Die Welt*, 3 December 1962; Max W. Kraus, interview, 6 July 1991; Egon Bahr, interview; Egon Bahr, "Als rasender Reporter im zerstörten Berlin," in Gustav Trampe, *Die Stunde Null: Erinnerungen an Kriegsende und Neuanfang* (Stuttgart: Deutsche Verlags-Anstalt, 1995), 293–300; Bahr, *Zu meiner Zeit*, 26–29; Wyden, *Wall*, 210f.

20. Olaf Meitzner, interview, Munich, 28 August 1992; Karl-Ulrich Gelberg, ed., *Kriegsende und Neuanfang in Augsburg 1945: Erinnerungen und Berichte* (Munich: Oldenbourg Verlag, 1996).

21. Inge Ungewitter, interview, Munich, 21 September 1992.

party members, promoters of racism or militarism, and those who had supported the NSDAP morally or materially were banned from the profession. The *Neue Zeitung*, however, hired a number of people whose records, according to the CIC, seemed tainted. Above all, quite a number of the staff members had been in the Hitler-Jugend (Hitler Youth), which had been mandatory, or the *Wehrmacht*. Some had voluntarily extended their services to the party. Editor Willi Rehm, born in 1910, a specialist in economic affairs, had applied to join the party and had frequently contributed to the *Völkischer Beobachter*. Months after he had begun to work for the *Neue Zeitung*, the intelligence center blacklisted Rehm, stating that "he certainly is not a man who should be connected with one of our overt [*official army*, J. G.-H.] publications." Habe nonetheless considered him "one of the outstanding and most constructive economic editors in Germany" and did not fire him.[22]

Walter Hagemann (born in 1900), employed to cover German politics, had worked as the chief editor of *Germania*, a Catholic paper tolerated by the Nazis until 1938. The CIC blacklisted Hagemann because he tried "to impress the German leadership with the fact that a good German Catholic can, at the same time, be a good Nazi." Habe again overrode CIC dictates and hired him. Hagemann then went on to become a professor of journalism at the University of Münster and published an analysis of the Nazis' press control.[23]

After five days of psychological testing, the CIC also blacklisted Hans

22. Johannes Schmitz, "DANA/DENA: Nachrichtenagentur in der amerikanisch besetzten Zone Deutschlands, 1945–1949" (Master's thesis, Ludwig-Maximilians-Universität, Munich, 1984), 49f.; Fred Bleyser, U.S. civ., to Capt. Peter Hart, Chief of Intelligence, 6870 DISCC, 26 January 1946, "Willi Rehm, editor of the *Neue Zeitung* in Munich," RG 260, OMGBY 10/117–1/6, BHStA; Erich W. Isenstead, Intelligence Officer, ICD/OMGBY, to Team Chief, Munich Detachment, 18 April 1946, "Willi Rehm," ibid.; Report to ICD/OMGBY, 8 April 1946, "Willi Rehm, Editor of the *Neue Zeitung* in Munich," RG 260, OMGUS 5/269–1/7, IfZ. Regarding the notion of a "civilian in the army," in the military there exist specialized positions that can be filled only by nonmilitary personnel. They receive "assimilated ranks" in order to facilitate their administration. I am indebted to W. Phillips Davison for this information.

23. Report to Captain Peter Hart, OMGBY/ICD, 7 February 1946, FO 1056/56, PRO; "Persons in Germany active in Propaganda, Press and Publication, Theatre and Film, Radio or Advertising, believed to be pro-Nazi in attitude," 7 September 1945, RG 331, Records of Allied Operational and Occupation Headquarters World War II, Entry 87, box 10, dec. file 091.412, NARA; Duncan Wilson, Controller "B" Group, Information Services Control Branch, Control Commission for Germany (BE), (British) to Major General W. H. A. Bishop, Chief, PR/ISC Group, Control Commission for Germany (BE) Berlin, 26 February 1946, FO 1056/57, PRO; Walter Hagemann, *Publizistik im Dritten Reich: Ein Beitrag zur Methodik der Massenführung* (Hamburg: Hansischer Gildenverlag, 1948); Frei and Schmitz, *Journalismus im Dritten Reich*, 181f.

Lehmann, born in 1909. His activities in the Third Reich appeared opportunistic, if not collaborationist, to the investigators. Lehmann had served as political editor for the *Leipziger Neueste Nachrichten*. Upon his return from the screening center, Habe told him: "Stay with us at this paper. If you go some place else, they will come running after you." Lehmann led the foreign policy section until February 1949.[24]

Walter Kiaulehn, born in 1900, was blacklisted for his work as assistant editor on economic matters at a publishing house, Deutscher Verlag. He was rumored to have written for *Signal*, a propaganda magazine geared toward exporting the Nazi "truth" to foreign countries. Kiaulehn published quite vociferous antifascist pieces in the cultural section, beginning in the fall of 1945.[25]

Elisabeth Noelle had been a political editor for *Das Reich* in Berlin, a weekly that regularly published editorials by Joseph Goebbels. Noelle had written reports on such topics as Jewish monopolies in the United States before her resignation in 1942. According to a newspaper article published in 1986, the CIC recommended that Ms. Noelle was "not to be employed." The *Neue Zeitung* did not heed this advice either.[26]

There remains little doubt that Hans Habe's tolerance vis-à-vis all these staffers stemmed from his own former involvement with Austro-Fascism in the 1930s. As the content analysis will show, throughout his editorship, the staff of *Neue Zeitung* showed great sensitivity when writing about the "gray area" of Germans between guilt and innocence. Much of this was certainly grounded in the fact that a number of editors had themselves experienced the gray area during the Nazi era.

The native German employees shared a common enthusiasm for their opportunities at the plant and their newfound freedom. "It came close to the miraculous," cultural editor Alfred Andersch remembered decades later. "Thirty-one years old, I found myself in a world which for twelve years I thought I would never be able to enter." The German employees assumed they were working for a "German newspaper" and retained fond memories

24. Hans Lehmann, interview, Stockdorf, 17 October 1992; Norbert Frei, *Lizenzpolitik*, 41.

25. "Persons in Germany active in Propaganda," 7 September 1945, RG 331, Entry 87, box 10, dec. file 091.412, NARA; Frank Klier to Ernst Langendorf, Chief Press Branch, OMGBY, 21 January 1947, RG 260, OMGBY 10/117–2/16, BHStA; Habe, *Im Jahre Null*, 122ff.; Herbert Stick, "Von einem, der sein Gesicht verlor," in *Die Weltbühne* (East Germany), (2 July 1952) 7: 27.

26. Frei and Schmitz, *Journalismus im Dritten Reich*, 110, 114ff.; Richard Albrecht, "Für alle Jahreszeiten: Elisabeth Noelle-Neumanns unbewältigte Vergangenheit," *taz*, 10 June 1986, p. 13.

of these early years. "I felt so free because for the first time in my life I did not have to be afraid anymore," said Hildegard Brücher.[27]

The German editors who belonged to the older generation (thirty-five or older) differed fundamentally from their younger colleagues. They had formed their political beliefs before the Nazis came to power and were politically more defined. Their literary expertise and political experience made them indispensable to the existence of the *Neue Zeitung*. Forty-five-year-old Erich Kästner assembled the material and a feature staff for a first-class cultural section. As a result of his popularity before the war, he attracted many readers who reportedly bought the paper just to read his essays.[28]

Equally vital to the endeavor was Else Reventlow, an unyielding Social Democrat. Married to a descendant of a Danish noble family, Reventlow had joined the SPD in 1918. She had passed the war partly in jail. Her political connections—she had meetings with SPD leader Kurt Schumacher and Ernst Reuter, the future mayor of Berlin—were key sources for the *Neue Zeitung*. Similarly, Hans Lehmann's knowledge of foreign affairs was crucial to the paper's success. Lehmann could write an article on the political situation almost anywhere in the world despite the lack of references.[29]

These older men and women shared firm, though varying, beliefs regarding Germany's future. Erich Kästner insisted on a nonpolitical stance but constantly denounced the Germans' blind submissiveness. An outright conservative, Hans Lehmann believed Germany had to undergo an extensive period of hardship under Allied occupation before the country would be accepted into the community of nations, led by a German-born person. Else Reventlow, conversely, strongly supported the Social Democrats and the nascent women's movement. More to the left were Alfred Andersch, the

27. Stephan Reinhardt, *Alfred Andersch: Eine Biographie* (Zurich: Diogenes Verlag, 1990), 114–31; Alfred Andersch, *Die Kirschen der Freiheit* (Stuttgart: Reclam, 1967); Gerhard Hay, "Literarische Positionen im München der Nachkriegszeit," in *Trümmerzeit in München: Kultur und Gesellschaft einer deutschen Großstadt im Aufbruch, 1945–1949*, ed. Friedrich Prinz (Munich: C. H. Beck, 1984), 209–19; Alfred Andersch, "Der Seesack," in *Literaturmagazin 7: Nachkriegsliteratur*, ed. Nicolaus Born and Jürgen Manthey (Reinbek b. Hamburg: Rowohlt, 1977), 117, 128; Hildegard Hamm-Brücher in Susanne Bittorf, "Die Insel in der Schellingstraße," broadcasted in Bayerischer Rundfunk, 25 September 1983, 10:07 P.M., manuscript, Hans-Joachim Netzer Collection, IfZ.

28. Kästner, *Der tägliche Kram*, 6; Alfred Andersch, "Fabian wird positiv," *Der Ruf: Unabhängige Blätter der jungen Generation* 1 (3) (1946):8.

29. Beatrice del Bondio-Reventlow, letter to the author, 21 February 1993; Employment Contract between Else Reventlow and Hans Wallenberg, POB, 1 November 1946 (Mrs. Reventlow had been hired on probation on 11 October 1945), Else Reventlow collection, Friedrich Ebert Stiftung, Bonn (hereafter cited as FES); interview with Hans Lehmann, interview; Frei, *Lizenzpolitik*, 41.

thirty-one-year-old communist youth leader from Munich, and Walter Kolbenhoff, a former KPD saboteur in the German army. Both had deserted the *Wehrmacht* during the German-Allied warfare in Italy in 1944, and both had found themselves in various reeducation camps in Louisiana, Rhode Island, and Massachusetts. They admired Franklin D. Roosevelt and preferred the American admixture of philosophy, sober pragmatism and basic optimism, over the cultural pessimism (*Kulturpessimismus*) of Heidegger and Spengler. Andersch returned from the United States not with a knapsack full of canned food, as did many of his fellow prisoners, but with loads of American books.[30]

These men and women used the paper as a tool to expound their respective convictions and believed they had a mission to educate their readers through writing. Erich Kästner, for example, wanted to urge the postwar world that "those who built dream castles now instead of shoveling away the debris should be thrashed by their fortune." The "debris" referred to the ruins of the German cities as well as the rubble in people's minds.[31] Walter Kolbenhoff felt an equally fervent zeal after his return from the POW camp: "I have to tell them that they should not despair, that they must start all over again." And Alfred Andersch added: "We need everyone with democratic convictions. We are about to build up a new German republic, and we do not want to make the same mistakes as the people in Weimar did."[32]

The younger Germans in the office had a more undifferentiated view of their job. To them, the paper was primarily an excellent training ground in journalistic expertise. Few believed they had a mission. Hans-Joachim Netzer, a former history and Spanish student assigned to the foreign policy section, would remember until the end of his life how his boss pestered him

30. Hans Lehmann, interview; Beatrice del Bondio-Reventlow, letter to the author, 21 February 1993; Walter Kolbenhoff, *Von unserm Fleisch und Blut* (Munich: Nymphenburger Verlag, 1947); Reinhardt, *Alfred Andersch*, 114–31; Alfred Andersch, *Kirschen der Freiheit*; Hay, "Literarische Positionen," 222; Alfred Andersch, "Der Seesack," 117, 128; Helga M. Novak, "Besuch bei Walter Kolbenhoff," *Literaturmagazin* 7, 283; Walter Kolbenhoff, *Schellingstraße 48: Erfahrungen mit Deutschland* (Frankfurt: Fischer Taschenbuch Verlag, 1984), 22, passim; Walter Kolbenhoff, Germering, letter to the author, 30 November 1991; Walter Kolbenhoff, interview, Germering, 22 February 1992.

31. Erich Kästner, "Der tägliche Kram," 91; Erich Kästner to his mother, 28 January 1946, in Kästner, *Mein liebes, gutes Muttchen, Du! Dein oller Junge: Briefe und Postkarten aus 30 Jahren* (Hamburg: Albrecht Knaus, 1981), 279.

32. Walter Kolbenhoff, interview; Walter Kolbenhoff, *Heimkehr in die Fremde* (Munich: Nymphenburger Verlag, 1949; repr. Frankfurt a.M.: Suhrkamp Verlag, 1988), 13, 27, 102f.; Andersch, "Der Seesack," 116, 127, 128; Helga M. Novak, "Besuch bei Walter Kolbenhoff," 279ff.; Bittorf, "Die Insel in der Schellingstraße"; Walter Kolbenhoff, *Schellingstraße 48*, 17–21, 189–226; Walter Kolbenhoff, interview.

with grammar and orthography.[33] Egon Bahr was notorious for his lengthy and detailed manuscripts, even when dealing with such insignificant incidents as a blown-up manhole at Nollendorfplatz in Berlin. "A second *War and Peace* we do not need," Peter Weidenreich finally told him. "Write what, when, where and why; okay?"[34]

For many of the younger German staff members, the émigré journalists in the plant also provided firsthand instruction in political and cultural currents of the last twelve years. "What did we know about Hemingway?" Hans-Joachim Netzer still marveled in 1991. "We had an incredibly pent-up demand, we had to read, read, read all the time." Inge Ungewitter revealed such an unfamiliarity with common cultural and political trends that her boss used to bellow: "We really have to do something about your flawless ignorance! You have to know at least some facts!"[35]

As in the case of the émigrés, the generational boundary within the group of "authentic" Germans ran between those who were now in their twenties and those who were over thirty-five, between Walter Kolbenhoff, born in 1911, and Egon Bahr, born in 1922. Those who had been twenty-five or older when the war broke out held firmer political beliefs than those who came of age during or after the war. Professionally, the older journalists often outranked the younger ones and had much more influence on the content of the paper. While the older editors often regarded the *Neue Zeitung* as a vehicle to promote their own beliefs, the young reporters saw it as a training camp.

This subtle differentiation is crucial for understanding the interaction among personnel at the plant. The older émigrés cooperated very closely with the older Germans who had stayed in Europe, often downplaying any differences. "It was a glorious but also humiliating moment," Habe said when later describing how he felt sitting opposite Erich Kästner in his *Neue Zeitung* office. "Although I was an American, I wanted to make it clear to him that I was not a 'real' American; he, in contrast, was German but thought it necessary to make it clear to me that he must not be counted among the 'typical' Germans."[36]

33. Hans-Joachim Netzer, interview, Munich, 13 December 1991; Netzer, "*Neue Zeitung*," 14f.

34. Peter Wyden, "Auf Egon Bahr warf man keine Tintenfässer," in *Das Undenkbare denken: Festschrift für Egon Bahr zum siebzigsten Geburtstag*, ed. Dieter S. Lutz (Baden-Baden: Nomos Verlagsgesellschaft, 1992), 69; Stefan Heym, "Schreiben Sie Was, Wann, Wo und Warum!" ibid., 65.

35. Hans-Joachim Netzer, interview; Inge Ungewitter, interview, Munich, 21 October 1992; Netzer, "*Neue Zeitung*," 14f.

36. Habe, *Im Jahre Null*, 89.

The evidence suggests that there was much less cooperation between the younger émigrés and the younger Germans. To the junior émigrés, their task was another army job; to the German reporters, it was political and cultural instruction. Some of the young émigrés made it clear that their German contemporaries were subordinates; for example, twenty-two-year-old Sergeant Peter Weidenreich threw ink pots at reporter Peter Bönisch, four years his junior, for an inappropriate remark. And when Bönisch asked him for a CARE parcel, Weidenreich raged at Bönisch for forgetting who he was.[37]

Nonetheless, in producing the *Neue Zeitung* émigrés and "authentic Germans" formed an almost seamless partnership. The entire venture "would not have been a success," Hans Wallenberg announced in October 1946, "if we few Americans . . . had made the mistake to rely solely on our own." Without Erich Kästner's fame or Else Reventlow's connections, without the expertise and authority of men such as Hans Habe or Hans Wallenberg, the *Neue Zeitung* might not have survived the first year.[38]

Any American editor would have viewed employment at the *Neue Zeitung* as a new job in a foreign language in an alien environment. For many of the émigrés and the older German editors, it was an exciting match with home-court advantage. They had spent most of their lives in Austria or Germany and were well acquainted with Central European culture, history, and mores. As journalists, many of them knew the kind of writing German readers appreciated. They also knew that a strictly American paper filled exclusively with U.S. news would fail in Germany. They were ideal agents for cultural transmission.

The portrayal of the men who criticized the *Neue Zeitung* during the following two years reveals that back in Washington, the War Department took little interest in the United States' foremost mouthpiece in Germany. In the eyes of most U.S. officials, material needs were more pressing than the dissemination of culture and information. In the winter of 1945, the ICD had not received any exact orders regarding American policy in Germany. In a bitter letter, Shepard Stone, former press officer in Bavaria, complained

37. Peter Bönisch and Peter Wyden, interviews; Hans Dieter Müller, *Der Springer-Konzern* (Munich: Piper, 1968), 94; Stefan Heym, "Schreiben Sie Was," 65ff.; Wyden, "Auf Egon Bahr warf man keine Tintenfässer," 69.

38. "Dank an die Mitarbeiter," *Neue Zeitung*, 21 October 1946, p. 11; "Festprogramm zur Einjahrfeier von *Die Neue Zeitung*, Else Reventlow collection, box 27, FES; Hans Lehmann, interview. For an organizational chart of the *Neue Zeitung* staff in 1945/46, see Herbet, *Die Neue Zeitung*, 74.

to General John H. Hilldring, chief of the Civil Affairs Division in the War Department, that any accomplishment by the ICD was "jeopardized by lack of interest and lack of adequate personnel and policy in Washington."[39] Even the department's leaders in the occupied zone, such as Eisenhower and Clay, did not extensively concern themselves with the *Neue Zeitung*. Most of its critics worked within the ICD, and the press branch in particular, which did not supervise the paper but competed against it.

Within the U.S. military government viewpoints on information policy varied considerably: Habe, who became chief of the Publishing Operations Branch (POB), was the most relentless opponent of the licensing process because he was convinced he could produce a far better newspaper than inexperienced antifascist German editors. The ICD press branch under Luther Conant was determined to create a licensed German press under close U.S. supervision as soon as possible. Robert Murphy, the State Department's political adviser and a staunch defender of the prevailing austerity policy in Germany, supported official Allied policy, i.e., the slow reconstitution of the German press for the dissemination of sober, factual news without any concessions to popular taste.[40] In this tangle of factions, Habe held the most trying stand; in contrast to Murphy, he agreed with the ICD press branch that the press should try to appeal to popular taste in order to attract readers. Simultaneously, he backed Murphy's viewpoint that the United States should have a proper voice in Germany as long as possible. In times of conflict he could always align himself with the party that supported one of his two major standpoints.

Top U.S. officials in Germany largely ignored the paper. In his 500-page autobiographical account of the occupation, Deputy Governor Lucius D. Clay devoted a scant twenty-five pages to the "appeal to the German mind" and only one paragraph to the *Neue Zeitung*.[41] Provisions of food, coal, and medications to the civilian population predominated his considerations. To be sure, Clay followed the daily press very closely. His wife, Marjorie, spoke German and often called matters printed in German papers to his attention. The deputy general received a daily summary of translations prepared by a bilingual press officer, and the *Neue Zeitung* was always part of it. He was very concerned about the paper's circulation. But Clay was a soldier, not an editor or writer. There is little evidence that in 1945 he would have liked to

39. Shepard Stone, New York, to John H. Hilldring, Washington, D.C., 26 February 1946, RG 165, Records of the War Department, Civil Affairs Division, Entry 463, 014 Germany, box 176, Sec. VI, NARA.

40. W. P. Davison to this author, 17 January 1992.

41. Clay, *Decision in Germany*, 281–305.

use the paper as a tool to mold public opinion.[42] To the contrary, when visitors from the U.S. Congress complained about the paper's independence during a visit to Germany, Clay fired back that the *Neue Zeitung*'s job was not to serve as the official mouthpiece of the military government. Instead, it was to represent a free newspaper according to good journalistic standards as a model for the German press.

Clay was a staunch defender of the idea that lasting spiritual and moral reform should come from within; U.S. officials could only assume a protective role, such as preventing the selection of former Nazi editors and the spread of fascist propaganda. Without freedom of the press, risky as such a privilege might seem in their situation, the Germans would not become wholehearted democrats. "There is no easy way to democracy," Clay wrote to ICD chief Robert McClure in December 1945. "The Germans must find it themselves."[43] In the early years of the occupation, the general's approach to the *Neue Zeitung* clearly reflected a laissez-faire attitude grounded in his suspicion of "carpetbaggers." An American Southerner, he hoped to dismantle the cumbersome bureaucracy of OMGUS as soon as circumstances would permit in order to return responsibility to the locals.

Officials in the ICD, above all its chief, Brigadier General Robert A. McClure, as well as the intelligence section doubted the Germans could correctly orient themselves. They insisted on a slow and careful process of licensing under U.S. supervision. In the eyes of the ICD, antifascist journalists still clung to authority and had no conception of freedom of speech. If one transferred control of the media to German authorities, this might plant the seeds for new "propaganda ministries."[44]

42. Jack M. Stuart, interview, New York, 12 August 1993; Robert L. Lochner, interview with author, Berlin, 10 April 1992. Robert L. Lochner, the son of the AP-correspondent Louis Lochner, served as Clay's personal interpreter in Frankfurt; OMGUS staff meeting, 11 December 1948, RG 260, Fg 112/15, IfZ; Habe later wrote to *Time* magazine that Clay had opposed any professional journalists in the *Neue Zeitung* since he preferred to exploit it as an official organ run by petty U.S. officers. "Hier irrt der General," *Hannoversche Allgemeine Zeitung*, 22 January 1950.

43. Robert L. Lochner, interview; Henric L. Wuermeling, *Die weiße Liste: Umbruch der politischen Kultur in Deutschland 1945* (Frankfurt: Ullstein, 1981), 252; OMGUS staff meeting, 11 December 1948; Clay, *Decision in Germany*, 281–305, esp. 286–87; Henry Kellermann, "Von Re-education zu Re-orientation: Das amerikanische Re-orientierungsprogramm im Nachkriegsdeutschland," in *Umerziehung und Wiederaufbau: Die Bildungspolitik der Besatzungsmächte in Deutschland und Österreich*, ed. Manfred Heinemann (Frankfurt: Klett-Cotta, 1981), 94; Wolfgang Krieger, *General Lucius D. Clay und die amerikanische Deutschlandpolitik, 1945–1949* (Stuttgart: Klett-Cotta, 1987), 170; Jean Edward Smith, *Lucius D. Clay: An American Biography* (New York: Holt, 1990), 332, 365–66, 369–70.

44. Hurwitz, *Stunde Null*, 45–46, 110, 115, 118f., 128f.; Wuermeling, *Die weiße Liste*, 55, 179, 252; William Paley, *As It Happened: A Memoir* (Garden City, N.Y.: Doubleday, 1979), 170.

Tensions between the ICD's press branch and Habe's POB reflected a struggle for power, influence, and independence. The conflict originated in the earlier antagonism between the leaders in the Psychological Warfare Division and Habe's Twelfth Army Group. Instead of cooperating, the two teams antagonized each other. As W. Phillips Davison, member of the Plans and Directives Section of the PWD, noted, "according to 12 AG [Army Group], those fellows up at headquarters were lazy so-and-so's who hadn't done anything to win the war and who had been wallowing in the flesh-pots of London and Paris while the poor men at 12 AG had been freezing in the trenches." At headquarters PWD, in contrast, officials believed that "the characters at 12 AG and Publishing Operations Branch were a lot of irresponsible whippersnappers who wanted to set up a lot of personal empires and live like oriental potentates, without any regard for the aims of the United States."[45] Press officers frequently complained that the *Neue Zeitung* stole readers, paper, and newsprint, thereby stalling the licensing of German newspapers.

Habe's immediate superior was Brigadier General McClure, an agreeable man with friendly eyes in a mousy face and thinning, sand-colored hair. The forty-eight-year-old son of a railroad manager from Illinois had passed the war as military attaché to the U.S. embassy and intelligence officer at the Allied Headquarters in England, and as chief of the Information and Censorship Section in the North African theater. In April 1944, he received an assignment as G-6 (Psychological Warfare) at the Supreme Headquarters of the Allied Expeditionary Forces. When the Supreme Headquarters were abandoned, McClure became director of the ICD.[46]

McClure did not want the job because he knew that for a military career this branch offered no opportunity for advancement. His activities, barely accepted even by the combat troops, would never catch a general's eye, never promote him to a higher rank. The closest he had ever come to intellectual duty was as an instructor at various army schools. Nonetheless, he

45. W. P. Davison, Santa Monica, Calif., to Harold J. Hurwitz, Berlin, 15 August 1955, courtesy of Harold J. Hurwitz, Berlin.

46. Typewritten biographical sheet, n. d., ISD Rep. Office, RG 260, OMGUS 5/242–1/4, IfZ; Robert A. McClure Papers, 1 box, United States Army Military History Institute, Carlisle Barracks, Carlisle, Penn.; Irving Dillard, "McClure, Robert," in *Dictionary of American Biography*, ed. John A. Garraty, supplement six, 1956–1960 (New York: Scribner's, 1980), 406–7; Colonel Alfred H. Paddock, *U.S. Army Special Warfare: Its Origins. Psychological and Unconventional Warfare* (Washington, D.C.: National Defense University, 1982), 17–20, 44–51; Peter Wyden, interview; William Konecky, interview; Toby E. Rodes, interview, Basel, Switzerland, 17 April 1994 (by telephone); W. P. Davison, letter to this author, 15 March 1994; *Papers of Dwight Eisenhower*, 6: 404.

gained a favorable reputation by never flaunting his authority, and "kept the peace in a family of prima donnas the like[s] of which has probably never been assembled." He always listened to Captain Habe's proposals, assisted with paper allocations, and occasionally even defended him against other press officers.[47]

But from the beginning, different perceptions of Germany's postwar treatment strained their relationship. In response to Habe's plans for a flashy army newspaper, McClure countered derisively that PWD would only publish notifications and directives: "The Germans do not have to form their own opinion—the Germans have to be told." Habe disagreed. The Germans deserved more sophisticated newspapers because they were a *Kulturvolk*, a civilized people. McClure retorted, "The Germans have ceased to be a civilized people."[48]

McClure was one of the few "authentic" soldiers in PWD and ICD, while most of his staffers were civilians from academia, the media, and the advertising business. In other words, Habe's problems were not caused by a clash between soldiers and thinkers but reflected conflicts among civilians thrown into a military bureaucracy and struggling for control. McClure's deputies came from the Anglo-American political scene or the media business. Richard H. R. Crossmann, in civilian life a university professor, an English labor politician, and later a member of parliament, represented the British Political Intelligence Department (PID).[49] McClure's second deputy was C. D. Jackson from New York. A dapper Princetonian, Jackson had begun to climb the corporate ladder at *Time*, Inc., in 1931 as an assistant to the media giant Henry R. Luce and eventually was appointed vice president. Before he joined the PWD in Europe, he had been the American codirector of the OWI Psychological War Branch in Algiers. In 1952 Jackson rose to prominence as vice president of *Time*, Inc., and temporary speech writer for Dwight D. Eisenhower in the presidential election. After Eisenhower's election, Jackson briefly joined the president's staff.[50]

47. Typewritten biographical sheet, n. d., ISD Rep. Office, RG 260, OMGUS 5/242–1/4, IfZ; Hurwitz, *Stunde Null*, 129; W. P. Davison to Hurwitz, 15 August 1955; and letter from W. P. Davison to the author, 2 December 1993 and 15 March 1994; Hurwitz, *Stunde Null*, 45–46, 93, 113, 129; Breitenkamp, *The U.S. Information Control Division*, 6f.

48. Habe, *Im Jahre Null*, 27–28, 56; Hurwitz, *Stunde Null*, 64–65.

49. Richard H. R. Crossman to German Planning Section, C. D. Jackson papers, 6 January 1945, box 4, Eisenhower Library, Abilene, Kansas (hereafter cited as DDEL); Hurwitz, *Stunde Null*, 27, 31, 46; Habe, *Im Jahre Null*, 26, 33f.; Richard Crossmann, "Psychological Warfare," *Journal of the Royal United Service Institution* 587 (August 1952): 329; Stephen Brooke, "Atlantic Crossing? American Views of Capitalism and British Socialist Thought, 1932–1962," *Twentieth Century British History* 2 (1991): 107–36.

50. "Notes on Organization of PWD SHAEF for Germany," 1 November 1944, C. D.

Son of a Jewish-Ukrainian cigar shop owner from Chicago, forty-four-year-old William Paley represented the Office of War Information (OWI). In 1928 he had assumed control of United Independent Broadcasting, including its Columbia network in New York, then a small radio venture, which Paley turned into one of the most influential broadcasting stations in the country: the Columbia Broadcasting System (CBS). In 1943 Paley was assigned to the PWD, first in North Africa, then in London, where he became chief of radio broadcasting. As a deputy to McClure in France, he supervised the preparation of guidelines for German postwar publications, media, film, theater as well as the Twelfth Army Group's radio propaganda.[51]

As early as 1944, McClure's assistants became apprehensive of Habe's publications. Jackson derided Habe's fancy information sheets as inappropriate for their purpose. Habe also fundamentally disagreed with William Paley on Germany's postwar treatment. The jaunty media man spoke no German, had a pronounced contempt for the local population, and a dogmatic view of ways to reform the media. Paley tended to regard the German civilian population as a monolithic entity and ignored its diversity. In an April 1945 memorandum he proposed that "considerable space [in the press] be devoted to atrocities . . . coldly treated within a framework of convincing and authoritative facts." He later boasted that within three months "we weeded the Nazis out of the communications media, pumped in fresh democratic ideas and personnel, and generally remade the German mind until we felt they could take over their communications themselves."[52] No doubt, Paley's views on reeducation were incompatible with Habe's approach.

---

Jackson papers, box 9, folder "McClure (Paris) I," DDEL; Jackson to McClure, 13 August 1944, ibid. Paley and Jackson remained on cordial terms long after the war. Lewis J. Paper, *Empire: William S. Paley and the Making of CBS* (New York: St. Martin's Press, 1987), 93, 96, 128–29, 231; Paley, *As It Happened*, 158f.; W. A. Swanberg, *Luce and His Empire* (New York: Scribner's, 1972), 110, 420; Robert T. Elson, *The World Of Time, Inc.: The Intimate History of a Publishing Enterprise*, (New York: Atheneum, 1973), 2: 29, 83, 107, 317, 365, 374, 378, 392; Blanche Wiesen Cook, "First Comes the Lie: C. D. Jackson and Political Warfare," *Radical History Review* 31 (1984): 42–71.

51. C. D. Jackson to Richard H. S. Crossman, 1 December 1944, C. D. Jackson papers, box 4, DDEL; Jackson to Robert McClure, "Aachen Newspaper," n.d., ibid., box 1, folder "Aachen-Paris" (correspondence from late 1944); Sally Bedell Smith, *In All His Glory: The Life of William S. Paley, the Legendary Tycoon and His Brilliant Circle* (New York: Simon & Schuster, 1990), 27f., 56–64, 206ff., 219; Paper, *Empire*, 93–99; Paley, *As It Happened*, 154–71.

52. Memorandum, 16 April 1945, quoted in Paper, *Empire*, 97; Smith, *In All His Glory*, 222. The records do not support Habe's claim that Paley was fully on his side, (Habe, *Im Jahre Null*, 55).

Habe's foremost intellectual opponent was Colonel Luther Conant, head of the PWD/ICD's press branch and in charge of licensing the local press. Tall, gray-haired, and in his mid-thirties, the colonel had been a liberal journalist in New York before joining the army. As a colonel, Conant was officially Habe's superior.[53] Yet the captain never accepted this chain of command. Habe denied that Conant's press team had anything to do with psychological warfare. As the war drew to its end, Conant, in turn, worried increasingly about Habe's power. On several occasions, the colonel tried to curtail the captain's editorial freedom by enforcing strict guidelines (which Habe ignored) and pushing for a directive that would forbid the appearance of army group papers wherever the press team had already installed a local publication. But apparently the colonel lacked endorsement from top officials to curb his subordinate.

The war's end brought their rivalry to a head. Conant represented the licensed press and urged Habe to stop treating readers as equals and to fill his publications solely with facts and news, rather than editorials and cultural contributions. Habe simply disregarded the advice. When Habe proposed the *Neue Zeitung*, Conant vehemently opposed the publication of a privileged newspaper because it would compete with the licensed press and thus his press branch, which supervised the German licensees.[54]

Opposition also came from lower ranks of the ICD. Primarily interested in the reconstruction of German information services, they regarded the *Neue Zeitung* "as a side show, and sometimes as an annoyance." These men were frequently civilians-turned-soldiers from academia, the media, or the advertising business who had some familiarity with Germany. Red-haired Arthur Eggleston, chief of the ICD press branch in Berlin, had come out of the *San Francisco Chronicle*. Some forty years old, he had served during the war with the PWD in London. Bernard B. McMahon, commanding officer of the 6870 District Information Services Control Command at Leonie castle near Starnberg Lake, was a former advertising man who had official jurisdiction over all information control activities in Bavaria. Since he was responsible for the provision of both the licensed and the U.S. press, McMahon and the *Neue Zeitung* clashed frequently over such matters as paper and newsprint allocations.[55]

53. W. P. Davison recalls that Conant always remained a civilian but may have been an "assimilated" colonel. W. P. Davison, letters to the author, 15 March 1994 and 11 April 1995; Toby E. Rodes, interview.

54. Hurwitz, *Stunde Null*, 49–50, 52f., 64–66, 72, 78, 112, 198.

55. W. P. Davison, letter to the author, 17 January 1992 and 15 March 1994; W. P. Davison, letter to the author, 15 March 1994; Max W. Kraus, letter to the author, 8 March 1994; Peter Wyden, interview; Jack M. Stuart, telephone interview; 20 March 1994; Toby Rodes, in-

In light of upper-level apathy and mid-level criticism, one wonders how Habe managed to initiate the venture. His success is linked to the involvement of a powerful man in occupied Germany: Robert Murphy, the State Department's political adviser to General Clay. Murphy had ties to Germany dating from the early years of his diplomatic career. Born in Milwaukee, he had been vice consul in Munich from 1921 to 1925. From 1942 to 1944 he served as member of the Allied Control Commission's Advisory Council for Italy before being assigned to Germany as Clay's political adviser.[56]

In early 1945 the State Department ordered Murphy to ensure that the PWD followed the formula of "unconditional surrender" and treated the civilian population appropriately. To comply with these instructions, Murphy pushed for tight control over the news media in occupied Germany.[57] Shortly after the *Neue Zeitung*'s publication had begun, he persuaded the State Department that the zonal newspaper should be converted into a daily with various local editions. The State Department consequently stated its intention to continue overt operations in Germany until at least 1 July 1946, if not for an indefinite period thereafter.

Murphy enjoyed a difficult position in occupied Germany. For one thing, the State Department's viewpoints on overt publications stood in sharp contrast to Clay's earlier directive to the ICD to leave the overt business by the end of 1945.[58] On a more general level, during World War II the State Department's (and Murphy's) role had been somewhat marginalized by the huge War Department. As a result, Habe and Murphy became linked together in a most paradoxical relationship. Habe opposed the austerity directive that prohibited U.S. soldiers from fraternizing with the locals and that ordered the official press to confront German readers with their collective

terview; Barbara Mettler, *Demokratisierung und Kalter Krieg: Zur amerikanischen Informations- und Rundfunkpolitik in Westdeutschland, 1945–1949* (Berlin: Verlag Volker Spiess, 1975), 151; Hurwitz, *Stunde Null*, 120f.

56. Biographical Note, Robert Murphy Collection, Herbert Hoover Institute for War, Revolution, and Peace, Stanford, Calif.

57. Hurwitz, *Stunde Null*, 64, 68f., 137; W. P. Davison to Hurwitz, 15 August 1955; Ulrich Bausch, *Die Kulturpolitik der US-amerikanischen Information Control Division in Württemberg-Baden von 1945 bis 1949: Zwischen militärischem Funktionalismus und schwäbischem Obrigkeitsdenken* (Stuttgart: Klett-Cotta, 1992), 31.

58. Robert M. Murphy to Colonel C. R. Powell, "Zonal newspaper," 18 October 1945, RG 260, OMGUS 5/241–1/7, IfZ; Memorandum "Information Control Policy in Germany" from C. R. Powell to Office of the Staff Secretary, OMGUS, 26 October 1945, RG 260, OMGUS 5/264–2/2, IfZ; Memorandum "Basic Policy for Information and Information Control Operations in Germany" from F. W. Marshall, Ltn Col, AGD, to Lucius D. Clay, 17 January 1946, RG 260, OMGUS 5/242–1/4, IfZ.

guilt. Murphy's explicit goal was to enforce this directive and to back official Allied policy through cautious reconstruction of the German news media with no concessions to popular taste. Both men opposed the quick establishment of a German press as advocated by the ICD press team, though for different reasons. Murphy did not believe in a "quick" democratization of twenty million Germans; Habe feared his loss of power.[59]

Murphy believed that the U.S. government should have an open channel to the German people in order to keep them informed about U.S. policy and news. This difficult task, he wrote to Clay in October 1945, could not be left to the Germans themselves, particularly not in light of the extremely different press concepts in the four occupation zones. America's voice in Germany was to reach local readers as well as the French, the British, and the Soviets. To Murphy, the *Neue Zeitung* offered a compelling tool to promote U.S. foreign policy while to the ICD press branch it represented a mongrel in the reconstruction of the German press. Ironically then, the foundation of the *Neue Zeitung* created a faction consisting of the State Department and the POB opposing the rest of the ICD, a unit of the War Department.[60]

Long after VE-Day Murphy maintained close contact with the POB. "By encouraging proper procedures in Bavaria," he said, "we might set a model for all Germany." He persuaded Clay that the *Neue Zeitung* was a "much better publication than other purely German controlled newspapers." It was imperative to contain the official media in Germany for direct communication to the German public, Clay agreed three days after the *Neue Zeitung*'s inauguration, because this heavy responsibility could not safely be left to the licensed press alone.[61]

* * *

59. Hurwitz, *Stunde Null*, 52f., 64, 71, 112f.; Kim, "*Neue Zeitung*," 33; Franz B. Gross, "Freedom of the Press and Military Government in Western Germany: The Origins and Developments of the New German Press, 1945–49," (Ph.D. dissertation, Harvard University, 1952), 6, 7.

60. Robert Murphy, telegram to Secretary of State, 28 September 1945, RG 59, State Department, General Records, box 6846, 1945–49, dec. file 862.911/9–2845, NARA; Colonel Powell, Acting Director of ICS, to Office of Staff Secretary, OMGUS, "Information Control Policies in Germany," 26 October 1945, quoted in Hurwitz, *Stunde Null*, 113; Memorandum from Press Control Officer to Chief, ICD/OMGBY, "Reactions to Impending Turnover," n. d., ibid.

61. Murphy, *Diplomat Among Warriors*, 295; OMGUS Staff Meeting, 21 October 1945, "Report of the Director of Information Control," RG 260, Fg12/2, IfZ; Memorandum "Policy—German Guilt," in "Basic Policy for Information and Information Control Operations in Germany," 17 January 1946; Leonard Ganse, Director, Legal Division, to POB, ISD, OMGUS,

The profiles of the men and women involved with the *Neue Zeitung* reveal a myriad of perceptions regarding information policy. To the older émigrés and native Germans at the plant, this paper represented a medium to accomplish their mission in the post-Nazi era. They had different visions regarding the nature of this task. Some focused their efforts on the promotion of socialism while others advocated a pluralistic society. Opinions converged on the need to eradicate submissiveness, implement "democratic values," such as a representative government, and develop a political consciousness among the German people. The younger employees saw their work either as a duty to be performed as ordered or as a stepping stone to a career in journalism. Top-level policy makers also exhibited markedly different viewpoints. The War Department tinkered with the venture while a high-ranking adviser urgently touted its value.

Most of the conflicts regarding the *Neue Zeitung* arose on the mid-level ranks of ICD. Besides fearing the paper's encroachment, many of the nonmilitary staffers could not fathom how it would fulfill any long-term goal. The ensuing debates around the content of the *Neue Zeitung*, then, were not merely about how to talk to the Germans but about who would do the talking.

---

"Opinion on Withdrawal from Publishing Operations," 22 December 1948, RG 260, OMGUS 22 December 1948, 5/243–2/6, IfZ; Peter Wyden, interview.

3

# CARROTS AND STICKS: CONTENT OF THE *NEUE ZEITUNG*, 1945–1947

ON 18 OCTOBER 1945 LOCALS CROSSING THE DOWNTOWN DISTRICT OF MUNICH were halted by a commonplace yet strange picture displayed at various newsstands. It depicted a man and a woman standing by a huge pile of rubble, their faces reflecting the utmost determination and their sleeves rolled up. "The Work Of Every Individual Matters—A Destroyed World Must Be Reconstructed," read the headlines. But the exotic part was the byline below: "General Eisenhower to the '*Neue Zeitung*'—Opening Words." The statement emphasized that this "American Newspaper for the German Population" would not be or look like a German newspaper. But what would the *Neue Zeitung* be or look like?

The *Neue Zeitung*'s layout reveals that it was not a conventional U.S. newspaper. An American newspaper, ideally, separates news and judgment and informs readers about current affairs in a nonbiased manner. The history of newsprint in Germany had a less detached or elevated role. In the nineteenth century struggles between the state and publishers encouraged the formation of politically outspoken and vociferous publications. These papers were the only public forum for free and liberal opinions. Until the end of the Weimar Republic, the interpretation of news rather than detached exposition of facts represented a priority for most German newspaper writers. In the eyes of American press officers, this lack of objectivity contributed to the rise of fascism in Europe.[1]

The *Neue Zeitung* did not always separate news and opinion. No separate editorial page existed for almost nine months. Editorials freely intermingled with factual reports, features, cartoons, announcements by the military government, and letters to the editor, often featured on the front page. On the front page of the first issue, three articles dealt with the black market and reeducation. Two of these essays reflected an editorial opinion, the third was the proclamation of General Eisenhower to the German population. Page two contained mostly political news, excerpts from other newspapers

1. Hurwitz, *Stunde Null*, 41f.

and a sensational blurb on the discovery of the NSDAP membership list. A column entitled "International Review" included a mixture of news about world politics and editorial opinion. Habe's "private" editorial column, entitled "*Tagebuch*" (diary), was placed on page three. This page predominantly treated national and international issues, including reeducation, denazification, and the notion of freedom. Like page two, page three contained: articles about politics, news, interviews, and political features. Business and sports news dominated page four. A supplement of two unnumbered pages was devoted exclusively to art features and culture. Political and economic essays on Germany clearly led this issue, followed by international political and economic reports and reeducation. More than thirty articles dealt with Germany, about a dozen covered foreign affairs, and a mere seven-liner informed readers about news from the United States.[2] In short, the *Neue Zeitung* looked much more like a daily from the Weimar period than a large American newspaper, because it heavily emphasized German news and opinion features. As the following content analysis indicates, it also often sounded like a German newspaper.

## AMERICANA

The editors' effort to cloak U.S. values in a German guise is most obvious in their handling of Americana. They chose not to emphasize American material lifestyles because the vast gulf between the prosperity of postwar America and the sense of hopelessness in defeated Germany would have made the contrast even more painful to their readers. When covering the United States they usually wrote from the perspective of a cosmopolitan observer and focused on the country's political significance, culture, way of life, and German-American mutual perceptions. European academics, POWs, and prominent émigrés enthusiastically recounted their experiences in U.S. cities, camps, and universities.[3]

Portraying American life to German readers represented a difficult task. The time between 1918 and 1945 had been neither a period of unlimited admiration of Americana nor a time of unmitigated anti-Americanism. On the one hand, a Eurocentric orientation had dominated the Nazi outlook. Goebbels's fierce anti-American campaign, started in 1937, had distorted

2. *Neue Zeitung*, Munich, 18 October 1945.

3. Arnold Sommerfeld, "Atomphysik in Amerika," *Neue Zeitung*, 18 November 1945, *Feuilleton;* "Hilfe hinter Stacheldraht," *Neue Zeitung*, 21 December 1945, *Feuilleton;* Alva and Gunnar Myrdal, "Kontakt mit Amerika," *Neue Zeitung*, 11 March 1946, *Feuilleton.*

the formerly positive image of the United States. Democracy and individualism became synonymous with the devil's work and symptomatic of a country that had no culture—because Americans danced to degenerate jazz music. At the same time, Nazi leaders had eagerly embraced many things American long after this anti-American propaganda had started. Historian Hans Dieter Schäfer and others have retraced the vast gap between National Socialist ideology and daily life. American movies and consumer products remained present in Germany even after the United States' entry into World War II. Mickey Mouse was so popular that it appeared on the coat of arms of a German battalion.[4] Film makers zealously studied and tried to copy successful American movies. While German youth secretly danced to swing tunes, jazz entertained German soldiers at the front.

This split perception was rooted in an equally paradoxical perception dating from the early days of the Weimar Republic when Germans of all strata had discussed the issue of "Americanization." Taylorism, mass production, fashion, and popular culture stirred curiosity, anxiety, and admiration among German observers. Union leaders and leftist politicians were among the staunchest advocates of the American way of life. Conservative upper and middle classes, the so-called *Kultur- und Bildungsbürgertum* (cultural and intellectual middle class) formed the most apprehensive faction against Americanization and a broader democratization. It was this latter group that the editors of the *Neue Zeitung* viewed as the most promising but also the most resistant factor in Germany's postwar democratization.

Postwar Germans knew little about the United States. Two-thirds of the population in the U.S. zone and Berlin did not have any contacts with American forces. Moreover, many locals hesitated to cooperate with the occupation power because they feared an eventual Nazi revival.[5]

4. Detlev Junker, "Hitler's Perception of Franklin D. Roosevelt and the United States of America," in *FDR and His Contemporaries: Foreign Perceptions of an American President*, ed. Cornelis A. van Minnen and John F. Sears (New York: St. Martin's Press, 1992), 145–156; Robert E. Herzstein, *Roosevelt and Hitler: Prelude To War* (New York: Paragon House, 1989), 3–10; Hans Dieter Schäfer, *Das gespaltene Bewußtsein: Deutsche Kultur und Lebenswirklichkeit, 1933–1945*, 3rd ed. (Munich: Carl Hanser Verlag, 1983), 114–62; Michael Kater, "Forbidden Fruit? Jazz in the Third Reich," *American Historical Review* 94, no. 1 (February 1989): 11–43; Victoria de Grazia, "Mass Culture and Sovereignty: The American Challenge to European Cinemas, 1920–1960," *Journal of Modern History* 61, no. 1 (March 1989): 53–87; Jan Kurz, *"Swinging Democracy": Jugendprotest im 3. Reich* (Münster: Lit Verlag, 1995); Philipp Gassert, *Amerika in Dritten Reich: Ideologie, Propaganda, und Volksmeinung* (Stuttgart: Franz Steiner Verlag, 1997).

5. "German-American Relations in Germany: Frequencies of Group Contacts," 13 November 1946, Report No. 27, Surveys Branch, Information Control Division, OMGUS, DK 110.001, 1, IfZ; Hans Wallenberg, "Totengräber des Vertrauens," *Neue Zeitung*, 6 May 1946, p. 2.

From a political point of view, the picture of the United States in the paper clearly reflected the voice of the military government. The *Neue Zeitung* repeatedly emphasized inter-Allied unity and the desire to bring about peace. U.S. politicians were presented as tough-minded but benign human beings working for Germany's economic and political rehabilitation within the community of nations. Doubts about the reliability of Allied and U.S. promises were quickly assuaged with articles on the unlimited wisdom and power of U.S. policy makers. Worries about the atomic bomb's destructive power were met with reassurances that U.S. leaders were attending to the issue. Americans would pursue a benevolent policy as long as the German people reciprocated with peaceful, democratic, and repentant behavior.[6]

The editors devoted considerable space and analytical creativity to familiarizing readers with American language, life, and culture, particularly high culture. In the first issue, émigré Arthur Steiner inaugurated a course for readers entitled "Everybody Learns English." "Students" were taught simple grammar rules, how to pronounce "th," and a phrase for translation. The column became so popular that the Soviet official army paper, the *Tägliche Rundschau*, copied the idea with a language course in Russian. A prize competition under the title "Who knows the truth?" promised 500 marks to readers who could answer tricky questions such as "How many stars are on the American flag?" or "Which are the four freedoms for all people that Roosevelt and Churchill stated in the 'Atlantic Charter?' "[7]

Two columns initiated in 1946, "Americana" and "The Scene in the United States," presented readers with interesting short stories and jokes. This included a wide array of topics ranging from U.S. women's preference for fat men and the invention of the car telephone in St. Louis to congressional elections, public opinion, America's first saint, or the importance of silkworm breeding in the New World. Starting in November 1946, a permanent correspondent regularly covered national and foreign politics.[8] American-born writers, in contrast, rarely received a chance to explain their own culture.

6. "Hoover kommt," *Neue Zeitung*, 11 March 1946, p. 4; "Der amerikanische Plan," *Neue Zeitung,* 15 July 1946, p. 7; "USA und Weltwirtschaft," *Neue Zeitung*, 5 August 1946, p. 7; "Die Szene in den Vereinigten Staaten," *Neue Zeitung*, 12 August 1946, p. 3; "Amerika kämpft für den Wirtschaftsfrieden der Welt," *Neue Zeitung*, 22 December 1946, p. 15; "USA-Aussenpolitik," *Neue Zeitung*, 20 January 1947, p. 7; "Fester Kurs," *Neue Zeitung*, 2 May 1947, p. 7.

7. "Jeder lernt Englisch," *Neue Zeitung*, 18 October 1945, *Feuilleton*; "Wer weiß die Wahrheit?" *Neue Zeitung*, 1 November 1945, *Feuilleton;* Arthur Steiner, *Jeder lernt Englisch: Der populäre Sprachkurs der* Neuen Zeitung, (Munich: *Die Neue Zeitung*, 1946); "Wir lernen Russisch," *Tägliche Rundschau*, 23 June 1946, p. 4.

8. "Die Szene in den Vereinigten Staaten,"*Neue Zeitung*, 15 July 1946, p. 5; *Neue Zeitung*, 29 July 1946, p. 5; *Neue Zeitung*, 23 September 1946, p. 5; Carl Misch, "Die Vereinigten Staaten nach den Wahlen," *Neue Zeitung*, 25 November 1946, p. 5.

Much of the *Neue Zeitung*'s coverage of Americana attempted to eradicate false images of the United States as a country with luxurious cities where the streets were paved with gold and everybody owned several refrigerators. "The fundamental error in the most recent European interpretations of America stems from the fact that in each case people only pick one particular aspect of America and then universalize it," "Spectator" noted in August 1947.[9]

Excerpts from J. C. Furnas's *How America Lives* introduced German readers into the homes of American middle-class families in Michigan, Arizona, and New York. These Americans were similar to millions of families in the western hemisphere. They liked to go dancing and to the movies. On weekends, they packed their kids into cars for a trip to the mountains. They adored sports, especially baseball, and attended church on Sundays.[10]

The *Neue Zeitung* continuously urged its readers to learn from the American example. A sense of gratification distinguished U.S. citizens in the international scene. Americans worked so hard because they were happy, and they were happy because they worked so hard. The Germans, Habe claimed, were constantly waiting for an outside force, such as the occupation armies or the state government, to step in and help them out, an attitude that turned them into a dependent, depressed, and subdued people.[11]

The *Neue Zeitung* made a determined effort to ameliorate its readers' bias against American cultural and academic achievements. Headlines such as "What Do People in America Read?" or "Does the American Have Any Sense of the Arts?" reminded Germans that the United States had a vibrant culture of its own. Editors showcased the vast array of museums, art galleries, public libraries, and newly published books in the United States. Many essays lauded American painters and literary figures as well as European film producers in Hollywood and theater reviews from New York.[12]

Such attention to achievement may sound obsequious, but the editors did not refrain from criticism. "Most Americans are anything but rich," Doug-

9. Hans Habe, "Gedanken unterwegs," *Neue Zeitung*, 5 April 1946, *Feuilleton;* Spectator, "Weltpolitische Rundschau," 11 August 1947, p. 5.

10. "USA: Städte nach dem Krieg," *Neue Zeitung*, 14 December 1945, *Feuilleton;* J. C. Furnas, "So lebt man in America," *Neue Zeitung*, 3 June 1946, *Feuilleton;* J. C. Furnas, "Familie Curry aus Snowflake," *Neue Zeitung*, 21 June 1946, *Feuilleton;* "Die Szene in den Vereinigten Staaten," *Neue Zeitung*, 19 August 1946, p. 5.

11. Hans Habe, "Briefe nach Deutschland (I)," *Neue Zeitung*, 10 June 1946, p. 2.

12. Arthur M. Schlesinger, "Die Wiederentdeckung Amerikas," *Neue Zeitung*, 3 May 1946, *Feuilleton;* "Amerikanische Bibliotheken," *Neue Zeitung*, 9 August 1946, *Feuilleton;* Hans Habe, "Was liest man in Amerika?" *Neue Zeitung*, 26 August 1946, *Feuilleton;* Karl [*sic*] Misch, "Hat der Amerikaner Kunstverstand?" *Neue Zeitung*, 19 May 1947, *Feuilleton.*

las Miller, former U.S. trade attaché in Berlin, expounded on 30 November 1945. Instead, they were "constantly worried about raising money for their house, food, and clothes." They were "nomads" living in remote rural towns or constantly roaming the streets in search of a better job, a better home, and a better future.[13] Nor were Americans portrayed as flawless. A letter from an African-American soldier, who was later killed in action, to his wife denounced fascism, racism, and anti-Semitism in the U.S. Army and severely criticized occupation politics. The editors condemned some of the most fundamental values of American democracy. "A wave of crime dashes across the country. Alcoholism begins to rage anew," decried an essay on life in California. "If a woman does not obey an adventurer anymore, he beats her to death and then cuts off her head. A young girl poisons herself because she does not have 'fun' anymore. Fun is a necessary elixir of life. Nobody really knows what it is."[14]

The editors also expressed dismay at the excesses of an unrestrained market economy. They sympathetically described the ongoing labor struggles and strikes in the U.S. postwar industry. Hans Wallenberg pleaded for a device to control the greed of American capitalists in order to preserve world peace.[15]

The largest number of articles and editorials explicated differing American and German perceptions of values and life. These essays reflected both the leftist heritage of some émigrés and the catalogue of American ideals they deemed worthwhile for transfer to Germany. While rejecting the notions of unlimited capitalism, economic individualism, and unrestrained freedom, the editors praised the educational advantages, the functional optimism and idealism, and the guaranteed right to the "pursuit of happiness" in the United States. "What is the basic difference between the American and the European spirit?" the pan-European specialist Richard Coudenhove-Kalergi asked. "The foremost difference is the gap between American optimism and European pessismism. European pessimism may be one of the reasons why Europe failed in its great effort to lead the world. American optimism will be a great plus for fulfilling this task." Europeans regarded the American belief in mankind's goodness as naive. Americans, in turn,

13. Douglas Miller, "U.S. und Vereinte Nationen," *Neue Zeitung*, 30 November 1945, p. 4; Hans Habe, "New York ist nicht America," *Neue Zeitung*, 15 July 1946, *Feuilleton*.

14. "Ein Toter schreibt," *Neue Zeitung*, 1 February 1946, p. 1; Adolf Keller, "Kalifornisches Klima," *Neue Zeitung*, 15 March 1946, *Feuilleton*.

15. "Die Streiklage," *Neue Zeitung*, 11 January 1946, p. 3; "Die Streikwelle ist nicht eingedämmt," *Neue Zeitung*, 21 January 1946, p. 2; "Die Szene in den Vereinigten Staaten," *Neue Zeitung*, 18 November 1946, p. 5; Hans Wallenberg, "Weltpolitische Rundschau," *Neue Zeitung*, 7 January 1946, p. 2.

found Europeans' cynicism and fear of the evil in mankind troublesome. "You cannot believe in democracy without being an optimist," Coudenhove-Kalergi continued. "Democracy is identical with the idea that people can live in freedom without abusing it." Germans had to recognize the "right to happiness" as a purpose in life, not as a side effect.[16]

Editors at the *Neue Zeitung* believed German resentment of the victors could be assuaged only through an understanding of America. The United States represented optimism, progress, and modernity—all this the Germans had hitherto rejected, not out of hatred but out of fear and ignorance. Knowing about America meant grappling with key values for the future. Dismissing America meant rejecting the last chance to join modernity and the community of nations.

In this regard, the *Neue Zeitung* may not have differed from any other U.S. information medium in postwar Germany. Yet the editors chose a unique approach for their message; they tried to see America through German eyes. Referring to key words of American pragmatism, such as happiness, optimism, and self-help, they deliberately accentuated those characteristics that would impress German readers just as much as they had impressed the émigrés years before.[17]

## DENAZIFICATION AND REEDUCATION

The *Neue Zeitung*'s coverage of reeducation issues employed the same diplomatic approach used in its portrayal of Americana. While criticizing the Germans' lack of individuality, the paper also reproached the original directive of "collective guilt," claiming that it blocked any positive understanding between occupiers and locals. They believed a stock of democratic "good Germans" existed. During the Nuremberg Trial in 1945–1946, they quite openly called for a reconciliation between German civilians and American officers.[18]

16. Graf Richard N. Coudenhove-Kalergi, "Der Optimismus Amerikas," *Neue Zeitung*, 21 December 1945, *Feuilleton;* Hans Habe, "Das Recht auf Glück," *Neue Zeitung*, 11 February 1946, p. 2. U.S. policy makers judged Coudenhove as undemocratic and anti-Anglo-American because he called for an independent Europe. I am indebted to Guido Müller for this information.

17. See also Jessica C. E. Gienow-Hecht, "When Spengler Saw Jefferson: The U.S. Army Newspaper *Neue Zeitung* and the Image of America in Postwar Germany, 1945–1947," in *Faces in the Mirror: American and European Reciprocal National Invention*, ed. Stephen Fender (Keele, UK: Keele University Press, 1996), 89–109.

18. The "Nuremberg Trial" led by the International Military Tribunal ended in November 1946. The term Nuremberg trials designates all trials held under American auspices in Nuremberg until 1949 against Nazis accused of war crimes. Jessica C. E. Gienow-Hecht, "Trial by

They emphasized the relevance of the Nuremberg Trial for the future of Germany and the development of international law to promote the idea of an "other," "good" Germany. "Maybe war could die out. Like the plague or the cholera," Erich Kästner marveled on 23 November 1945. "And then friends and admirers of warfare could die out. Like bacteria. And later generations would laugh about those times when men were once slaughtering each other. Could this become true? Could they laugh about us one day?"[19]

The editors turned the question of guilt into the central focus for reeducation. Many articles echoed the American prosecutor Robert Jackson's statement that only Nazis, not the entire German nation, were on trial. They underscored his assertions by declaring the international community's complicity: the Allies, too, had helped to prepare the way for a situation where the German people became victims of a National Socialist conspiracy. "If I had a brother who had deprived somebody of his property and someone came and said I was guilty, then this would be an unjust charge," Kästner explained in an essay entitled "Guilt and Debt." "But if somebody said because I was the thief's brother I should help to return the stolen good or its material value to the person that has been robbed, I would answer without any hesitation: 'I will do so.' I would have to reject the guilt but not the debt."[20] It was the Germans' responsibility to pay the bill for Nazi atrocities, not because they had all actively participated in the genocide, but because they were Germans.

Numerous letters to the editor and an opinion poll taken by the *Neue Zeitung* in February 1946 revealed that many readers doubted the legitimacy of an international court in which the victors judged the losers after having vanquished them militarily. Apathy or helplessness characterized the German response to the trial. "Our feelings, overly stressed by the sorrows of the war, are burnt out," a young actress told the *Neue Zeitung*. "We need a break." Others questioned their ability to have prevented the Nazi atroci-

Fire: Newspaper Coverage of the Nuremberg Trial, 1945–46," in *Studies in Periodical and Newspaper History 1995 Annual*, ed. Michael Harris and Tom O'Malley (Westport, Conn.: Greenwood Press, 1997), 167–83; Klaus-Jörg Ruhl, *Die Besatzer und die Deutschen: Amerikanische Zone, 1945–1948* (Düsseldorf: Droste, 1980), 137. Bradley F. Smith, *Reaching Judgment At Nuremberg* (New York: Basic Books, 1977), xiii.

19. Erich Kästner, "Streiflichter aus Nürnberg," *Neue Zeitung*, Munich, 23 November 1945, *Feuilleton;* "Beweise in Nürnberg," *Neue Zeitung,* 26 November, 1945, p. 1; Hans Habe, "Nürnberger Tagebuch," ibid, p. 3

20. Louis Lochner, "Über die Anklagerede," *Neue Zeitung*, 26 November 1945, p. 3; Erich Kästner, "Schuld und Schulden," *Neue Zeitung*, 3 December 1945, *Feuilleton;* Ann Tusa and John Tusa, *The Nuremberg Trial* (New York: Atheneum, 1983; repr. 1984), 155; Eugen C. Gerhart, *America's Advocate: Robert H. Jackson* (Indianapolis, Ind.: Bobbs-Merrill, 1958), 355.

ties. "*Ich bin ja nur ein kleiner Mann* [I am just an ordinary citizen]," rang in American interrogators' ears long before the war ended. It was the standard excuse of most POWs and of most civilians, and it likewise became the standard excuse at Nuremberg. The ordinary citizen, supposedly, had not known much about anything beyond his garden fence and had just followed orders without reflecting upon the consequences.[21]

The *Neue Zeitung* focused its reeducation efforts on the mentality of the German individual, these "ordinary citizens" popping up by the millions in postwar Germany. Ordinary citizens, Habe wrote on 18 October 1945, had deliberately rejected their responsibility to think, had abandoned what Descartes called "human dignity," and had silently supported National Socialism. Confronted with reality, the ordinary citizen now stuck his head in the sand, dismissing as propaganda what was presented to him as the postwar heritage of Hitler's Thousand-Year Reich.[22]

Despite the editors' critical assessment of the German character, their treatment of denazification received hardly more attention than news coverage. A few editorials in 1946 implored municipal administrators to apply the standards of the *Säuberungsgesetz* (cleansing law) more rigorously once the responsibility for denazification had been put into German hands. One article, by Jewish émigré Leopold Goldschmidt, even imputed that Germans denounced alleged party members, while another labeled German *Mitläufer*, Hitler's willing executioners, as individually "harmless." "Cleansing itself," Goldschmidt remarked in February 1947, "is not sufficient." Inner reorientation was more important, which explains why the paper focused more on reeducation than on denazification.[23]

21. Hans Habe, "Er hat es nicht gewußt," *Neue Zeitung*, 28 October 1945, p. 3; Hans Habe, "Das Spiel der Dilettanten," *Neue Zeitung*, 11 November 1945, p. 3; "Beginn in Nürnberg," *Neue Zeitung*, 23 November 1945, p. 1; Hans Habe, "Erwachter Individualismus," *Neue Zeitung*, 10 December 1945, p. 5; "Nürnberg und kein Interesse," *Neue Zeitung*, 8 February 1946, p. 3; "Die Parteiführer nach Nürnberg," *Neue Zeitung*, 21 December 1945, p. 3; William J. Bosch, *Judgment on Nuremberg: American Attitudes Toward the Major German War-Crime Trials* (Chapel Hill, N.C.: University of North Carolina Press, 1970), 4ff., 50, 54, 131, 142; Konrad Kellen, interview.

22. Hans Habe, "Ich bin ja nur ein kleiner Mann," *Neue Zeitung*, 18 October 1945, p. 3; Stefan Heym, "Fassungsvermögen," *Neue Zeitung*, 21 October 1945, p. 2; Otto Graf, "Der Einspruch," *Neue Zeitung*, 14 December 1945, p. 3.

23. "Die Säuberungsaktion von deutscher Seite," *Neue Zeitung*, 11 November 1945, p. 5; "Dachau auf der Anklagebank," *Neue Zeitung*, 18 November 1945, p. 3; "Säuberungsprozeß im Beamtentum," *Neue Zeitung*, 26 November 1945, p. 3; Ernst Müller-Meiningen, Jr., "Über die Parteigenossen," *Neue Zeitung*, 11 February 1946, *Feuilleton;* "Unterzeichnung des Säuberungsgesetzes," *Neue Zeitung*, 8 March 1946, p. 1; "Reserviert für Nazis," *Neue Zeitung*, 29 April 1946, p. 7; "Innere Abkehr," *Neue Zeitung*, 1 November 1946, p. 3; Walter Kolbenhoff, "Ein kleines oberbayerisches Dorf," *Neue Zeitung*, 20 December 1946, *Feuilleton;* Leopold Goldschmidt, "Innerpolitische Rundschau der 'NZ'," *Neue Zeitung*, 17 January 1947, p. 7; 28 February 1947, p. 7.

Moreover, the editors admitted that the American military government had committed errors in the process of reeducation and denazification. They questioned the decision of the U.S. military headquarters to transfer the lower level of administration to German authorities in November 1945, because they feared that local legislative bodies would fall prey to immaturity, corruption, abuse, and political failure. On similar grounds, the paper protested the scheduling of the first postwar elections for January 1946.[24]

The *Neue Zeitung* devoted much space to criticism of the U.S. occupation raised by influential Americans such as Republican Senator Wayne L. Morse from Oregon. Morse visited Germany in the late fall of 1946 and reproached the United States for not sending enough able personnel to Europe and for assigning too much responsibility to the Germans. In August 1947 the paper published James Warburg's provocative essay, "Our Job in Germany." Warburg declared that U.S. policy makers were obsessed with the destruction of Nazi Germany but failed to clarify their objectives for the postwar period.[25]

Such outspoken criticism had mixed consequences. Though true to the point, it disregarded that Americans were right in trying even though they found it impossible to purge a society with so many "willing executioners." On the other hand, the editors' faultfinding encouraged many readers to respond with letters to the *Neue Zeitung.* In January 1947 Wallenberg installed a regular column named "*Klärende Aussprache*" (heart-to-heart talk), devoted to German opposition and criticisms of OMGUS measures. The column quickly developed into a forum for readers disgusted with the military government. According to Hans Habe, the paper received some ten thousand letters in reaction to the article "Erroneous Solidarity" that condemned the alliance between former Nazi leaders and nonparty members. Most letters criticized the paper's distinction between "good" and "bad" Germans because too many people inhabited the gray zone. Habe welcomed this outspoken critique as a manifestation of democratic freedom and willingness to think.[26]

24. The *Länderrat* (provinces' council) in Stuttgart was the first institution of a German assembly to work as a counterpart to the U.S. military government. Hans Habe, "Das Vertrauen," *Neue Zeitung,* 21 October 1945, p. 3; Hans Habe, "Inflation der Zeugen," *Neue Zeitung,* 17 December 1945, p. 2; Hans Habe, "Politische Reife," *Neue Zeitung,* 8 November 1945, p. 3; "Die ersten freien Wahlen in Großhessen," *Neue Zeitung,* 21 January 1946, p. 1; Wolfgang Benz, "Die Entstehung der Bundesrepublik," in Benz, *Die Bundesrepublik Deutschland,* 1:23.

25. "Senator Morse über Weltprobleme," *Neue Zeitung,* 29 November 1946, p. 1; Spectator, "Weltpolitische Rundschau der 'NZ,' " *Neue Zeitung,* 25 August 1947, p. 5.

26. Hans Wallenberg to Arthur Eggleston, 12 January 1947, RG 260, OMGUS 5/241–1/11, IfZ; Adolf Arndt, letter to the editor, "Mißverstandene Solidarität," *Neue Zeitung,* 10 December 1945, p. 4; Hermann Nowack, Gilching, letter to the editor, "Mißverstandene Solidari-

"The German Memorandum: Victors of the world, come to an agreement!"

*This cartoon by Helmut Beyer was published in the* Neue Zeitung *on 17 March 1947. It alludes to the Moscow Peace Conference and reflects the newspaper's German bent. The German "Michel" is a stereotypical character representing the common man.*

---

tät," 17 December 1945, p. 3; Hans Habe, "Erzwungene Solidarität," *Neue Zeitung*, 4 January 1946, p. 2; "Klärende Aussprache," *Neue Zeitung,* 14 February 1947, p. 6; Hanns Schmidt, Munich, "Ansicht des 'kleinen Mannes,' " *Neue Zeitung,* 2 May 1947, p. 7; letters to the editor: Heinz von der Daele, Ditzingen, "Die andere Seite," 16 September 1946, p. 7; Werner Hammel, Gladenbach, "Da hilft keine Aufklärung," 21 October 1946, p. 11; Wilhelmine Veit, Stuttgart, "Die Sorgen möchte ich haben," 16 December 1946, p. 7; Friedrich Didjurgelt, Hamburg, "Es wird geschimpft," 28 March 1947, p. 6; Oscar Hesse, Mannheim, "Es wird nicht geschimpft," ibid.; Habe, *Im Jahre Null*, 98.

In general, the staffers of the *Neue Zeitung* sympathized with Germany. Articles expressed the hope that the country "once again will stand before the world" as a nation whose "intellectual history, industriousness, thoroughness, talents, idealism, science, poetry, and music will remain just as important as the achievements of the Americans, the Russians, the British, or the French." In fact, German authors wrote most of the articles on reeducation. Appealing to icons of German culture such as Goethe's *Faust,* and employing an array of stock phrases, such as *das deutsche Volk*, "national talent," and "German idealism and industriousness," these writers detailed the shortcomings of the German character.[27] By stressing the positive heritage of the "good Germans" and by leaving much of the debate on reeducation to Germans themselves, the émigrés repeatedly displayed deep concern for their readers. The editors never regarded their role as didactic. They acted out of a desire to promote democracy in their former homeland. In doing so, they often articulated sentiments shared by their cowed compatriots. In February of 1947, for example, the editors urged that the U.S. delegation to the Moscow conference should include a group of German notables.[28]

Nonetheless, two distinctive "American" beliefs guided the paper's approach to reeducation: first, an optimism that, despite all evil, the good in every human being would eventually prevail; and second, a trust in political individualism and the conviction that individuals find their identity above all through themselves, not through their government. The greatest achievement of the *Neue Zeitung*'s reeducational endeavor may have been that it inspired readers to discuss and to think critically about themselves and their occupiers.

## CULTURE

To the staff of the *Neue Zeitung*, German *Kultur* offered the most viable tool for the democratization of the German middle class, whose resistance to modernity had characterized public debates since the late nineteenth century. *Kultur* would attract this target audience to the program called "democracy" because it constituted their most cherished and unshattered ideal.

27. Leopold Goldschmidt, "Innerpolitische Rundschau der 'NZ,' " *Neue Zeitung*, 11 November 1946, p. 7; Arnold Weiß-Rüthel, "Die psychologischen Ursachen," *Neue Zeitung*, 17 January 1947, p. 3; "Klärende Aussprache," *Neue Zeitung*, 14 February 1947, p. 6; Leopold Goldschmidt, "Innerpolitische Rundschau," *Neue Zeitung*, 28 February 1946, p. 7.

28. "Nach einem Wahlkampf," *Neue Zeitung*, 2 December 1946, p. 7; "Die Stimme Deutschlands," *Neue Zeitung*, 17 February 1947, p. 7.

Only a thorough investigation of German *Kultur* could induce the desired political transformation. In this respect, the *Neue Zeitung*'s coverage of culture clearly resembled a German *Feuilleton* in the Weimar tradition more than its American counterpart. Highbrow essays explicating philosophical ideas, literature, opera, and theater outnumbered those on popular culture. The émigrés drew on their deep ties to European culture. The recently hired German author Erich Kästner in the cultural section, reinforced this tendency by demanding a "nonpolitical democracy."[29]

According to the *Neue Zeitung*, the country's current political problem lay in the attitude of individual citizens: Germans had always suffered from a certain sense of a special mission, which had compelled them to develop a culture apart from the rest of the world. Rather than looking to the future, Germans were fascinated by the past and celebrated poetic and artistic achievements of long ago. The Nazis carried this predilection to an extreme. Fueled by Oswald Spengler's "decline of the West" theme, this pessimistic focus on the past had bred intolerance, misunderstanding, and a stubborn resistance to anything new. According to the editors, these effects manifested themselves most obviously in the realm of art. Goebbels's artistic credo defining "beautiful" and "degenerate" art had stifled individual opinion and creativity. In fact, it had led to the negation of the individual.[30]

Many Germans feared that accepting Western democracy implied a denial of German culture. Numerous letters to the U.S. radio station RIAS indicated it lost many listeners because of its "Western" music program. Listeners felt they had to choose between Bing Crosby merged with democracy or Tchaikovsky coupled with communism. During an Augsburg exhibition of abstract art in early 1946 young Germans yelled "What filth!" and "These artists should be done away with. Concentration camp!" while some

29. Wilhelm Dultz, "Unpolitische Demokratie," *Einheit: Theoretische Zeitschrift des wissenschaftlichen Sozialismus* 2, no. 8 (August 1947): 798–800; Hay, "Literarische Positionen," 214.

30. Bernd Kellermann, "Unbeliebtheit—warum?" *Neue Zeitung*, 28 October 1945, *Feuilleton;* Hans Habe, "An Haupt und Gliedern," *Neue Zeitung,* 22 February 1946, *Feuilleton;* Erich Fromm, "Kleinbürgertum und Autorität," *Neue Zeitung,* 1 February 1946, *Feuilleton;* Alfred Döblin, "Die beiden deutschen Literaturen," *Neue Zeitung,* 8 February 1946, *Feuilleton;* Döblin, "Abschied und Wiederkehr," *Neue Zeitung,* 8 March 1946, *Feuilleton;* "Spengler und die Tatsachen," *Neue Zeitung,* 15 March 1946, *Feuilleton;* Albert Schweitzer, "Kulturerneuerung," *Neue Zeitung,* 6 January 1947, p. 3; Hans Habe, "Freiheit des Geschmacks," *Neue Zeitung,* 21 December 1945, p. 3; "Säuberung im deutschen Kunstleben," *Neue Zeitung,* 12 July 1946, *Feuilleton;* Franz Roh, "Über den Bildungsdünkel besonders vor Kunstwerken," *Neue Zeitung,* 18 November 1946, *Feuilleton;* Conrad Westphal, "Gedanken über die 'entartete' Kunst," *Neue Zeitung,* 12 September 1947, p. 3.

even threatened to "shoot the painters who did this." Their attitude, Erich Kästner marveled, reflected a deeply-embedded fear of modernity. Since the beginning of the world, the young always had passionately defended progress and invention. These youths, however, exhibited the most conservative disposition possible.[31]

Foremost on the editors' agenda was the refinement of their readers' perception of international art. "Art" meant more than beautiful pictures or heroic sculptures. It implied the right to display individual feelings, tastes, and opinions and, at the same time, a respect for the feelings, tastes, and opinions of others. The function of art, according to the French philosopher Henri Bergson, cited in October 1946, was "to eliminate . . . all that hides the reality from us. Instead, it attempts to let us look into the face of reality." A well-functioning democracy required tolerance of all artistic movements. It inspired discussion, criticism, and courage. In other words, art was democracy and democracy was art.[32]

All Germans, the *Neue Zeitung* stressed, should frequent galleries and exhibitions. The number of viewers determined a show's success. It did not matter "if Mrs. Brameshuber tells her friend that she has no use for Bonnard or the much discussed Picasso." The simple act of attendance provided instruction through osmosis. The people who looked at a picture by the American painter Grant Wood without threatening to kill the artist would be less inclined to start another war than those who could not do this.[33]

31. Erich Kästner, "Die Augsburger Diagnose," *Neue Zeitung*, 7 January 1946, *Feuilleton;* Hans Habe, "Tagebuch der Kultur," *Neue Zeitung,* 18 January 1946, *Feuilleton;* D. G. White, *U.S. Military Government in Germany: Radio Reorientation* (Karlsruhe: U.S. European Command, Historical Division, 1950), 114–17.

32. Henri Bergson, "Der Gegenstand der Kunst," *Neue Zeitung*, 18 October 1946, *Feuilleton;* Maxwell Anderson, "Wir haben eine Hoffnung," *Neue Zeitung,* 4 January 1946, *Feuilleton;* Franz Roh, "Die Erziehung zur neuen Kunst," *Neue Zeitung,* 28 January 1946, *Feuilleton;* Edwin Redslob, "Die erwachende Kunst," *Neue Zeitung,* 4 March 1946, *Feuilleton;* Roh, "Die andere Wirklichkeit: Was ist Surrealismus?" *Neue Zeitung,* 11 March 1946, *Feuilleton;* Kenneth Clark, "Kunst und Demokratie," *Neue Zeitung,* 27 May 1946, *Feuilleton;* Hans Lilje, "Die Krisis des modernen Menschen," *Neue Zeitung,* 13 June 1947, *Feuilleton;* Theodor Steltzer, "Das Problem des modernen Menschen," *Neue Zeitung,* 8 August 1947, p. 5; Philipp Lersch, "Ruf nach Verinnerlichung," *Neue Zeitung,* 25 August 1947, *Feuilleton;* Franz Werfel, "Von der Glückseligkeit durch die Kunst," *Neue Zeitung,* 8 September 1947, *Feuilleton;* André Maurois, "In der Zeit der Prüfung," *Neue Zeitung,* 15 September 1947, *Feuilleton.*

33. Walter Schinke, Chemnitz, "Gegen den Expressionismus," letter to the editor, *Neue Zeitung*, 15 April 1946, p. 4; Natalja Berhaus, Munich, "Kunst und keine Kunst," letter to the editor, *Neue Zeitung,* 16 September 1946, p. 7; Erich Kästner, "De gustibus est disputandum," *Neue Zeitung,* 9 August 1946, *Feuilleton;* Hans Trillitzsch, Spalt, Mittelfr., ". . . non est disputandum," letter to the editor, *Neue Zeitung,* 26 August 1946, p. 7; Heinz Berggruen, "Moderne Kunst im Fragebogen," *Neue Zeitung,* 28 February 1947, *Feuilleton;* Bruno E. Werner,

According to the *Neue Zeitung*, Germans worshiped their traditional ideal of high culture just as much as Americans glorified their democratic tradition. What democracy meant to Americans, *Kultur* meant to the Germans: a higher purpose that required consensus, a strong faith, and a set of traditional icons. Symbols of democracy, such as Thomas Jefferson and the Declaration of Independence, paralleled in significance icons of *Kultur*, such as Friedrich Schiller and his famous poem "Die Glocke" (The Bell), untouchable and almost sacred to many Germans. On the other hand, democracy meant just as much to Germans as culture meant to Americans; it was a tool, a commodity to try, to use, and to destroy if it turned out to be useless or unfashionable.[34]

The prominent coverage of German culture and American values was rooted in the editors' assumption that *Kultur*, once cleansed from Nazi slang and conformity, would serve as a remedy to avoid a replay of Weimar. One of the reasons for the rise of Nazism had been the fractured nature of Germany's social and political landscape, and the lack of voters' trust in their government. *Kultur* would form the bond to unite both antimodern and prodemocratic elements in Germany. If Germans were to be democratized, they had to appreciate democracy just as much as *Kultur*. Time and again, the editors urged their readers to change their attitude and take political culture as seriously as *Kultur*. Any democratic institution, the *Neue Zeitung* argued, such as equal opportunity schools, parties, and a parliament, would prove useless as long as the German people lacked a common *faith* in the political system. Highbrow *Kultur* thus became the vehicle for the democratization of Germany.[35]

---

"Ein Vorhang geht auf," *Neue Zeitung,* 14 March 1947, *Feuilleton;* Julian Huxley, "Weltgemeinschaft der Kunst," *Neue Zeitung,* 18 August 1947, *Feuilleton.*

34. "Selbstkritik," *Neue Zeitung*, 3 November 1947, p. 5; Erich Kästner, "Pfiffe im Kino," *Neue Zeitung,* 8 November 1945, *Feuilleton;* Walter Kain, "Mangelnder Idealismus," letter to the editor, *Neue Zeitung,* 11 February 1946, p. 3; Hans Habe, "Was liest man in Amerika?" *Neue Zeitung,* 26 August 1946, *Feuilleton;* Karl Misch, "Hat der Amerikaner Kunstverstand?" *Neue Zeitung,* 19 May 1947, *Feuilleton;* Werner Richter, "Der Präsident," *Neue Zeitung,* 22 February 1948, p. 3; Max W. Kraus, "Die Präsidentenwahl (I)," *Neue Zeitung,* 6 June 1948, p. 7; "USA feiern Independence Day," *Neue Zeitung,* 4 July 1948, p. 2; Johannes Urzidil, "Tradition und Wechsel in USA," *Neue Zeitung,* 18 August 1948, p. 3; Joan Parlowe, "Fernsehen wird Volksvergnügen," *Neue Zeitung,* 4 November 1948, p. 4.

35. Hans Habe, "'Außerhalb der Grenzen'," *Neue Zeitung*, 18 October 1945, p. 3; "Kluge Entscheidung," *Neue Zeitung,* 23 September 1946, p. 7; "Ein Ruhepunkt," *Neue Zeitung,* 25 April 1947, p. 7; Winfried Martini, "Die Lehre von Weimar," *Neue Zeitung,* 5 September 1947, p. 5; Hans Nawiasky, "Kein Zurück zu Weimar," *Neue Zeitung,* 29 September 1947, p. 5; "Lieber Wähler!", *Neue Zeitung,* 25 April 1948, p. 5; "Menschenrechte," *Neue Zeitung,* 9 October 1948, p. 7; "Staatsidee wurde in Bonn erläutert," *Neue Zeitung,* 11 September 1948, p. 7; Gienow-Hecht, "Art Is Democracy and Democracy Is Art," 32–33.

*This cartoon, with the attribution of "Vicky," a British cartoonist, appeared in the* Neue Zeitung *on 18 January 1946. It alludes to the ironic fact that while Germany produced world-famous composers and writers—the foundation of* Kultur*—it also gave assent to the rise of Adolf Hitler and Nazism.*

## WOMEN

The editors' coverage of women's postwar societal role reflected an approach resembling the one applied to *Kultur.* Traditional ideals acted as advance troops for democratic principles. The *Neue Zeitung* portrayed women as loving mothers, daughters, and wives but also encouraged them to become active in the job market, in politics, and reconstruction. The two roles were not mutually exclusive but mutually dependent on each other. Marriage was the microcosm of postwar society. A woman could not be a responsible citizen or even a professional politician if she was not a good wife and vice versa.

The reason for an intensified coverage of this issue was that shortly after New Year's Eve 1946, U.S. military government officials urged Hans Habe to print more women's features. With women outnumbering men, often at a ratio of 3:2, postwar women had become the largest political and professional group. Leading women in American politics, such as Clare Boothe Luce, urged Assistant Secretary of State John H. Hilldring to include German women in the political process.[36]

Under Hitler's rule, women had no role in society outside the home. With the motto: "The man is the organizer in life, the woman is his assistant and his tool," the Nazis had driven women increasingly out of the public sphere, out of the marketplace, politics, academia, and the legal system. Family politics devolved on an increase in the fertility rate; every child born of a German mother, Hitler maintained, demonstrated "a battle that she wins for the existence or nonexistence of her *Volk*."[37]

The editors sought to shatter this stultifying image by emphasizing women's responsibility for Germany's part in the war as well as for its political future. The paper described the fate of female guards who had served in concentration camps and indicted women who had received the motherhood cross for "delivering new blood" to the Führer.[38] Their culpability for the Third Reich's horrors equaled that of their fathers, sons, and husbands.

The editors concurrently revived a number of traditional values downplayed in fascist as well as communist ideology, such as mutual love and marital bonds. Immediately after the war, divorce rates skyrocketed, climaxing in 1948 with 87,013 divorce cases. The city of Hannover alone recorded 1,443 divorce cases within three months. The *Neue Zeitung* strongly encouraged alienated couples to renew their relationship because marriage formed a microcosm of society.[39]

36. "Report on Temporary Duty with the Information Control Division, Bavaria, Dealing with Women and Youth Affairs," by ICD/OMGUS, 2–16 January 1946, RG 260, OMGBY 10/116–3/6, BHStA; "Minutes of the ICD-DISCC Meeting on 22 January 1946, Robert McClure presiding, ibid.; Clare Boothe Luce to John H. Hilldring, 26 July 1946; J. H. Hilldring to Brig. General George F. Schulgen, Acting Chief, Civil Affairs Division, War Department, 6 August 1946, RG 165, Entry 463, dec. file 014, Sec. XII, box 2344, NARA.

37. Ute Frevert, *Frauengeschichte: Zwischen bürgerlicher Verbesserung und neuer Weiblichkeit* (Frankfurt a.M.: Suhrkamp Verlag, 1986), 207ff., 225, 242; Maruta Schmidt and Gabi Dietz, eds., *Frauen unterm Hakenkreuz* (Berlin: Elefanten Press, 1983).

38. "Tag der Frauen im Belsen-Prozeß," *Neue Zeitung*, 21 October 1945, p. 3; "SS-Aufseherinnen im Verhör," *Neue Zeitung,* 4 November 1945, p. 2; "Das freie Wort," *Neue Zeitung,* 28 January 1946, p. 3; Erich Kästner, "Nochmals: Das Mutterkreuz," *Neue Zeitung*, 28 January 1946, p. 3.

39. Else Reventlow, "Über die Scheidungs-Epidemie," *Neue Zeitung*, 21 October 1945, p. 3; "Geschlechtsmoral im Abstieg,' " *Neue Zeitung,* 8 November 1945, p. 3; Manfred Hausmann, "An einen Heimgekehrten," *Neue Zeitung,* 3 December 1945, *Feuilleton;* "Die deutsche Scheidungsepidemie," *Neue Zeitung,* 21 January 1946, p. 4; Robert G. Moeller, *Protecting Motherhood: Women and the Family in the Politics of Postwar West Germany* (Berkeley, Calif.: University of California Press, 1993), 29.

The *Neue Zeitung* simultaneously encouraged women to enter the political arena and fight for their suffrage. National Socialism had rendered the ballot worthless while all established women's institutions were placed under a central Nazi women's organization (Nationalsozialistische Frauenschaft). German men were sharply divided on this issue. Some advocated the abolition of suffrage because "the votes of women in 1933 brought Hitler the majority he needed." Others stated that women, "the greatest flops of the last twelve years," were too emotional to be able to make a political decision. Representatives of the Christian Social Union wanted to see more democratic education among women before admitting them to the polls. Communists advocated the unrestricted right to vote for women. Both Socialists and Christian Democrats agreed that women bore the responsibility for Hitler's victory because in the elections of 1933, a majority of women had voted for the NSDAP. Social democratic editor Else Reventlow, an active member of the nascent women's movement, strongly opposed this argument on the grounds that women had the suffrage in Weimar and constituted more than half of the population. She encouraged women to join unions, universities, and independent associations and to form their own political circles. Throughout the world, women were gaining political, individual, and professional power. They became police officers, deans, professors, diplomats, prosecutors, and even state presidents.[40] Why not in Germany?

During 1946 the *Neue Zeitung*'s encouragement of female political activism was increasingly prompted by the East German communists' efforts to organize women politically. U.S. investigators noticed the strong appeal of SED (Sozialistische Einheitspartei Deutschlands) propagandists to this constituency. East German communists regularly portrayed Western women as

40. Henry P. Pilgert, *Women in West Germany* (n. p., Historical Division, Office of the Executive Secretary, Office of the U.S. High Commissioner for Germany, 1952), 3ff., 32, DK 157.009, IfZ; "Minister äußern sich über Wahlrecht," *Neue Zeitung*, 1 November 1945, p. 3; "Polemik über Frauenstimmrecht," *Neue Zeitung*, 30 November 1945, p. 5; "Wahlbeteiligung war Wahlerfolg," *Neue Zeitung*, 25 January 1946, p. 2; "Arbeit der Frauen," ibid.; Else Reventlow, "Organisierte Frauen," *Neue Zeitung*, 1 March 1946, p. 3; "Japans Frauen im Jahre 1946," *Neue Zeitung*, 12 April 1946, p. 3; Else Reventlow, "Frauen in der Politik," *Neue Zeitung*, 10 May 1946, p. 5; "Arbeit der Frauen," *Neue Zeitung*, 15 July 1946, p. 7; "Die Szene in den Vereinigten Staaten," *Neue Zeitung*, 21 October 1946, p. 9; Egon Jameson, "Geschichten ohne Politik," *Neue Zeitung*, 4 November 1946, p. 6; letters to the editor: Theodor Klüber, Schliersee, "Frauen-Wahlrecht," *Neue Zeitung*, 11 November 1945, p. 6; Horst Milchereit, "Frauen und Politik," 10 December 1945, p. 4; Hilda Gobien, "Frauen und Politik," 18 January 1946, p. 3; Ruth v. Mäsegg, Munich, "Frauenfrage und Wahl," 8 July 1946, p. 4; Elisabeth Meyer-Sprekkels, Fürth i.B., "Staatsbürger zweiter Klasse?" 14 March 1947, p. 6.

oppressed "slaves," doubting there could be equality in a capitalist economy. Moreover, socialist leaders viewed the nucleus of the family as a danger to the state. Giving women a day-long job with equal pay meant providing them with a semblance of equality while estranging them from their role as wives, mothers, and family members.[41]

To counter Soviet zone propaganda and, at the same time, to promote political activism by women, the *Neue Zeitung* appropriated contrasting models. Its argument for women's rights took exactly the opposite stand from the communist perspective. In the postwar world, a woman's role would be defined precisely by her "otherness" rather than equality. The major asset of influential women such as Eleanor Roosevelt lay in their willingness to compromise and their suspicion of male aggressiveness. For centuries, men had caused wars and sorrow.[42] For the first time in history, women had a chance to counterbalance men's desire for armed dispute.

The notion of a mother and a wife moored this credo. Only a mother would sacrifice herself in order to prevent her son from going to war. She acted as "the heart of society," a core of peace amidst conflict. Headlines such as "Mother of the POWs," "World Mothers League Founded," or "Women Want Peace" conflated the concerns of a mother and a politician. War brides, female exiles, and mothers of POWs served a political function. Their work as mediators and ambassadors abroad helped to mitigate international conflict and contributed to mutual understanding.[43]

This combination of the traditional and the innovative woman fulfilled three goals simultaneously: it repudiated political propaganda, encouraged family planning, and inspired economic reconstruction. This approach was pursued with the same zeal by *Neue Zeitung* staffers as the dissemination of political messages through the traditional icon of the model wife and mother.

As in the case of *Kultur*, the *Neue Zeitung* women's issues reflected the marriage of conservative images and political messages. The notion of "equal but different" was not an innovation of the editors but had already

41. "Communist Appeal to Women," Daily Brief, 29 May 1946, Political Affairs Section, OMGBY/ICD, Intelligence Branch, RG 260, OMGBY 10/86–2/20, BHStA; " 'Offene' Worte in der Ostzone," *Neue Zeitung*, 25 August 1947, p. 2; "Das Trojanische Pferd," *Neue Zeitung*, 14 March 1947, p. 7.

42. Hans Habe, "Eleanor Roosevelt," *Neue Zeitung*, 11 January 1946, p. 1; Martha Maria Gehrke, "Moskau: Die Konferenz ohne Frauen," *Neue Zeitung*, 25 April 1947, p. 6.

43. "Deutsch-amerikanische Heiraten erleichtert," *Neue Zeitung*, 13 December 1946, p. 1; "Die tiefere Bedeutung," *Neue Zeitung*, 22 December 1946, p. 13; Irmgard Litten, "Mutter der Kriegsgefangenen," 16 May 1947, p. 6; "Weltbund der Mütter gegründet," ibid., 6; "Frauen fordern Frieden," *Neue Zeitung*, 26 May 1947, p. 5.

marked the *Mütterlichkeit* (motherhood) discourse among German middle-class feminists since the late nineteenth century. As Robert Moeller has shown, notwithstanding the fact that most women could never hope to become wives and mothers since there were not enough men left, after World War II this ideal took on a new meaning as the family became the nucleus of resistance against communism.[44]

Interestingly, the editors never exploited the enormous problem of rape in the Soviet zone nor the effect this had throughout the rest of Germany. This is curious because such an investigation might have tempered the editors' zeal to win women for the cause of democracy. Norman Naimark has argued that women in the Soviet occupation zone did not typically vote for the SED because of its coalition with the Soviets—who were responsible for two million rapes—and because of the party's reluctance to let women in and move up the career ladder.[45] But the editors of the *Neue Zeitung* bowed to the provision of the Potsdam Agreement, which forbade any public criticism of another Allied power. As earlier events had shown, American press officers cracked down much more severely on licensed editors criticizing the Soviets, British, or French than on those who lambasted the United States.[46]

## YOUTH AND EDUCATION

The editors also deployed the forces of tradition in their coverage of youth and education. They emphasized the importance of higher education because of its historic links to *Kultur* and social prestige while rejecting John Dewey's traditional belief in children as the key to the future. *Kultur* implied a refined, advanced education instilled through universities. The editors thus extended their argument that the path to Germany's democratization led through the realm of *Kultur.*

The U.S. military government initially neglected issues concerning youth and education. Under Nazi rule, the majority of school teachers and university professors had been members of the National-Sozialistische Deutsche Arbeiterpartei (NSDAP). In the fall of 1945 the U.S. military government

44. Moeller, *Protecting Motherhood*, 5; Irmgard Roebling und Wolfram Mauser, eds., *Mutter und Mütterlichkeit: Wandel und Wirksamkeit einer Phantasie in der deutschen Literatur. Festschrift für Verena Ehrich Haefeli* (Würzburg: Königshausen & Neumann, 1996), 12–14. For a similar assessment of women's role in the United States, see Elaine Tyler May, *Homeward Bound: American Families in the Cold War Era* (New York: Basic Books, 1988).

45. Norman M. Naimark, *The Russians in Germany: A History of the Soviet Zone of Occupation, 1945–1949* (Cambridge, Mass.: Belknap Press, 1995), 69–140.

46. See also chapter 5.

simply reopened schools with the pre-1933 system and allowed them to function with nonparty members for two years before initiating reforms. Extracurricular activities, such as the organization of sports games and youth groups, intensified somewhat in response to the Soviets' establishments of mandatory youth groups similar to the Hitler-Jugend. U.S. reformers agreed that they would assist and advise, but the German states had to construct their own educational system rather than copy the American model.[47]

As with women's issues and Americana, the editors of the *Neue Zeitung* covered youth and education topics in a variety of special columns. The special column "Klärende Aussprache," begun in November 1946, gave a voice to critical and frustrated young people. A baseball column familiarized young Germans with America's favorite sport.[48]

The *Neue Zeitung* superficially encouraged U.S. efforts to reeducate the German youth and presented the education debate. The various German states had very different ideas about how to reconstruct the schools, none of which corresponded to the American school model: while Bavarian representatives strongly fought for the reestablishment of a stratified system and the preservation of corporal punishment, Hesse and Württemberg-Baden demanded a more progressive system, including a comprehensive school and the elimination of school tuition. Editors paid tribute to the American example and the American effort to reach out to young Germans. Long essays celebrated the network of youth hostels in the United States, the German-American theater in Schwetzingen, and the U.S. youth group program. Upon the request of both German and American children, the paper even matched up cross-Atlantic pen pals.[49]

47. Tent, *Mission on the Rhine*, 39, 130f., 250ff., 315; Henry P. Pilgert, *The West German Educational System* (Historical Division, Office of the Executive Secretary, Office of the U.S. High Commissioner for Germany, 1953), 4–10, 78f.; Robert Murphy, confidential cable to Secretary of State, 12 August 1946, RG 84, Office of the Political Adviser Berlin, classified cables sent to the State Department 1945–49, box 6, Washington National Research Center (hereafter cited as WNRC); Tent, *Mission on the Rhine*, 130f., 250ff., passim.

48. POB/ICD to James Clark, Deputy Chief, ICD, OMGBY, "After Action Report for month of January 1947," 14 February 1947, courtesy of Harold J. Hurwitz; "Die neuen Schulbücher," *Neue Zeitung*, 17 May 1946, *Feuilleton;* Martha Maria Gehrke, "Es kommt auf die Persönlichkeit an," *Neue Zeitung,* 21 February 1947, *Feuilleton;* Leopold Goldschmidt, "Innerpolitische Rundschau," *Neue Zeitung,* 25 April 1947, p. 7; "Klärende Aussprache," *Neue Zeitung,* 15 November 1946, p. 6; see also the section "Reeducation" in this chapter.

49. Artur Holde, "Künstlerische Arbeit in Schulen der USA," *Neue Zeitung*, 15 July 1946, *Feuilleton;* "Amerikanische Freunde der deutschen Jugend," *Neue Zeitung,* 12 August 1946, p. 2; "Jugendherbergen hüben und drüben," *Neue Zeitung,* 26 August 1946, p. 5; "Schwetzinger Theater der Jugend eröffnet," *Neue Zeitung,* 16 September 1946, *Feuilleton;* "Das Jugendprogramm," *Neue Zeitung,* 20 September 1946, p. 5; "Volksbildung in Deutschland und USA,"

Nonetheless, from the outset a deep pessimism colored the *Neue Zeitung*'s youth coverage. The Nazis had had the tightest grip on adolescents not through the schools but through extracurricular youth groups. Mandatory membership in the Jungvolk (Youth Volk) or Jungmädel (Young Girls) began at the age of ten, followed by participation in the Hitler Youth or the Bund Deutscher Mädel (German Girls' League) at the age of fourteen. All the flags, songs, speeches, marching, mass hypnosis were aimed at estranging the child from the family and bringing him or her under the party's direct control. Despicable though their ends were, the Nazis succeeded in creating one of the most dynamic, almost irresistible youth movements in the world, thus effectively using pageantry to promote patriotism. The editors of the *Neue Zeitung* recognized the attractiveness of such a movement, particularly because postwar youth had to live in a grey, apparently meaningless world. Hans Habe dismissed scout groups, one of the pillars of American youth life, as unfit for Germany because "a tradition lasting centuries dictates that a dozen young people cannot go for a walk without marching, cannot have an open fire without marveling about a warlike bivouac, and cannot wear a uniform without longing to become a sergeant major."[50]

The *Neue Zeitung* found suspicions held by modern youths against the adult world a burden and a barrier to change. The education system's ties to the Nazis stymied the situation. "Today, the youth stands alone because the older generation tries to deny its responsibility," wrote a boy from Fürth to the editors; "I lack belief in all human beings." The older generation parried with accusations of fanaticism, nihilism, self-pity, delinquency, and political apathy.[51]

The *Neue Zeitung*'s pessimism contrasted with the typically American buoyant faith in the potential of childhood for a society's future. The "cen-

---

*Neue Zeitung,* 27 September 1946, *Feuilleton;* "Briefwechsel mit US-Jugend," *Neue Zeitung,* 24 January 1947, p. 5; N. B. Lincoln, The Open Road Publishing Company, to Major General F. L. Parks, Chief of Public Information Division, War Department Special Staff, 21 May 1947, RG 260, OMGUS 5/241–1/11, IfZ; Tent, *Mission on the Rhine.*

50. Hans Habe, "Lieber andere Pfade," *Neue Zeitung,* 15 February 1946, p. 3; Luise Rinser, "Sachlichkeit als Erziehungsziel," *Neue Zeitung,* 14 January 1946, *Feuilleton;* Arthur Steiner, "Sport ohne Militarismus," *Neue Zeitung,* 21 October 1945, p. 4; Harald Scholtz, *Erziehung und Unterricht unterm Hakenkreuz* (Göttingen: Vandenhoeck & Ruprecht, 1985).

51. "Junge Menschen über ihre Not," *Neue Zeitung,* 1 April 1946, *Feuilleton;* "Klärende Aussprache," *Neue Zeitung,* 17 January 1947, p. 6; "Klärende Aussprache," *Neue Zeitung,* 31 January 1947, p. 6; Fred Thide, "Staat ohne Jugend," *Neue Zeitung,* 28 February 1947, p. 6; " '. . . kam ein junger Mann zu mir!' " *Neue Zeitung,* 13 December 1946, p. 6. For a comprehensive study of German postwar youth, see Karl-Heinz Füssl, *Die Umerziehung der Deutschen. Jugend und Schule unter den Siegermächten des Zweiten Weltkriegs, 1945–1955* (Paderborn: Schöningh, 1994).

tury of the child" had become an inferno for all European children who suffered death or lost their youth to the war; the landscape of their imagination no longer included building dream castles or living happily ever after. Instead, they had transformed into little adults, executors of the political system at the age of ten. All the reports covering juvenile delinquency, refugee babies, and the fate of homeless street children reiterated the same message: these children had already seen too much. "This youth is an endangered youth," lamented a November 1946 article. "A youth that has been acquainted with the hardships of life so early can no longer be educated."[52]

Identifying the university and not the school as the last stronghold for influence, editors of the *Neue Zeitung* echoed a conservative creed current before the war. The German solution, Hans Habe believed, lay in the training of a "spiritual aristocracy," an idea that can be traced back to German eighteenth-century school concepts. Extensively chronicling the denazification of higher education, the *Neue Zeitung* often served as a mediator between furious prospective university students who asked for better professors, and the military government. According to the editors, universities should open their doors to all segments of society to recruit the country's best intellects. They should become a haven for democratically inclined professors who could instruct future citizens in the art of discussion, tolerance, and constructive criticism.[53]

52. H.R., "Der Weg zurück ins Leben," *Neue Zeitung,* 15 November 1946, p. 6. See also "Klärende Aussprache," *Neue Zeitung,* 15 November 1946, p. 6; Walter Kolbenhoff, "Das große Erlebnis," *Neue Zeitung,* 18 April 1947, p. 7; Leopold Goldschmidt, "Innerpolitische Rundschau der 'NZ,' " ibid., p. 7; Ernst Penzoldt, "Das Recht auf Jugend," *Neue Zeitung,* 9 June 1947, *Feuilleton;* Luise Rinser, "Mut zum Experiment," *Neue Zeitung,* 23 September 1946, *Feuilleton.*

53. Hurwitz, *Stunde Null,* 138; Jutta-B. Lange-Quassowski, *Neuordnung oder Restauration: Das Demokratiekonzept der amerikanischen Besatzungsmacht und die politische Sozialisation der Westdeutschen: Wirtschaftsordnung—Schulstruktur—Politische Ordnung?* (Opladen: Leske Verlag + Buderich, 1979), 25; "Studienplanung—aber wie?" *Neue Zeitung,* 10 May 1946, *Feuilleton;* Georg Hohmann, "Menschenwert und Menschenwürde," *Neue Zeitung,* 12 July 1946, *Feuilleton;* Arnold Bauer, "Über die demokratische Geistesbildung," *Neue Zeitung,* 30 August 1946, *Feuilleton;* E. Y. Hartshorne, "Die Krise der deutschen Hochschulen," *Neue Zeitung,* 29 November 1946, p. 6; Eduard Brenner (Rector of the University of Erlangen), "An die Akademische Jugend," *Neue Zeitung,* 6 December 1946, *Feuilleton;* "Zukunft der deutschen Hochschulen," *Neue Zeitung,* 4 January 1947, p. 5; "Der neue Rektor in München," *Neue Zeitung*, 11 February 1946, p. 5; Hans Wallenberg, "Umbau des Studiums?" ibid., p. 3; 18 February 1946, *Feuilleton;* 4 March 1946, p. 3; "Warum keine ausländischen Professoren," *Neue Zeitung,* 6 January 1947, p. 6; "Studenten nehmen Stellung," *Neue Zeitung,* 7 March 1947, p. 6; Karl Jaspers, "Die Verantwortlichkeit der Universitäten," *Neue Zeitung,* 16 May 1947, *Feuilleton;* Alfred Rauschenbach, Erlangen, "Studenten in Quarantäne?" letter to the editor, *Neue Zeitung,* 11 August 1947, p. 5.

As in its coverage of *Kultur* and women, the *Neue Zeitung* once again appealed to middle-class values rooted in Germany's pre-1933 history when it infused its message with a bicultural background. The editors underlined the conservative ideal of a university-trained, intellectual leadership. Abandoning the optimistic belief in childhood and innocence, the editors transferred John Dewey's idea of a citizen's education into the arena of higher education. The postwar generation had never had a youth and could therefore not be treated as such. The only hope to rescue and transform them into democratic citizens lay in appealing to their intellect as young adults.

In their coverage of Americana, reeducation, culture, women, and youth between 1945 and 1947, *Neue Zeitung* editors posited core American values such as public discussion, tolerance, compromise, individualism, personal and economic self-sufficiency, self-consciousness, optimism, separate gender roles, and the pursuit of happiness, draped in traditional German clothing. In their review of Americana, they deliberately wrote from a foreign perspective, thus facilitating their readers' grasp of the "American way of life," while simultaneously castigating the economic pitfalls of an unrestrained capitalist society. In their coverage of reeducation they appealed to the "good" Germans while admitting faults on the part of the U.S. military government. In their analysis of culture, they linked Germans' admiration for high *Kultur* to political behavior, portraying democracy as an "art." In their coverage of women's affairs, they strongly encouraged economic and political activism along with a traditional family model as a symbol for the new democratic postwar citizen. And in their coverage of youth and education they abandoned the American belief in children as a key to a better future but suggested that the seeds of German democracy lay in the academic training of an intellectual leadership.

The central theme uniting all these topics was the presentation of democratic behavior in terms of *Kultur, Bildung*, and gender. It was aimed at a very specific audience, namely the *Bildungsbürgertum*, the bulwark of resistance against the "encroachment" of modernity. This group, according to the editors, formed the largest intellectual potential but also the biggest obstacle to Germany's political reorientation.

The licensed press reflected some of the *Neue Zeitung*'s key themes. While local editors did not have the means to cover Americana and international affairs, they often aligned with the *Neue Zeitung*'s viewpoints on reeducation, *Kultur*, women, youth, and education. For example, the regional newspaper *Südost-Kurier* in the southeastern corner of the U.S. occupation zone strove to reconcile the principles of democratic journalism with the demands of a public accustomed to standard parochial, and often biased, newspapers. Editors there occasionally reprinted news from the U.S. army paper. The social democratic editor in chief, Josef Felder, featured many of the same items. The United States played a small role in the paper's columns while the future of German *Kultur* loomed large. Similar to Hans Habe, the *Südost-Kurier* concluded that a new cultural elite had to create a viable postwar version of *Kultur*.[54]

The *Südost-Kurier* likewise applauded the *Neue Zeitung*'s appeal to women as the greatest democratic potential in Germany. And no section reflected a consensus between the *Südost-Kurier* and the *Neue Zeitung* as much as the articles on "Youth and Education," which portrayed young people's pessimism, disillusion, and deep apprehension vis-à-vis the adult world. If parents and teachers again instituted corporal punishment in order to discipline the children, if adults continued to believe that age was a sign of merit and youth an indication of immaturity, Germany could again fall prey to a dictatorship.[55]

In conclusion, the *Neue Zeitung*'s coverage did not merely reflect a concession to German taste but the editors' own preferences as well. With roots in both camps, the émigrés thought that German readers would appreciate the philosophical implications of American values much more than straight presentation of features, news, and viewpoints from America. The public response would prove that they were right.

54. "Die genierten Gazetten," *Südost-Kurier,* 14 September 1946, p. 2; H. W., "Mutter Cabrini," *Südost-Kurier,* 8 June 1946; "Die Vorraussetzungen für ein demokratisches Deutschland: Dr. Schumachers aufsehenerregende Rede auf dem SPD Kongress," *Südost-Kurier,* 17 May 1946, p. 3; "Was heisst Demokratie?" *Südost-Kurier,* 25 May 1946, p. 3; "Tribüne der Demokratie: Aus dem Leben der Parteien," *Südost-Kurier,* 29 May 1946, p. 3; J. Felder, "Was geht hier vor?" *Südost-Kurier,* 5 June 1946, p. 1; "Den Sinn verstanden?!—'Nein!' " *Südost-Kurier,* 18 August 1946, p. 1; Heinrich Haug, "Kultur des Geistes," *Südost-Kurier,* 24 May 1947, p. 1; Fritz Nomitz, "Was wird aus der Kunst?" *Südost-Kurier,* 17 August 1946, p. 2; Wilhelm Hofmockel, "Ein Emigrant gibt Antwort," *Südost-Kurier,* 5 October 1946, p. 8; Hofmockel, "Sozialismus und Kultur," *Südost-Kurier,* 24 May 1947, p. 5; Frei, *Lizenpolitik*.

55. Helga Schneemann, "Die Frau im Aufbruch," *Südost-Kurier,* 8 June 1946, p. 8; Therese Widman, "Ach, was kümmert mich der Landtag!" *Südost-Kurier,* 26 June 1946, p. 8; "Die Frau als Trägerin des demokratischen Gedankens," ibid.; Pieter Bö, "Väter und Söhne?" *Südost-Kurier,* 26 July 1946, p. 7; Erwin Hosemann, "Lohnt es sich noch zu leben, zu arbeiten? Aus dem Aufsatzheft eines Schülers," ibid.; Heinrich Haug, "Das Thema hat gezündet," *Südost-Kurier,* 27 July 1946, p. 1; E. H., "Es gibt keine Tatzen mehr," *Südost-Kurier,* 26 June 1946, p. 8; H. H., "Geht es ohne Stock?" *Südost-Kurier,* 24 May 1947, p. 2. Letters to the editor: Susanne Zimmer, "Dankbar, wenn mein Junge ein paar hinter die Ohren bekäme. . . ," *Südost-Kurier,* 29 March 1947, p. 6; Josef Resch, Traunstein, "Möglichst bald wieder 'Prügelstrafe,' " ibid.; H. Frotzheim, Altötting, "Nicht das richtige!" ibid.

# 4

## CULTURE OR *KULTUR*? GERMAN AND AMERICAN PERCEPTIONS

GOTTFRIED STROHSCHNEIDER CONSIDERED HIMSELF A LUCKY MAN. DISmayed by the lack of highbrow publications in his hometown, the twenty-six-year old student from Greifswald in the Soviet zone had bribed the caterer of the express train Berlin-Stralsund with a bag of potatoes to have him bring the newest editions of the *Neue Zeitung* every week. Now friends, family members, and even the security guard at the local train station enthusiastically shared with Gottfried the semiweekly copies of the "American Newspaper for the German Population."[1]

From its inception, the *Neue Zeitung* proved enormously successful among German readers. Within three months, in January 1946, circulation jumped from 500,000 to 1.6 million copies per issue.[2] While German readers overwhelmingly welcomed its style, content, and message, American observers disapproved of it. Members of the Information Control Division criticized the *Neue Zeitung* for exactly the same reasons that earned it readers' praise.

Officially priced at twenty pfennig per issue or 2.95 reichsmark per month, the *Neue Zeitung* "was eagerly bought and widely influential" from the beginning. A small-town newspaper distributor claimed that he had a waiting list for the *Neue Zeitung* of more than a hundred people, "many of whom called every day to see if a new consignment had arrived." Munich students modeled their school magazine along the model of the *Neue Zeitung*. A survey reported that almost half the adult population in the American zone, approximately ten million people, read the *Neue Zeitung*. Decades later, one reader still remembered: "We bought it [the paper] from our spare money, and we gave it as a gift when we were invited somewhere." Eventually, the *Neue Zeitung* would be read in all four zones of Germany as well as in Austria, Switzerland, and across the Atlantic where scattered

1. Gottfried Strohschneider, interview, Gauting, 13 February 1994.

2. OMGBY Weekly Government Report No. 38 for week ending 31 January 1946, RG 260, OMGBY 13/142–2/4, BHStA.

issues of the paper still pop up in the records of the World Jewish Congress in New York.[3]

But the supply never met the demand. Had there not been such a drastic paper shortage, Habe's early estimates of 2.25 million could have been met. At the same time, the *Süddeutsche Zeitung* reached a circulation of 375,000 copies per issue; all licensed and official papers had a combined circulation of some four million copies per issue in the U.S. zone.[4] Surveys indicated that 4.4 million copies of the *Neue Zeitung* could have been sold in Berlin and the three Western zones. Some distributors whose requests had been turned down offered to deliver the necessary paper themselves. Hans Habe remembered that he had to establish a separate division devoted to writing apologies to the three to four million readers the plant was unable to supply. On the black market the price of the *Neue Zeitung* jumped to eight marks—or one egg. According to William Konecky, after six months of existence, the paper registered a net profit of fifty million marks even though it did not carry advertisements.[5]

Who were these six to ten million readers? What did they like about the *Neue Zeitung*? And why were they so responsive to the paper, as thousands of letters to the editor testify? The earliest reader survey, dated February 1946, revealed that the paper was more widely read in Bavaria (66 percent of all newspaper readers) than in Hesse (50 percent), a bulwark of Social Democracy, or Württemberg-Baden (26 percent). The primary readership included Catholics, upper-class people, and educated groups, POWs, and

3. The rule to estimate the number of readers is to multiply the circulation by five. Reader's recollection, "Die Insel in der Schellingstraße"; "Public Relations," Historical Report Eastern Military District and Headquarters of the Third United States Army, 15 October to 14 November 1945, RG 260, OMGBY 13/147–2/15, BHStA; "Information Control," Monthly Report No. 5, OMGUS, 20 December 1945, RG 260, DK 101.006, 3, IfZ; "Reactions to the *Neue Zeitung*," Information Control Intelligence Summary No. 31, 16 February 1946, RG 260, OMGUS 5/234–2/3, IfZ; Maren Roth, "Zur Problematik der Reeducation in Bayern (mit Methoden der Oral History): Politischer Anspruch und Schulrealität. Das Beispiel des Theresien-Gymnasiums in München" (Masters thesis, Ludwig-Maximilians-Universität, Munich, 1996), 87; World Jewish Congress Collection, Series H, box H149, American Jewish Archives, Cincinnati, Ohio; Eva Fischer, interview, Berlin, 4 January 1993.

4. "Historical Report, May 1946," OMGB Land Director, Information Control, RG 260, OMGBY 13/142–2/1, 13/143–2/5, 13/147–2/19, 13/147–2/21, 13/147–2/22, BHStA; Habe, *Im Jahre Null*, 95, and *Ich stelle mich*, 493.

5. "Public Operations Branch," OMGBY Historical Report, July 1946 to June 1947, RG 260, OMGUS CO-580/2, BHStA; Summary of Activities, OMGBY, 28 June 1946, RG 260, OMGUS 13/141–2/5, BHStA; Alpha Lörrach, Lörrach/Baden, to Verlagshaus der Amerikanischen Armee, Munich, 15 June 1947, RG 260, OMGUS 5/260–2/1, IfZ; William S. Konecky, interview; Habe, *Love Affair*, 109; Habe, *Im Jahre Null*, 95.

former Nazi party members. City residents were more likely to read it than rural people.[6]

Significantly, two thirds of those surveyed who identified themselves had a higher education. A random list of one hundred writers of letters to the editor shows among other professions writers, journalists, merchants, ministers, a teacher, a lawyer, an engineer, a doctor, an officer, a policeman, a bank director, a construction businessman, and a student. Of those who disclosed their gender, more than 60 percent of the writers were men, and less than 20 percent identified themselves as women.[7]

In other words, the paper reached primarily the conservative, Catholic, educated middle classes. As Mary Nolan has shown, this group traditionally represented the social strata most resistant to modern developments. They interpreted American materialism and consumption as the future enemy if not the antithesis of German *Kultur* and *Geist* (spirit, intellect), and many insisted that the latter should be protected from the former. Yet as numerous letters to the editors revealed, people with little education also appreciated the paper. In the Upper Franconian town of Kronach, for example, farmers, craftsmen, homeworkers, and housewives violently denounced a dealer's attempt to distribute the paper among the more educated city dwellers only. One should not underestimate the intellectual ability of workers and housewives, wrote a woman from Coburg. "As for myself, I am glad that the *Neue Zeitung* introduces me to big politics, . . . the significant function of the economy and all modern problems of art."[8]

6. Readership figures are notoriously difficult. The paper's popularity in predominantly Catholic Bavaria where it was published probably accounted for its largely Catholic readership. POWs were most likely attracted to the supplement *Rat und Tat* (Advice and Action) inserted into some 100,000 copies of the *Neue Zeitung*. "Reactions to the *Neue Zeitung*," Information Control Intelligence Summary No. 31, 16 February 1946, RG 260, OMGUS 5/234–2/3, IfZ; Office of Military Government in Bavaria, "Weekly Reports," Nos. 38–45 (24 January to 21 March 1946); Nos. 46–54 (22 March to 23 May 1946), RG 260, OMGBY 13/142–2/4, BHStA.

7. "Germany: Letters and Reports, 1945–46, on current affairs and conditions in Bavaria and in Germany generally addressed to the editors of the of *Die Neue Zeitung*, of Munich," 1 box, New York Public Library, Rare Books and Manuscripts Division (hereafter cited as NYPL).

8. Mary Nolan, *Visions of Modernity: American Business and the Modernization of Germany* (New York: Oxford University Press, 1994), 111–21; Adelheid von Saldern, "Überfremdungsängste: Gegen die Amerikanisierung der deutschen Kultur in den zwanziger Jahren," in *Amerikanisierung: Traum und Alptraum im Deutschland des 20. Jahrhunderts*, ed. Alf Lüdtke, Inge Marßolek, and Adelheid von Saldern (Stuttgart: Franz Steiner Verlag, 1996), 213–44; Andreas Bauer, Kronach, "Die *Neue Zeitung*," letter to the editor, *Neue Zeitung*, 1 March 1946, p. 3; Gerda Bombe, Coburg, "Niveau der *Neuen Zeitung*," letter to the editor, *Neue Zeitung*, 18 February 1946, p. 4.

This opens the question of what these readers thought and appreciated about the paper. Two opinion polls among German editors—whom U.S. press officers had licensed for the journalistic trade—and readers, conducted by the ICD in January 1946, revealed two sets of opinions about the *Neue Zeitung*. Both readers and licensed editors agreed that the paper offered good international coverage. Two out of three readers preferred the paper to any other because it was more factual and presented a greater variety of material or had better national and international coverage.

Yet on all other points, readers and licensed editors sharply disagreed. Analysis of these conflicting viewpoints reveals that the marketing success of the *Neue Zeitung* was a result of the fact that the paper disregarded the orders from the ICD. German editors almost unanimously complained about the paper's non-American layout and content. Many editors could not define the political standpoint of the paper. They used adjectives such as "cloudy," "zigzag course," and "ill-defined" when trying to judge the *Neue Zeitung*'s agenda. Some accused the *Neue Zeitung* of displaying too much "*Kurfürstendamm Kultur*" (pseudosophistication) and not enough Americana. One asserted that readers would accuse the licensed media of being much more anti-German in their coverage of denazification, propaganda, or German guilt than the *Neue Zeitung*. Another suggested that the paper might learn something from the licensed press, such as following military government orders more closely.

Readers, in contrast, showed an overwhelming approval of these characteristics, often comparing the *Neue Zeitung* to highbrow papers of the Weimar Republic. Many expressed a strong inclination to buy the *Neue Zeitung* only because of its cultural section. Half the readers believed the newspaper presented a German point of view. Two out of five thought it was published by Germans rather than Americans. A small group of interviewees did not even like to see signed articles by "non-Germans." None of them asked for more features dealing with the American way of life, culture, politics, or history.[9]

In sum, then, German readers did not want more reports about American culture and politics in their zonal paper while licensed editors wanted more information on this point. Licensed editors blamed the paper for not supporting their own standpoint on denazification and reeducation, while read-

9. "Meinung von deutschen Schriftstellern über *Die Neue Zeitung*, 26 January 1946, RG 260, OMGBY 10/76–2/1, BHStA; Hans-Joachim Heller to Capt. H. Peter Hart, Chief, Intelligence Section, OMGBY, ICD, "Attitude of German Editors towards the *Neue Zeitung*," 26 January 1946, RG 260, OMGBY 10/117–1/2, BHStA; "Reactions to the *Neue Zeitung*," Information Control Intelligence Summary No. 31, 16 February 1946, RG 260, OMGUS 5/234–2/3, IfZ.

ers were not very interested in reading more about those issues. Finally, some licensed editors felt that the *Neue Zeitung* sympathized with German readers while licensed papers were seen as representatives of the occupation forces. In short, readers' approval and editors' blame focused on the same issue: the interest of Habe's staff in German matters and their alleged indifference toward the nation that they were supposed to represent. In this respect, the surveys confirmed the ICD's worst suspicion: despite its masthead, "An American Paper For the German Population," the paper was popular because of its Germanophile approach.

The "mountains" of letters to the editor reflected the enormous approval of the *Neue Zeitung* and defied the argument of some critics that people bought it merely to obtain wrapping paper or wallpaper. Estimates vary, but at the end of the paper's first year, an official report counted a total of 140,000 letters. In September 1947 ten employees were exclusively occupied with reading letters to the editor.[10]

Why did people write so many letters? German newspaper readers had traditionally been very reluctant to communicate with the press. Twelve years of Goebbels's censorship had discouraged readers from registering their opinions publicly in regional papers. Said one reader, "When I read the title 'The Free Word' [in the *Neue Zeitung*] for the first time, I thought: what is that? There is no free word—except that they put you into jail afterwards." Most readers professed genuine enthusiasm over their newly won privilege to voice their daily political and social concerns. Readers specifically liked to criticize the occupation through the *Neue Zeitung*. To them, the mailbox of the U.S. plant was not just a way to challenge the local magistrates but served as a direct channel to celebrities such as members of the U.S. Senate or even President Harry Truman.[11] It must have been downright exhilarating to sound off to an editor, and even more so when he or she represented the United States of America.

In 1946 the Nuremberg Trial was the hottest topic among all letters; 26

10. Erich Kästner to his mother, 28 January 1946, in Kästner, *Mein liebes Muttchen*, 279; Richard L. Merritt, *Democracy Imposed: U.S. Occupation Policy and the German Public, 1945–1949* (New Haven: Yale University Press, 1995), 303; Hans Wallenberg, "Dank an die Mitarbeiter," *Neue Zeitung*, 21 October 1946, p. 11; Hans Wallenberg, interview by Alfred Fischer; Hurwitz, *Stunde Null*, 262; John H. DeForrest, POB, to James Clark, Deputy Chief, OMGBY/ICD, "Statistical and Analytical Report for the Month of April, 1947," 14 May 1947, RG 260, OMGBY 10/66–1/39, BHStA.

11. Walter Jähel, Bayreuth, letter to the editor, "Das freie Wort," *Neue Zeitung*, 18 November 1945, *Feuilleton*; Hal Godshaw, survey officer, Information Services Control Section U.S. Hq. Berlin District, to Information Services Control officer, 18 July 1945, Rep. No. 3, courtesy of Harold Hurwitz, Berlin; Conrad Willeke, Munich, "Offener Brief an den Herrn Präsidenten Truman," date illegible (July 1946), RG 260, OMGBY 10/110–2/6, BHStA.

percent of all letters dealt with this topic. Second in popularity were letters regarding the German-American relationship (16 percent); denazification and denunciation (12 percent); critique of the *Neue Zeitung* (6 percent); refugees and women's problems (5 percent each); postwar hardships, student and university matters (4 percent); Hitler's personality (4 percent); youth problems, Germany's fate, and politics (3 percent each); concentration camps, agriculture, cultural affairs, athletic meetings, and Austria's stake in National Socialism (2 percent each); the Berlin situation, church matters, forced labor, taxes, foreigners in Germany, and miscellaneous matters (3 percent).[12]

Few of these letters were openly hostile. They suggest indignant citizens insisting on their legal rights in a letter to their favorite paper, rather than Germans addressing the mouthpiece of the nation against which they had gone to war. It appeared as if readers viewed the paper as mostly concerned with their own personal well-being rather than impersonal propaganda forced on them by a military government. In that respect, they confirmed the ICD's gravest misgivings, namely, that the *Neue Zeitung* was a highbrow paper, did not sufficiently promote features from the United States, and that readers regarded it as their channel to the military government rather than vice versa. In short, it was not an American but a German paper for the educated, conservative upper and middle classes whose distress at the "encroachment" of mass culture and modern values, including individualism, had climaxed in the 1920s.

American officials such as ICD chief Robert McClure disapproved of the *Neue Zeitung*'s approach. They interpreted indications of the newspaper's success as reasons to halt its publication. The ICD complained about the absence of laudatory features on U.S. culture and history. In its opinion, Habe's policy denied the righteous mission the U.S. forces had in the war and portrayed American culture and history as inferior to German *Kultur*.

Starting even before the publication of the first issue, the ICD poured out analyses discrediting the *Neue Zeitung*. Press officers and visitors from the United States remarked that it did not look at all like an *amerikanische Zeitung*. If it was supposed to be an American newspaper, they reasoned, then it should look like one.[13]

Oddly enough, it was not the political section but the cultural section that caused Habe the most trouble with his superiors and the ICD. In a detailed

12. "Germany," NYPL.

13. J. H. Hill, USFET/ICD, "Control of the German Press: A Study of Nazi Methods in Relation to Democratic Objectives," 22 September 1945, RG 260, OMGBY 10/116–3/5, BHStA; W. P. Davison, letter to the author, 2 December 1993.

examination, Lieutenant W. Phillips Davison, chief of Directives and Planning in the division's headquarters, pointed out that the paper, instead of being a vehicle for American views and American life, had gone to the opposite extreme: only 40 percent of its articles involved straight reporting. Commentaries, cultural articles, and pictures formed the bulk of the paper. Davison complained that few stories could be identified as having been written by Americans because most authors carried "Germanic" names. "Feature" material was devoted almost entirely to German *Kultur*, and material on life and culture in the United States was lacking. In that respect, Davison went on, "the *Neue Zeitung* is unwittingly supporting the old Nazi slogan that America is a land of barbarians, looking only to Europe—and principally to Germany—for culture and art."[14]

Davison was the first to express the fears underlying all the subsequent efforts of U.S. officials to change the *Neue Zeitung*: American observers suspected that Germans, even if they had been crushed politically and militarily, would still look down on American GIs culturally. Davison implied that suggestions about the superiority of German culture would make the acceptance of democratic values more problematic and identified the paper's orientation as a "Nazi slogan."

In late November 1945 Habe received an order to devote half of the *Neue Zeitung* to Americana and to print at least two American authors for every German writer. He ignored it. McClure subsequently confronted him with a list of authors publishing in the *Neue Zeitung*. Some 74 percent, the general said, were Germans. When Habe discovered Carl Sandburg and John Steinbeck in the inventory, he pointed out that both belonged to the writers' elite in the United States. McClure was perplexed: "That's right," he said, "but Sandburg and Steinbeck have German names—the Germans will take them for Germans."[15]

McClure's views were typical of those of many American observers and created a serious dilemma. With the exception of a scattering of academicians, most OMGUS officials were not part of a U.S. elite but professional soldiers, administrators, and the like. Their less-than-sophisticated conception of culture derived from the fact that they had never seriously reflected on the amorphous nature of American civilization. Instead, they stressed monotonously that the paper was American and should not confuse German culture and American life. They were determined to promote "the

14. W. P. Davison to Arthur Eggleston, "Die *Neue Zeitung*," 19 November 1945, RG 260, OMGBY 10/116–3/5, BHStA.

15. Charles A. H. Thomson, Lt. Col., to Arthur Eggleston, Berlin, 28 November 1945, RG 260, OMGUS 5/242–2/7, BArch; Habe, *Love Affair*, 18f.; Habe, *Im Jahre Null*, 91.

American view" and "American features" vigorously, long before the existing tensions among the four Allies became an issue of public discussion. But the same officers never clarified what they meant by "American." Confusing "American" with "democratic," they regarded the customs, the products, and the journalistic practices of the United States as pillars of democracy. They felt they had fought the war for the American way of life. They failed to see that by catering to German *Kultur*, the editors successfully communicated some uniquely American values.

Shortly before Christmas 1945 the first open clash between Habe and the ICD occurred. According to Habe, Hans Wallenberg wrote an editorial in the *Neue Zeitung*'s issue of 21 December in which he indirectly blamed the Soviet military government for employing former Nazis. Immediately thereafter, a furious Brigadier General McClure sent a colonel to Munich to reproach Habe for his anti-Soviet editorial policy. "The Russians are our Allies, the Germans are our enemies," the colonel complained. "You have gone native." During the following three months, Habe was charged with abusing his position and his influence in the *Neue Zeitung*, disregarding the nonfraternization law, criticizing the military government and the Nuremberg trials, and siding with the Social Democrats.[16]

All these criticisms were true to a point. The paper did carry more editorials and emphasized cultural features more than U.S. dailies, and it did display an increasing skepticism of the military government. But those developments did not occur because the editors disdained Americana. It was their belief that German readers would not subscribe to a paper that was written solely from a victor's perspective. A successful paper, they believed, had to cater to traditional cultural preferences. "Unless the Germans become Americans, the American paper will not really touch them," the émigré Enno Hobbing wrote to his superior. "It will impress them from then to then [*sic*] and it will perhaps interest them but it will not be a decisive factor in their lives."[17]

U.S. officials had little sympathy for this view. In February 1946 Alfred Toombs sharply criticized the paper. Toombs, the influential chief of the Intelligence Section of the ICD, was known for his uncompromising attitude toward the Germans. He remonstrated that many readers did not know what point of view the *Neue Zeitung* expressed and might not even under-

16. Habe, *Im Jahre Null*, 101f.; H. W., "Über die Prügelknaben: Die Hintergründe des Separatismus," *Neue Zeitung*, 21 December 1945, p. 1; Habe, *Ich stelle mich*, 493ff.

17. Undated manuscript by Enno Hobbing, re.: Memorandum by Wayne Jordan, visiting expert, OMG Hesse, "Program for Training German Newspapermen," 16 August 1948, courtesy of Harold Hurwitz, Berlin; Hurwitz, *Stunde Null*, 105.

stand its highbrow articles. Toombs recommended a reconsideration of the *Neue Zeitung* directives on the grounds that "many items appearing in the newspaper might have unfortunate results among the German people who are always looking for indications of inter-Allied disunity."[18]

On 11 February 1946, the *Neue Zeitung* failed to pay homage to Abraham Lincoln on the occasion of his birthday. A furious Robert McClure cabled to Munich: "Birthday would have been [an] excellent opportunity to drive home some lessons on American democracy." McClure did not specify exactly what Lincoln should symbolize for the defeated Germans in 1946. Subsequently Leon Edel, deputy chief of the Press Control Branch, suggested the appointment of a special Americana editor for the *Neue Zeitung* who would force the inclusion of "historical material, anniversaries, and exploitation to the full of American angles in the day-to-day news."[19]

A few days later B. N. Karvid, acting deputy of the ICD, listed a whole array of complaints in a new report. Karvid blamed the editors for their criticism of President Truman's domestic political difficulties. There were also a few "makeup" flaws the investigator did not like: the use of Gothic headline type certainly violated a directive. Karvid believed that the front page should be much "newsier," like the Anglo-American model. More important, he complained that the *Neue Zeitung* displayed a much less energetic attitude than the majority of licensed papers concerning denazification and collective guilt.[20]

The worst complaint was still to come. A five-page memorandum written in early April 1946 by Bernard Lewis, a U.S. civilian, to McClure enumerated what all the preceding analysts did not dare to say. "Who and what Americans are is a life-and-death matter to Germans because it determines how much they eat, how much freedom they have, possibly how much they suffer." But the lack of articles on Americana in the columns of this paper echoed Joseph Goebbels's propaganda tune that "Americans are money-hungry barbarians with no cultural life of their own." This, in turn, enforced the Germans' "national feeling" that their life and culture was superior to any other way of life.

18. Alfred Toombs, Chief of Intelligence Branch, to Col. C. R. Powell, Deputy Director of Division, "Scrutiny of *Neue Zeitung*," 18 February 1946, RG 260, OMGUS 5/241–1/7, IfZ; Hurwitz, *Stunde Null*, 124.

19. Robert McClure, Bad Homburg, cable to OMGUS press section, Munich, 16 February 1945, RG 260, OMGBY 10/117–2/5, BHStA; Leon Edel, 1st Lt., AUS, Dept. Chief, Press Control Branch, to Colonel Kinard, "Americana in *Neue Zeitung*," 21 February 1946, RG 260, OMGUS/ISD 5/241–1/7, BArch.

20. B. N. Karvid, Captain C. E., Acting Deputy of ICD, to Chief, Information Control Division, OMGBY, Press Section, 25 February 1946, "Consolidated Scrutiny Report on *Die Neue Zeitung*," RG 260, OMGUS/ISD 5/241–1/7, BArch.

The paper had used traditional German format, Lewis continued, despite the fact that "American [newspaper] make-up has been scientifically demonstrated to be the best in the world." Ignoring American superiority meant ignoring the reason for which Allied troops had stormed the beaches of Normandy. "A quarter of a million American lives were not lost, and untold billions of dollars spent, for us now to fear German public opinion. We did not fear German reaction to American ideas and life while our troops were hammering at Germany's front lines. Why now, with victory in our hands, should we be afraid to tread on Germany's ideological toes?" OMGUS, Lewis concluded, should abandon the *Neue Zeitung* and start a new newspaper with a different name.[21]

ICD officials wanted to exploit the paper as a mouthpiece, not as a critical journal. They did not want coverage of quarrels on the U.S. home front or of strikes in American mines. They objected to any stories about the underside of American life in a paper that was designed to "bring the true story of America" to the Germans.

In this context, it is worthwhile to look at the Red Army's official paper, the *Tägliche Rundschau*, for a comparison. Published in the Soviet zone since 15 May 1945, this newspaper constantly announced its intention "to make the German people familiar with the truth about the Red Army and the Soviet Union," including the great achievements of Russian life and culture and the Russian language. The sixteen-page edition of 7 November 1945, for example, reserved most of the space for the celebration of the twenty-eighth anniversary of the October Revolution. The progress of communism, celebrations of Lenin and Stalin, of Russian history and institutions dominated this issue.[22]

As relations between the western Allies and the Soviets grew more tense, U.S. press officers publicly denounced the Russians' paper as propaganda. One wonders, though, if the concept of the *Tägliche Rundschau* was not much closer to the ICD's vision of an "official mouthpiece" than the *Neue Zeitung* (both newspapers were, ironically, printed on the presses of Goebbels's notorious *Völkischer Beobachter*).[23] If one replaced the essays on

21. Bernard Lewis, U.S. civ., to Robert McClure, "Suggested Changes in *Die Neue Zeitung*," 26 April 1946, RG 260, OMGUS/ISD 5/241–1/7, IfZ.

22. "Die Zeitung der Roten Armee in Berlin," *Tägliche Rundschau*, 15 May 1945; "Wir lernen Russisch" *Tägliche Rundschau*, 23 June 1946, p. 4; *Tägliche Rundschau*, 7 November 1945, p. 1. For more on Soviet cultural policy in the Eastern zone, see David Pike, *The Politics of Culture in Soviet-Occupied Germany, 1945–1949* (Stanford: Stanford University Press, 1992); Jens Wehner, *Kulturpolitik und Volksfront: Ein Beitrag zur Geschichte der Sowjetischen Besatzungszone Deutschlands, 1945–1949* (Frankfurt a.M.: Peter Lang, 1992).

23. Günter Raue, *Im Dienste der Wahrheit: Ein Beitrag zur Pressepolitik der sowjetischen Besatzungsmacht, 1945–1949* (Leipzig: Karl-Marx-Universität, 1966), 74.

Lenin and Stalin with essays on Lincoln and Washington, those on the October Revolution of 1917 with others on the War of Independence in 1776, and articles on Russian history and institutions with American features, one would have an ideal model of the type of paper Eisenhower and McClure wanted.

For the victors, the *Neue Zeitung* was supposed to be a reinforcement of their conquest and their mission in Germany. U.S. officials like Eisenhower, McClure, and Joseph T. McNarney, the U.S. military governor, believed that America was vital not only for Germany's material well-being but also for its spiritual future. The defeated people would be attracted to Western civilization only if they embraced America's political ideology and popular culture.

In addition to their ideological antipathy, the licensing team of the ICD had very practical reasons to resent Hans Habe, who some now referred to as the "damned Hungarian." The paper "soaked up paper stocks, dominated the newsstands, and had a slick appearance that made the licensed newspapers look amateurish by contrast." According to them, Habe's sharp criticism of the licensed press and his high-pressure salesmanship had prompted many poor farmers to subscribe to the *Neue Zeitung* and abandon the rural local papers.[24]

The editorial board of the *Neue Zeitung*, however, felt that it was much more important to investigate the advantages and shortcomings of German history and culture in order to discover the reasons for "the German catastrophe." Features from America were considered to be useful, but not essential for a discussion of the country's future.

Hans Habe did not simply disregard his superiors' orders, he openly resented them. Taking his editorial independence away was, as one of his staffers once put it, "like depriving Rembrandt of his painting colors." More important, the Americans' dogmatic ideas regarding the implementation of democracy abroad seemed naive to him, and he bombarded the ICD headquarters in Bad Nauheim with critical memoranda. In a paper entitled "The 5 Mistakes of U.S. Policy in Germany," Habe vehemently attacked the

24. Carl Hermann Ebbinghaus, interview; Hans-Joachim Heller to Capt. H. Peter Hart, Chief, Intelligence Section, OMGBY, ICD, "Attitude of German Editors towards the *Neue Zeitung*," 26 January 1946, RG 260, OMGBY 10/117–1/2, BHStA; "Reactions to the *Neue Zeitung*," Information Control Intelligence Summary No. 31, RG 260, OMGUS 5/234–2/3, IfZ; J. L. Edel, Deputy Chief, Press Control Branch, memorandum to Colonel Kinard, 13 February 1946, RG 260, OMGUS/ISD 5/241–1/7, BArch; B. N. Karvid, Captain C. E., Acting Deputy Director of Division, to Chief, ICD, OMGBY, Press Section, "Letter-Directive, Permitting Criticism of One Licensed Paper by Another," 25 February 1946, RG 260, OMGBY 10/117–2/5, BHStA.

corruption of U.S. occupation soldiers, the Nuremberg Trial, and the Americans' determination to promote their ideas without regard to circumstances abroad: "We brought democracy to the Germans like a suit from a ready-to-wear clothes shop that you pick from a catalogue—with no regard to the owner's size and body shape."[25]

American officers criticized the paper for exactly the reasons for which Germans liked it: because the *Neue Zeitung* emphasized *Kultur*, criticized American policy, and looked like a German and not an American newspaper. Officials believed that by sympathizing with the Germans and by downplaying the efforts of the ICD press branch, the *Neue Zeitung* ridiculed the entire U.S. position in Germany. Military Governor McNarney was particularly appalled by the paper's single-handed course. A soldier at heart without much political astuteness and cultural interest, he often differed with his deputy, Clay, over occupation matters. "Who is in charge of occupation policy?" McNarney yelled when Max Kraus and Hans Habe published a series of complaints of former POWs on occupation policy. "I or Major Habe?"[26]

The conflict between Habe and his bosses came to a sudden halt in March 1946. While OMGUS officials continued to bicker over the *Neue Zeitung*'s independence, across the ocean media giant Henry Luce was eager to obtain a base in Europe. Luce's agents targeted the *Völkischer Beobachter* plant in Munich, the largest and most modern one on the continent. Luce wanted to print the European editions of both *Time* and *Life* there, and he offered Habe, Wallenberg, and Konecky $50,000 per year as starting salary plus all personal expenses for a five-year period. The three men were delighted, but kept the deal secret until contracts were signed.

Secretary of State James Byrnes had arranged the sale. It is not clear why he wanted to sell the plant but one may infer that he preferred to see the information program in private rather than governmental hands. C. D. Jackson, McClure's former aide at the Psychological Warfare Division, represented *Time* and *Life*. In March 1946 Habe, Wallenberg, and Konecky went to Washington and New York to formalize the contract. Unexpectedly, the deal did not materialize. Byrnes was unable to tell Jackson how the publishing company could convert marks into dollars. Jackson got cold feet and withdrew the offer.[27]

25. Habe, *Stunde Null*, 128; "Verfrühte Demokratie?" *Badische Zeitung*, 4 October 1946, p. 3; Wyden, "Die bunte Truppe von Camp Shapiro."

26. Habe, *Im Jahre Null*, 135f.; "Ehemalige Kriegsgefangene haben das Wort," *Neue Zeitung*, 11 March 1946, p. 3–4.

27. William S. Konecky and Kurt Wittler, interviews; Willi Schlamm, memorandum to Henry Luce, "Notes on the New Magazine," n.d. (March 1946), RG 59, State Department General Records, 1945–49, box 5020, dec. file 811.917/3–2146, NARA; Robert T. Elson, Bu-

For Major Habe, the deal had offered a glittering opportunity to advance in one of the largest magazine businesses in the world. He never published this course of events but recorded that a break between his supervisors and himself occurred over the famous speech made by Winston Churchill in Fulton, Missouri. The former British premier accused the Soviet Union of "communist imperialism" and conjured up the notion of an "Iron Curtain." At first Habe had been unwilling to publish the complete transcript without official authorization. After all, a few weeks before, his superiors had almost court-martialed him for printing anti-Soviet editorials. Subsequently the ICD in Bad Nauheim and "Washington" bombarded him with directives that were often contradictory. Frustrated with his work, he left the paper and the army with a citation of the oak-leaf cluster to the Bronze Star Medal.[28]

As his successor, Habe suggested Wallenberg, the émigré journalist of the Ullstein Publishing House in Berlin. After VE-day, Wallenberg had become chief editor of the *Allgemeine Zeitung*, the U.S. army paper in Berlin. Then in late November 1945 Wallenberg had replaced Stefan Heym as editor of the "*Weltpolitische Rundschau*" (International Political Review) of the *Neue Zeitung* in Munich.[29]

The German staff liked Wallenberg. Some called him a disguised Berlin metro rider; others described him as "incredibly hardworking," "a terrific journalist," or "one of the world's greatest worriers." Short and agile, with little hair left but a sizable belly, Wallenberg was a prime example of the ubiquitous editor, half wizard, half ferret, who could smell the news before it had even happened. "He gave us fire," remembered the famous theater critic Friedrich Luft, who launched his career under Wallenberg in Berlin. "He constantly bombarded us with topics and ideas, half of which you could use for sure."[30]

---

reau Chief, *Time* Inc., Washington, D.C., letter to William Benton, Assistant Secretary of State, 21 March 1946, ibid.; Henry R. Luce, "Time Inc. Abroad," 1945, memo, C. D. Jackson papers, box 57, "Luce 43–45," DDEL; Jackson, memo to Luce, "Establishing and Explaining Time International," 6 September 1945, ibid.; Elson, *The World of Time Inc.*, 172–73, 206–7, 260–61. The records of Henry Luce are not accessible to the public. Robert E. Herzstein, Luce's biographer, and the archivists of *Time*, Inc., in New York have confirmed this information.

28. Habe, *Im Jahre Null*, 106; Habe, *Ich stelle mich*, 499; Habe, *Love Affair*, 110; Hurwitz, *Stunde Null*, 108f.; "Citation" in Hans Habe Collection, box 11, MBU. William Konecky, too, decided not to return to Germany. Instead, he spent four months playing golf in Arizona, then started a publishing firm for art and children's books in New York. Konecky, interview by author.

29. Matz, *Zeitungen der US-Armee*, 96.

30. Hans Lehmann, Konrad Kellen, Peter Wyden, Hans-Joachim Netzer, Walter Kolbenhoff, Carl Hermann Ebbinghaus, and Max Kraus, interviews; Friedrich Luft, "Erinnerung an Hans Wallenberg," *Welt am Sonntag*, 17 April 1977.

The transition from Habe to Wallenberg did not bring about the change many ICD officials had expected. The new editor in chief appreciated German *Kultur* as much as his predecessor. He did not change the coverage of the *Feuilleton* nor increase Americana significantly. When McClure ordered the new editor in chief to establish an editorial page, Wallenberg complied grudgingly.[31] Throughout 1946 and 1947, ICD officials continued to criticize the paper and the editor in chief continued to ignore their advice. In September 1946 the paper even reprinted John Hersey's essay on the bombing of Hiroshima without permission from the ICD or the original publisher.[32]

In early 1947 criticism regarding "un-American" features in the paper intensified markedly. ICD investigators complained about the paper's questionable use of sources. They also reprimanded the editors for not using the newswire services that the ICD had recommended, such as the U.S. controlled DENA (Deutsche Nachrichtenagentur) in Bad Nauheim. Instead, the *Neue Zeitung* relied on a private newswire service whose stories were not officially released or confirmed. Wallenberg, just like Habe, was denounced as a highbrow intellectual not interested in the broader public.[33]

31. OMGB/ID, "Reaction on the change in the editorship of *Neue Zeitung* (interrogation, reports)," "Brief from Berlin, 28 August –3 September: Reactions to New Editorial Page of *Neue Zeitung*," RG 260, OMGBY 10/71–1/8; "Reactions to *Neue Zeitung* Editorials," Information Control Intelligence Summary, week ending 12 October 1946, RG 260, OMGUS 5/234–2/4, IfZ; Lucius Clay to Hans Wallenberg, 15 October 1946, RG 84, Office POLAD Berlin, classified general correspondence, 1946, dec. no. 891, box 123, WNRC; Brigadier General Robert McClure to Col. B. B. McMahon, 17 July 1946, quoted in Norman, *Our German Policy*, 37.

32. David E. Warner, Chief, Press Section, RO, memorandum to Lt. Col. R. B. McRae, Chief, Reorientation Branch, CAD, "Report on a Survey Trip to Germany, Austria, and Venezia Giulia," n.d., RG 260, OMGUS 5/242–2/15, IfZ; Edward T. Peeples to Editors, *Neue Zeitung*, "Employment of Research Personnel," 13 May 1947, RG 260, OMGUS 5/315–3/12, IfZ; "Cumulative Annual History Report of Publications Control Branch," ICD, 1 July 1946–30 June 1947, RG 260, OMGBY 10/66–1/39, BHStA; "Hiroshima," *Neue Zeitung*, 9 August 1946, p. 3; John Hersey, "Hiroshima," repr. from *New Yorker* in *Neue Zeitung*, 16 September 1946, *Feuilleton*; Lucius Clay, cable to the War Department, Civil Affairs Division, 14 September 1946; cable from J. G. Nyland, Maj. GSC, Administrative Officer, cable to OMGUS, Berlin, 25 September 1946; J. G. Nyland, cable to Robert McClure, 9 October 1946, RG 165, documents of the War Department, Civil Affairs Division, Entry 463, 0007, Sec. IV, box 225, NARA; Hurwitz, *Stunde Null*, 122.

33. "Functional Program for Period January 1 to June 30, 1947 (revised 1 April)," Information Control, Annex A, RG 260, OMGBY 10/112–3/1, BHStA; Hans-Joachim Netzer and Ernst Wynder, interviews; letter to this author from Andreas Gregoriades, Geneva, 6 December 1992; Erich Kästner, Munich, to Dolf Sternberger, Heidelberg, 20 December 1945, Archiv Dolf Sternberger, Deutsches Literaturarchiv, Schiller-Nationalmuseum, Marbach am Neckar, (hereafter cited as DLS); John Stuart, Chief Press Control Officer, DENA, to Arthur Eggleston,

Still, the ICD hesitated to alter the *Neue Zeitung* radically because it did not yet regard the newspaper as a top priority. "Everyone had their hands full already," W. Phillips Davison recalls, "so the *Neue Zeitung* was sometimes seen as a low priority. It was going to disappear in a few years anyway, and the licensed press was supposed to be permanent." Moreover, there was no consensus about what a democratic model newspaper for Germany should look like. Press officers often expressed rather exotic notions regarding Germany's future media. Democracy in the press, as one said, could be achieved only by having more active verbs in the headlines.[34] Furthermore, press guidelines from the State and the War departments to the ICD (and the *Neue Zeitung*) often came late or got lost. And even if they arrived at their point of destination, they often struck U.S. officials in Germany as utterly ineffective. OMGUS officials generally regarded the occupation as a local operation and often resented the interference of the State Department and its representatives in Germany. Furthermore, the ICD was ideologically committed to the First Amendment everywhere.[35] But the most important reason for not taking drastic measures was the newspaper's enormous popular success. Officials, such as the political adviser Robert Murphy, felt that the paper's positive attributes outweighed its liabilities.[36]

The public response proved the success of the editors' carrot-and-stick method. Readers liked the *Neue Zeitung*'s emphasis on German internal affairs and *Kultur* along with features from America. They approved of Habe's and Wallenberg's encouragement of a mutual dialogue and felt that this paper was like a hand reaching out to help Germans get back on their feet.

American officials like Alfred Toombs did not approve of the editors' ap-

---

"*Neue Zeitung* credits," 28 April 1947, RG 260, OMGUS 5/241–1/11, IfZ; Ernest H. Mayer, Circulation Manager, POB, OMGBY/ICD, to Arthur Eggleston, OMGUS/ICD, "Readers Survey," 18 March 1947, RG 260, OMGUS 5/241–1/11, IfZ.

34. W. P. Davison, letters to this author, 17 January 1992 and 11 April 1995; W. P. Davison to Harold Hurwitz, Berlin, 15 August 1955, letter courtesy of Harold Hurwitz.

35. Abijah U. Fox, "Military Government for Germany—Speech—October 1945," Abijah U. Fox Papers, box 7, HSTL; "Germany," Department of State Policy Statement, 26 August 1948, *Foreign Relations of the United States 1948*, vol. 2, *Germany and Austria* (Washington, D.C.: United States Government Printing Office, 1973), 1318; Jack M. Stuart, Robert L. Lochner, and Jack M. Fleischer, interviews; T. B. Wenner, "Free Speech and Press in Germany, under Potsdam; Interzonal Transmission of Newspaper in Germany," 22 July 1946, memorandum, RG 84, POLAD (Political Adviser) Berlin, classified general correspondence, 1946, dec. file 891, box 122, WNRC.

36. U.S. Civil Censorship, 19 August 1946, "SPD Official and Editor of *Südost Kurier* Praise Non-Partisan Newspapers," RG 84, POLAD Berlin, classified general correspondence, 1946, dec. file 891, box 122, WNRC.

proach. They interpreted signs of the *Neue Zeitung*'s success as reasons for its discontinuation, and they complained about the absence of laudatory features on U.S. culture and history. They sensed that Habe's approach downplayed the United States' mission in the war while glorifying German *Kultur.* It is ironic that the *Neue Zeitung* could attract readers' curiosity and successfully accomplish its mission only if its editors deliberately "disregarded" orders from their superiors.

Since the editors were accomplishing the real mission of U.S. occupation policy by conveying American values and ideas to their German readers, they were not literally disregarding orders. Instead, they were pursuing the same goal through more adroit tactics. Individual U.S. officials like Murphy and Clay may have grasped this point. As indicated earlier, Clay believed that OMGUS should not actively control the press as long as the latter did not violate the Potsdam Agreement. Murphy, in contrast, firmly advocated a strong U.S. mouthpiece in Germany as a tool of foreign policy. And both men were keenly aware of the paper's influence on public opinion. Thus because of their tolerance—or lack of interest—the *Neue Zeitung* was allowed to continue.

# 5

# FEAR NOT THE SED: THE WAR OF WORDS, 1945–1947

IN THE EARLY AFTERNOON OF 21 AUGUST 1946, TWO UNIFORMED MEN ENtered the newsstand of Mr. Hahn at Frankfurter Allee in East Berlin. They briefly identified themselves as a German policeman and a Russian officer and, by order of the Russian commandant, seized ninety-seven copies of the *Neue Zeitung*. On that day, all over East Berlin, Soviet officials confiscated copies of the "American Newspaper for the German Population." At a newsstand at Alexanderplatz, the owner hid most of his copies under the counter. When a customer asked for the *Neue Zeitung*, the newsdealer pulled one out from under the table, whispering, "Put it away quickly and don't show it to anyone, otherwise I'll have trouble with the Russians."[1]

In the developing conflict between the Western and Soviet occupation powers, during the years 1946–1947, the *Neue Zeitung* changed from an almost accidental byproduct of U.S. press policy to a viable instrument for the dissemination of information in both East and West Germany. Once U.S. officials became aware of the potential propaganda power of the *Neue Zeitung* in the unfolding Cold War, they began to think that the political and ethnic background of the émigrés might interfere with the paper's job of reeducating German readers. The rising tide of anticommunism went hand in hand with a lingering anti-Semitic attitude when U.S. observers began to wonder if a German émigré could convey American values to the country where he or she had been born.

Conflicts in the Allied Control Council and the Kommandantura, a board of the four Allied commanders of the Berlin sectors to ensure the uniform treatment of all zones in the metropolitan area of Greater Berlin, foreshadowed a breakup of the Allied alliance. Delegates increasingly fought over the unresolved question of reparations, the subsequent dismantling of East German industry by the Soviets, and the disputes over denazification, travel conditions, and the interzonal exchange of goods and news. Fearing

1. OMGUS Berlin District, ICD, "Confiscation of *Die Neue Zeitung*," 11 [21] August 1946, RG 260, OMGUS 5/246–2/12a, IfZ.

the spread of communism in Germany, in the summer of 1946 General Clay begged Secretary of State James Byrnes to give his famous Stuttgart speech to assure the country of America's long-lasting political protection. The plans in mid-1946 for the merger of the British and the American zones into one economic entity, "Bizonia," as well as the announcement of the Truman Doctrine in March 1947, sent clear signals to the Soviets regarding U.S. interest in the economic reconstruction of Germany.[2]

U.S. officials feared allowing these internal disputes to escalate into a public confrontation. As Harold Hurwitz has shown, throughout 1946 military government officials like Clay wanted to keep up the illusion of unity among the Western Allies and the Soviet Union. They dreaded that open friction would disrupt inter-Allied harmony and thwart Germany's economic and political reconstruction. Therefore, the Information Control Division (ICD) enforced the Potsdam Agreement as well as Directives No. 4 and No. 40 of the Allied Control Council which forbade any criticism of the occupying powers.[3]

In line with the "doctrine of harmony," the editors of the *Neue Zeitung* refrained from criticizing the Soviet military government or Stalin. "We *liked* the Russians," recalls Sergeant Peter Weidenreich, chief of the *Neue Zeitung*'s Berlin bureau. "Indeed, our policy directives in military government *ordered* us to get along with these new neighbors." Weidenreich and his friends from the U.S. press corps were quite amused by Russian soldiers walking around and asking every American for "Uhri, Uhri" (*Uhr* being the German term for watch). "I would have loved to run stories about such local color in our paper. We did not. It would have been unfriendly, hence contrary to American policy." Young reporter Egon Bahr had a similar experience. When he heard through the grapevine that the Soviets had discovered uranium in the Erzgebirge and were ready to exploit it for military purposes, his boss, Enno Hobbing, bribed him and the informer with a carton

2. Barbara Ann Chotiner and John W. Atwell, "Soviet Occupation Policy Toward Germany, 1945–1949," in *U.S. Occupation in Europe After World War II: Papers and Reminiscences from the April 23–24, 1976, Conference Held at the George C. Marshall Research Foundation, Lexington, Virginia*, ed. Hans A. Schmitt (Lawrence, Kans.: The Regents Press of Kansas, 1978), 47f.; General Lucius D. Clay, New York, N.Y., 16 July 1974, oral history interview by Richard D. McKinzie, HSTL; Krieger, *Lucius D. Clay*, 160–66, 196, 204–206.

3. Harold J. Hurwitz, *Die Eintracht der Siegermächte und die Orientierungsnot der Deutschen, 1945–1946* (Cologne: Verlag Wissenschaft und Politik, 1984), 130; Hurwitz, "Antikommunismus und amerikanische Demokratisierungsvorhaben in Deutschland," *Aus Politik und Zeitgeschichte* 29 (1978): 29–46; Jean Edward Smith, "The View from USFET: General Clay's and Washington's Interpretation of Soviet Intentions in Germany, 1945–1948," in Schmitt, *U.S. Occupation in Europe*, 67–69; Hurwitz, *Stunde Null*, 122, 325ff.

of cigarettes to keep quiet until the news was officially confirmed.[4] The editors of the *Neue Zeitung* came to perceive inter-Allied conflicts from quite a peculiar standpoint: while the tone of the *Neue Zeitung* was clearly anticommunist from the beginning, it was not anti-Soviet.

Editor in chief Hans Wallenberg made no secret of his anticommunist inclinations. His faith in the Social Democrats was not merely grounded in ideology. He also resented the communists' acceptance of former members of the NSDAP who simply changed political camps in order to continue their old principles under a new banner. Wallenberg's criticism of the KPD (Kommunistische Partei Deutschlands) began around New Year's Eve 1946 when several articles charged that all parties looked alike and were failing to focus on basic issues. The paper deplored the proposed merger of the SPD and KPD in Berlin as "absurd."[5] Once the proposed merger had been frustrated by a majority of the SPD in April 1946 and the communists in the Eastern zone formed the Sozialistische Einheitspartei Deutschlands (SED), the *Neue Zeitung* incessantly blamed the communists for their totalitarian strategies and antidemocratic politics.

To Wallenberg and many other editors of the *Neue Zeitung*, Germany's future lay in pan-Europeanism and German reunification. Their hero was Kurt Schumacher, head of the SPD, and the first German politician who officially visited a foreign country, Great Britain, in September 1946. The editors of the *Neue Zeitung* repeatedly praised the Social Democratic leader for his frankness and political skills. Far more frequently than other German politicians, he was allowed to voice his opinion in the columns of the paper.[6]

Wallenberg's sharp criticism intensified with the approach of the Berlin election in the fall of 1946. Under the headline "Bread and Politics," he denounced the SED's distribution of food in procommunist townships as "hunger propaganda" and "the veggie war." He concluded that while playing the Allies out against each other, the SED "throws itself at the Russian occupation power with a frenzy that is obviously designed to create the impression that it is much closer to the Soviet Union than the Allies themselves."[7]

4. Wyden, *Wall*, 181, 185ff.; Bahr, *Zu meiner Zeit*, 42.

5. Spectator, "Innerpolitische Rundschau der 'N.Z.,' " *Neue Zeitung*, 31 December 1945, p. 2; "Wahlbeteiligung—achtzig v.H.?" *Neue Zeitung*, 4 January 1946, p. 1; "Das Lebensproblem der SPD," *Neue Zeitung*, 25 February 1946, p. 3; "Kritik an der Berliner SPD," *Neue Zeitung*, 4 March 1946, p. 3; Spectator, "Innerpolitische Rundschau," *Neue Zeitung*, 22 February 1946, p. 2; "Erfolg der Agilen," *Neue Zeitung*, 28 March 1947, p. 7

6. Kurt Schumacher, "Deutschland und die Demokratie," *Neue Zeitung*, 22 March 1946, p. 3; "Der gordische Knoten," *Neue Zeitung*, 29 November 1946, p. 7; "Deutscher Internationalismus," *Neue Zeitung*, 17 January 1947, p. 7.

7. Hans Wallenberg, "Brot und Politik," *Neue Zeitung*, 2 August 1946, p. 7.

Time and again, Wallenberg reinvented this parallel between the SED and the Nazis. To him, the enemies in 1946 were not the Soviets but those Germans who once again were eager to please an authority and to follow orders without questioning them. The point was not that they were communists but that, in fact, they were Nazis and *Mitläufer* in disguise.[8]

"Fear not!" Wallenberg titled his most influential editorial, on 14 October 1946, in which he urged the Berlin people to participate in the elections. "In these days, the eyes of the world are focused on Berlin. On five continents, men are passionately debating the local elections in Berlin." The author declared that no occupation power, including the Soviets, could approve of a campaign designed to frighten voters. "If on 20 October the people of Berlin will renounce the fear, they will make the largest contribution to the reconstruction of democracy in Germany."[9]

Wallenberg's column had an enormous impact. Numerous Berlin newspapers and magazines reprinted the editorial. Even *The New York Times* analyzed it. The text was featured on a placard on advertising pillars throughout the city and was distributed as flyers to people in the streets. Decades later, books and dailies still commemorated the *Neue Zeitung*'s address to the people of Berlin. On election day, approximately 48 percent of the Berliners voted for the Social Democrats.[10]

Although the *Neue Zeitung* regularly criticized the SED, until the summer of 1947 the paper never openly ascribed the party's faults to the influence of Soviet authorities. In fact, the *Neue Zeitung*'s attitude toward the Soviet occupation power remained remarkably sympathetic. Like Clay, the paper openly supported the alliance of the four Allies. The German people's hope for a rupture between the Soviets and the Western Allies was still very much alive, Stefan Heym wrote in the very first issue of the *Neue Zeitung*, "particularly among people who still adhere to the old Goebbels argument that East and West cannot get along with each other." Nothing could be further from the truth, Heym continued, the great powers would never act independently from each other.[11]

8. "Zur Erinnerung," *Neue Zeitung*, 20 September 1946, p. 5. Interestingly, recent scholarship has argued along the same lines: Wilfried Loth, *Stalins ungeliebtes Kind: Warum Moskau die DDR nicht wollte* (Berlin: Rowohlt Berlin, 1994).

9. Hans Wallenberg, "Fürchtet Euch nicht!" *Neue Zeitung*, 14 October 1946, p. 7.

10. Quarterly Historical Report OMGB, 1 October–1 December 1946, RG 260, OMGUS 540/2, BHStA; Hans Wallenberg, interview by Alfred Fischer; Axel Springer, " 'Zum 65. Geburtstag von Hans Wallenberg," *Die Welt*, 27 November 1972, p. 4; W. Joachim Freyburg and Hans Wallenberg, eds., *Hundert Jahre Ullstein, 1877–1977* (Berlin: Ullstein, 1977), 3: 544–547; "48 Prozent der Berliner Wähler für die SPD," *Neue Zeitung*, 25 October 1946, p. 1.

11. Stefan Heym, "Weltpolitische Rundschau der 'N.Z.,' " *Neue Zeitung*, 18 October 1945, p. 2; "Berlin—neue Phase," *Neue Zeitung*, 28 October 1946, p. 7; "Die Wirkung

With front page headlines such as "The Three Powers Have Always Found A Solution," or "Allied Friendship: American-Russian Rally in New York," the editors sought to create the notion of unity and understanding among the occupation powers. A lengthy essay on 18 March 1946 downplayed the consequences of Churchill's speech at Fulton, pointing out that he had spoken as a private person, not as prime minister. Headlines such as "Russia Wants No Isolation" created the notion of cooperation and harmony. Twice—in November 1946 and in January 1947—the *Neue Zeitung* portrayed Stalin as a kind, peace-loving, and understanding man. Both Stalin and Byrnes, the paper emphasized shortly before the latter's resignation, agreed that German unity was their common end.[12]

Life under Soviet rule was not too bad, either, as many articles stated. As a POW returning from Russia reported in March 1947, the Soviets were a pragmatic and progressive people who had a far more liberal view of gender equality than Western politicians. Erich Kästner urged a revision of German children's literature, praising Soviet youth books that consciously discouraged elitism and class rivalry.[13] Moreover, the editors admired the Soviets' efforts to reestablish a glamorous cultural life in the city of Berlin. "They took care of the theater. They took care of people who should perform. They took care of the music," Friedrich Luft, chief editor of the Berlin cultural section, marveled decades later. "These were highly educated people. . . . [They] consulted us and wanted to know what and where to organize."[14] Long after most Western journalists had ceased to cover cultural events in East Berlin, editors of the *Neue Zeitung* regularly crossed the sector line in order to report on plays, musical events, and movies performed in the Soviet zone.

---

draußen," ibid.; "Das Ende eines Blocks," *Neue Zeitung*, 6 December 1946, p. 7; "Eile oder Weile?" *Neue Zeitung*, 16 December 1946, p. 7; "Das beste Dementi," *Neue Zeitung*, 6 January 1947, p. 7; "Peinlich," *Neue Zeitung*, 27 January 1947, p. 7; "So nicht," *Neue Zeitung*, 24 March 1947, p. 7; Hurwitz, *Eintracht der Siegermächte*, 130.

12. "Die Politik Rußlands," *Neue Zeitung*, 8 November 1945, p. 1; "Alliierte Freundschaft," *Neue Zeitung*, 18 November 1945, p. 1; "Weltpolitische Rundschau," *Neue Zeitung*, 18 March 1946, p. 2; "Stalin-Interview stark beachtet," *Neue Zeitung*, 1 November 1946, p. 2; "Stalins Antworten," ibid., p. 5; "Zwei-Zonen-Hetze," *Neue Zeitung*, 27 January 1947, p. 7.

13. Franz X. Jürke, "Die Kriegsgefangenen in Rußland," *Neue Zeitung*, 14 March 1947, p. 5; Erich Kästner, "Die Klassiker stehen Pate," *Neue Zeitung*, 21 October 1946, p. 6; Erich Kästner, "Sowjetrussische Kinderbücher," *Neue Zeitung*, 28 October 1946, p. 4.

14. Friedrich Luft, *Die Stimme der Kritik: Gespräch mit Hans Christoph Knebusch in der Reihe "Zeugen des Jahrhunderts"* (Göttingen: Lamuv Verlag, 1991), 44, 56ff.; Friedrich Luft, "Erinnerung an Hans Wallenberg," *Welt am Sonntag*, 17 April 1977; Hans Heinz Stuckenschmidt, *Zum Hören geboren: Ein Leben mit der Musik unserer Zeit* (Munich: Piper, 1979), 181f.

Criticism of Soviet policy in the columns of the *Neue Zeitung* appeared exclusively in quotations or reprints from other papers. Such reports portrayed the lackluster denazification efforts in the Eastern zone, the treatment of POWs in Soviet camps, the unjust Eastern border of Germany, the dismantling of German industry, and shortcomings of Soviet negotiation tactics.[15] Given the deplorable condition of Soviet occupation policies, according to the historian Norman Naimark, it might seem surprising that the editors refrained from condemning these policies. However, in the light of top officials' reluctance to publicly sever ties with the Soviets, this policy makes sense. The editors lacked either permission or information about the facts to write about them.

The *Neue Zeitung*'s tactic to cover but not to comment on Allied tensions changed with the Conference of Foreign Ministers in Moscow from 10 March to 24 April 1947, where Anglo-American delegates called for a higher level of German production in order to speed up the country's economic recovery. French and Soviet delegates rejected the proposal and voted for limited reparations from Germany's present production. The new U.S. secretary of state, George C. Marshall, and the British foreign secretary, Ernest Bevin, believing that the Soviets wanted to gain politically from the stalemated Allied negotiations, decided to continue moving unilaterally toward lifting the level of industry in Bizonia.[16]

The *Neue Zeitung*'s coverage during these months clearly reflected this shift in American foreign policy. Editorials now dealt directly with Soviet foreign policy. On 14 July 1947 the paper openly accused the Soviet Union of thwarting a common Allied policy in Central Europe, oppressing all states in their sphere of influence, and obstructing the Marshall Plan. Proposed in June 1947 by Secretary of State Marshall, this plan would contribute raw materials, food, and investments worth some $17 billion to Western Europe between 1948 and 1952. Like many U.S. policy makers, Marshall believed that Germany's rehabilitation was the key to Europe's economic and political stability. European stability, in turn, would relieve the United States of the financial burden of the occupation.[17]

15. "Gefährliches Gefälle," *Neue Zeitung*, 19 August 1946, p. 7; "Tor zur Hoffnung," *Neue Zeitung*, 13 September 1946, p. 5; "Bilanz von Paris," *Neue Zeitung*, 18 October 1946, p. 5; "Die Demontagen in der Sowjetzone," *Neue Zeitung*, 28 October 1946, p. 8; "Die Abtransporte von Facharbeitern," *Neue Zeitung*, 1 November 1946, p. 2; "Das Säuberungschaos in der Ostzone," *Neue Zeitung*, 31 January 1947, p. 5; "Deutliche Antwort," *Neue Zeitung*, 3 March 1947, p. 7.

16. Naimark, *The Russians in Germany*; Krieger, *Lucius D. Clay*, 166–78; Bruce Kuklick, *American Policy and the Division of Germany: The Clash with Russia over Reparations* (Ithaca, N.Y.: Cornell University Press, 1972), 234f.

17. Spectator, "Das Weltecho der Truman-Rede," *Neue Zeitung*, 17 March 1947, p. 7; "Der Viermächtepakt," *Neue Zeitung*, 18 April 1947, p. 7; "Das magere Resultat," *Neue Zei-*

Soviet officials rejected the Marshall Plan. Foreign Minister Molotov cautioned Western representatives that the plan would violate the autonomy of European states and might depart from previous agreements regarding Germany. Reparations were the most vital point on the Soviets' agenda and more important than Germany's economic recovery. During the war, the USSR had lost 31,850 industrial enterprises, 2,890 machine-tractor stations, 61 of the largest power stations, and almost half of its kolhozes. The Yalta Agreements targeted approximately $10 billion in reparations for the Soviet Union. If industrial production did not yield this amount, dismantling German factories would. When the United States initiated the Marshall Plan, portending the abandonment of reparations, the rift between the Soviet and the Western occupation powers widened considerably.[18]

The *Neue Zeitung* did not attribute ideological motivations to the Soviets' resistance: if Soviet Foreign Minister Molotov only *understood* the goodwill on the part of the West, the Eastern block could be helped. Instead, they blamed the widening rift between East and West on the East German communists. According to the paper, they were abusing socialist principles for fascist purposes and recruiting former Nazis—the same Nazis that had chased the émigrés into exile years ago. While the United States and the Soviet Union were still searching for common ground, the SED was driving a wedge between the two Allies in order to prevent German reunification. According to the *Neue Zeitung*, SED leaders were keenly aware that they would not succeed in a parliamentary system in a reunited Germany. They gambled that in a separate state and under the auspices of the Soviet Union they could build a strong socialist system.[19]

The *Neue Zeitung*'s interpretation of the split among the Allies resulted

---

*tung*, 25 April 1947, p. 7; Spectator, "Weltpolitische Rundschau," *Neue Zeitung*, 28 April 1947, p. 7; "Kein westdeutscher Staat," *Neue Zeitung*, 2 May 1947, p. 1; Carl Misch, "Amerikas Deutschlandpolitik in Moskau," *Neue Zeitung*, 2 May 1947, p. 6; "Die Wandlung in Europa," *Neue Zeitung*, 14 July 1947, p. 5; Krieger, *Lucius D. Clay*, 290ff.; John Gimbel, *The American Occupation of Germany: Politics and the Military, 1945–1949* (Stanford, Calif.: Stanford University Press, 1968), 148–51; Michael J. Hogan, *The Marshall Plan: America, Britain, and the Reconstruction of Western Europe, 1947–1952* (Cambridge: Cambridge University Press, 1987), 26–134; Charles Maier, *In Search of Stability: Explorations in Historical Political Economy* (New Rochelle, N.Y.: Cambridge University Press, 1987), 121–53.

18. Melvyn P. Leffler, *A Preponderance of Power: National Security, the Truman Administration, and the Cold War* (Stanford, Calif.: Stanford University Press, 1992), 5, 153f., 184–86, 218f.; Woodford McClellan, *Russia: The Soviet Period and After*, 3d ed. (Englewood Cliffs, N.J.: Prentice Hall, 1994), 169f., 178; Clay, *Decision in Germany*, 124.

19. "Nationalismus in der UdSSR," *Neue Zeitung*, 29 August 1947, p. 1; "Die Kunst des Möglichen," *Neue Zeitung*, 12 September 1947, p. 5; "SED-Parteitag eröffnet," *Neue Zeitung*, 22 September 1947, p. 2; "USA glauben nicht an Sozialismus," ibid.; "Vor der Weltöffentlichkeit," ibid., p. 5.

"Just because of the design, should I refuse such a gift? Nowadays . . ."

*This cartoon by Helmut Beyer, published in the* Neue Zeitung *on 18 July 1947, reflects German ambivalence toward the Marshall Plan.*

in a fierce dispute between Soviet and American press officers over what was fit to print. American reporters frequently published objective quotations under the protection of the First Amendment of the U.S. Constitution. For a Soviet press officer, in contrast, mere publication of an anticommunist quotation meant taking an anti-Soviet position.[20] The *Neue Zeitung*'s increasing propensity to print critical quotations or present facts about either Stalin's foreign policy or the SED offended the Soviets, who consequently restricted the paper's circulation in their zone.

20. Raue, *Im Dienste der Wahrheit*, 55, 76.

Inter-Allied conflicts over the *Neue Zeitung* escalated as early as January 1946. During the previous fall, the initial agreement to publish a four-power newspaper in Berlin had failed. In consequence, the American military government urged the Allied Control Council to encourage the interzonal exchange of information materials. On 31 December 1945 the Munich printing plant started shipping 200,000 copies of the *Neue Zeitung* to Berlin twice a week. These copies were supposed to replace the only U.S. Army Group paper in the city, the *Allgemeine Zeitung*, which had been closed on 11 November 1945 because of Soviet protests.[21]

A few days later, however, the SMAD (Soviet Military Administration) placed a ban on the *Neue Zeitung*. A public notice posted in the Eastern sector prohibited the reading and the purchase of the paper. At a meeting of the Informal Quadripartite Information Control Committee on 7 January 1946, ICD representatives reminded their Soviet colleagues of the provision of the Potsdam Agreement regarding freedom of the press. The Soviet delegate replied that there had never been an agreement regarding the exchange of newspapers among the four zones.[22]

The following month, Sergei Tjulpanov, chief of the Soviet information control, assured the American delegation that his government favored interzonal exchange in principle but reserved the right to exclude certain newspapers. When reminded of the ban against the *Neue Zeitung*, the colonel added that he was willing to lift it at once. The promise, however, was never fulfilled. Even worse, during the same month, the French military government also ordered postal services in the Saar to block and confiscate newspapers coming from other parts of Germany.[23]

The inter-Allied conflict over the *Neue Zeitung* intensified in May 1946 when the Polish Mission in Berlin denounced the paper's reprint of a British article on the expulsion of Germans from Polish territories. A second dispute evolved during the same month over a *Neue Zeitung* article that criticized Polish leaders for their political incompetence and questioned the va-

21. Hurwitz, *Eintracht der Siegermächte*, 86, 99; Gesine Frohner, "Die *Allgemeine Zeitung*: Portrait einer Zeitung für die Berliner Bevölkerung" (Master's thesis, Freie Universität Berlin, 1966).

22. Robert A. McClure, report to Lucius D. Clay, "Functional Program Control," 28 January 1946, RG 260, OMGUS 5/242–1/4, IfZ.

23. Robert D. Murphy, confidential telegram to Secretary of State, 15 February 1946, RG 84, Office of the Political Adviser in Germany, Berlin, classified cables to the State Department, box 4, WNRC; Sergej Tjulpanov, *Deutschland nach dem Kriege, 1945–1949: Erinnerungen eines Offiziers der Sowjetarmee*, trans. and ed. Stefan Doernberg, 2d ed. (Berlin: Dietz Verlag, 1987), 49, 56, 248, 293, 313; "German Propaganda Banned from the Saar," 24 April 1946, RG 226, Records of the Strategic Services Unit, War Department, M 1656 #1, NARA.

lidity of the Polish western borders along the Oder-Neisse line.[24] The essay offended Soviet authorities, too, because it disregarded Soviet interests, which favored the border and a Russia-friendly Poland that would serve as a buffer zone between Germany and the Soviet Union.

A few weeks later, Soviet authorities suggested limiting the exchange of newspapers, much to the fury of the U.S. political adviser. "The Russians want to prevent the circulation in their Zone of those papers which present a political, economic, or social point of view out of line with basic tenets of Marxian Communism, or that have been most critical of Soviet policies," Murphy's assistant, T. B. Wenner, angrily stated. He noted that the Soviets had broken the Potsdam Agreement and the doctrine of Allied unity because the *Tägliche Rundschau* "has been attacking, slurring, or by innuendo casting reflection upon the U.S. and Great Britain." Simultaneously, the Berlin SED evening paper *Vorwärts* frequently featured headlines such as "Inconsistencies of the U.S. Occupation Authorities," "Street Battles between Danes and Americans," or "Ten Million Americans Have No Right To Vote."[25]

In mid-July 1946 Soviet press officers reportedly increased the circulation of their paper, the *Tägliche Rundschau*, to over a million copies daily. News dealers were not allowed to sell any other newspapers before the last *Tägliche Rundschau* had been sold. In various cities in the Eastern zone, licensed editors reported that Russian censors altered practically everything they wrote and discouraged the sale of West Berlin publications by making house searches and arrests of people possessing such newspapers.[26]

In late summer 1946 the Soviet military government relaxed its attitude briefly. At a commandants' meeting on 9 August it confirmed an "agreement on control of cultural affairs," which guaranteed free interzonal distribution

24. Robert Murphy, Berlin, confidential telegram to Secretary of State, Berlin, 2 May 1946, RG 84, Office of POLAD Berlin, classified cables to the Department of State, 1945–49, box 5, WNRC; Max Kraus, interview, 14 July 1991; Hurwitz, *Eintracht der Siegermächte*, 139; "Polen Land zwischen Ost und West," *Neue Zeitung*, 24 May 1946, p. 2.

25. T. B. Wenner, "Free Speech and Press in Germany, under Potsdam. Interzonal Transmission of Newspapers in Germany," 22 July 1946, RG 84, POLAD Berlin, classified general correspondence, 1946, dec. file 891, box 122, WNRC; Memorandum, August 1946, RG 260, OMGUS 5/241–1/7, IfZ.

26. Office of Strategic Services, Report July–August 1946, 26 August 1946, RG 226, Entry 108A, box 28, Wash-Reg-INT 39, LB 400, NARA; "Germany (Russian Zone and Berlin) Political: Current Newspaper Situation, March–April 1946," 26 April 1946, RG 226, Entry 108A, box 27, Wash-Reg-INT-39, LB 225, NARA; "Germany/Russian Zone and Berlin: Current Newspaper Situation, March–April 1946," 26 April 1946, RG 226, Strategic Services Unit, M 1565 #2, NARA; "Germany (Russian Zone) Political: Press Notes, July–August 1946," 26 August 1946, RG 226, Entry 108A, box 28, Wash-Reg-INT-39, LB 400, NARA.

of Allied approved newspapers throughout Berlin. Less than two weeks later, however, in an action covering the entire Russian sector of Berlin, East-German policemen under Soviet orders seized copies of No. 66 of the *Neue Zeitung*. This issue contained electoral instructions by the president of the Berlin SPD, Franz Neumann, and an interview with the political adviser of the State Department, Robert Murphy, emphasizing the need for free interzonal exchange of newspapers.[27]

On 23 August 1946, Major General Frank A. Keating, the American commander of Berlin, vigorously protested the massive confiscation of the *Neue Zeitung* and the U.S. licensed *Tagesspiegel*. The Soviet commander of Berlin, Major General Kotikov, defended the measure on the grounds that both papers had carried unauthorized criticism of an occupation power. Subsequently, General Clay brought up the subject of freedom of the press in the Coordinating Committee meeting and urged the Soviets to punish the respective editors in the Eastern zone for their false reports.[28] The Potsdam Agreement, he reminded the Soviets, obliged them to take measures against licensed editors scolding an Allied power.

U.S. officials were still reluctant to let the dispute break out openly. They repeated their protest behind closed doors at the Information Committee meeting on 9 September 1946, warning that if all Allies engaged in mutual confiscation, it would undermine the objectives of Allied occupation. Internal conflicts, Keating added, would only discredit the occupation powers "in the minds of the people of a country with which the Allies are still technically at war."[29]

27. F. N. Leonard, U.S. Civilian, Chief of Branch, OMGUS, Berlin District, ICD, to Director, OMGUS, Berlin District, "Agreement on citywide distribution of newspapers," RG 260, OMGUS 5/246–2/12a, IfZ; OMGUS Berlin District, ICD, "Confiscation of *Die Neue Zeitung*," 11 [21] August 1946, RG 260, OMGUS 5/246–2/12a, IfZ; Memorandum "Die *Neue Zeitung*: Comments on a Confiscation," 26 August 1946, RG 260, OMGUS/ISD 5/241–1/7, IfZ; "Das Interview mit Botschafter Murphy," *Neue Zeitung*, 19 August 1946, pp. 1, 5.

28. "Information Control," Bi-Monthly Report of the Military Governor No. 15, OMGUS, 1 August to 30 September 1946, 1, RG 260, DK 101.006, IfZ; Robert A. Murphy, telegram to Secretary of State, 26 August 1946, RG 84, Office POLAD Berlin, classified cables to Department of State, 1945–49, box 6, WNRC; Frank L. Howley, Colonel, CAV, Director, to Deputy Military Governor for Germany, OMGUS, "Confiscation of Newspapers," 29 August 1946, courtesy of Harold J. Hurwitz, Berlin; Hurwitz, *Stunde Null*, 327f.

29. A. V. Chukayeff, Secretariat, Information Control, to Mr. R. M. Barry, Secretariat, Political Directorate, "Seizure of the American licensed newspapers *Der Tagesspiegel* and *Die Neue Zeitung* in the Soviet Sector of Berlin," "Protest on Seizure of *Der Tagesspiegel*, *Die Neue Zeitung* in Russian Sector of Berlin," 13 September 1946, RG 84, Office POLAD Berlin, classified general correspondence, 1946, box 122, dec. file 891, WNRC; Director, Office POLAD, memorandum to Major General Frank A. Keating, Acting Deputy Military Governor for Germany, 27 November 1946, RG 84, Office POLAD, Berlin, classified general correspondence, 1946, dec. file 891, box 123, WNRC; Hurwitz, *Stunde Null*, 328.

At the heart of the matter lay a different understanding of administrative jurisdiction between U.S. and Soviet press officers. As with their standpoint regarding reparations and dismantling, Soviet officials argued that the distribution of newspapers was a zonal matter, falling under the jurisdiction of the Soviet military governor. Anglo-American officials, in contrast, regarded the circulation of news publications as a policy matter covering all of Germany and thus falling under the control of the Allied Control Council. They reinforced this argument by pointing to the universal principle of freedom of speech.

Throughout the winter of 1946–1947, both the Soviets and the Americans claimed that the other power violated Directives No. 4 and No. 40, the Potsdam Agreement, and the doctrine of inter-Allied harmony. The Soviets blamed the *Neue Zeitung* for multiplying the numbers of German POWs in their sphere of influence, downplaying the denazification efforts of the Russian military forces, and spreading rumors on kidnapping and starvation in the Eastern zone. U.S. officials, such as Robert Murphy and Frank Keating, in turn, protested the Soviet ban on Western journalists and newspapers in their zone.[30] Another Directive (No. 55), signed in June 1947, did not terminate the quarrel.

These disputes between Soviet and American representatives led to a change in the development of the *Neue Zeitung*. Until August 1946 the paper had mostly been a concern of the ICD. But as tensions worsened over reparations, dismantlement, Berlin, and the exchange of information material, U.S. officials, such as H. Freeman Matthews, chief of the division for West European affairs in the State Department, began to consider using the *Neue Zeitung* for propaganda purposes against the Soviet Union.[31]

In December 1946 Robert Murphy asked James Byrnes if it was time to counter Soviet propaganda. The secretary of state, however, urged caution. As Robert Messer has shown, for a brief time Byrnes, in an effort to internationalize control over atomic energy and the use of the A-bomb, turned

30. Heath, telegram to Secretary of State, 29 March 1947, RG 84, Office POLAD, Berlin, classified cables to Department of State, 1945–49, box 8, WNRC; Muccio/Wenner, telegram to Secretary of State, 12 February 1947, RG 84, Office POLAD, Berlin, classified cables to the State Department, 1945–49, box 8, WNRC; Lucius D. Clay, message to the War Department, 1 March 1947, OMGUS 5/246–2/12a, IfZ; Allied Control Authority, Control Council, Directive No. 55, "Interzonal Exchange of Printed Matter and Films," 25 June 1947, signed by R. Noiret, M. I. Dratvin, F. A. Keating, B. H. Robertson, RG 260, OMGUS 3/429–2/39, IfZ; Hurwitz, *Stunde Null*, 331f.; Norman M. Naimark, "The Soviet Gulag in Eastern Germany, 1945–50," in *The Soviet Empire Reconsidered: Essays in Honor of Adam B. Ulam*, ed. Sanford R. Lieberman, David E. Powell, and Carol Saivetz (Boulder, Colo.: Westview Press, 1994), 83.

31. H. Freeman Matthews to Secretary of State, 6 November 1946, courtesy of Harold J. Hurwitz, Berlin; Smith, "The View from USFET," 67.

from a "less coercive" to a more positive approach vis-à-vis the Soviets.[32] The United States' only objective should be "to correct" false statements of the Soviet-controlled German media, Byrnes advised Murphy.

Byrnes and Murphy did agree, however, that certain propaganda material should be used in official organs such as the *Neue Zeitung.* Starting in December 1946 Hans Wallenberg in Munich and Enno Hobbing of the Berlin bureau, as well as selected German radio stations and the newswire service DENA, received special secret instructions regarding what they should publish. In early 1947 the Publishing Operations Branch of the ICD received $1 million dollars to employ correspondents in London, Paris, Zurich, Prague, and the United States.[33]

Finally, in the spring of 1947 the ICD installed a Berlin edition of the *Neue Zeitung* as an American counterweight to the Soviet official paper *Tägliche Rundschau* and to influence public opinion in case the city was cut off from Western newspapers. "The United States is placed in an unfavorable light when the frequency of its official publication for the German population is compared with that of the daily *Tägliche Rundschau,*" W. Phillips Davison, chief of the Plans and Directives Section of the ICD, pointed out in September 1946. Byrnes' Stuttgart speech had defined U.S. policy more clearly, "and it is primarily the responsibility of U.S.-published organs to expand this policy."[34]

The paper, entitled *Berliner Blatt,* consisted of a special four-page supplement inserted into the main editions published in Munich and Frankfurt. There were approximately one hundred thousand copies per issue. Enno Hobbing, hitherto chief of the paper's local bureau and one of Berlin's shrewdest, most outspoken postwar journalists, became chief of the *Berliner Blatt.* The grandnephew of a famous Berlin publisher, Hobbing had emi-

32. Robert L. Messer, *The End of an Alliance: James F. Byrnes, Roosevelt, Truman, and the Origins of the Cold War* (Chapel Hill: University of North Carolina Press, 1982), 141; Robert Murphy, cable to James Byrnes, 28 December 1946, RG 165, Entry 463, 014, Sec. XVII, box 236, NARA.

33. Cable from James Byrnes to Robert Murphy, 30 December 1946, ibid.; "Information Control," Quarterly Historical Report, OMGB/ICD, Press Control, 1 January–31 March 1947, RG 260, OMGUS CO-547/1, BHStA; John DeForrest to Chief, OMGUS/ICD, Press Control, 9 July 1947, "Dollar Credits for Publishing Operations Branch," RG 260, OMGUS 5/241–1/11, IfZ.

34. Hans Wallenberg to Director, Office of Director of Information Control, OMGUS, "Berlin Supplement *Neue Zeitung,*" 1 December 1946, RG 260, OMGUS/ISD 5/241–1/11, BArch; "Public Operation Branch," OMGBY Weekly Detachment Report, No. 97, Week ending 20 March 1947, RG 260, OMGBY 13/142–2/9, BHStA; W. P. Davison, Chief Plans & Directives Branch, to the Director of Information Control, "Increase in Frequency of *Die Neue Zeitung,*" 19 September 1946, RG 260, OMGUS/ISD 5/241–1/7, BArch.

grated with his parents to the United States in 1927 at the age of seven. With its highbrow approach and a strong emphasis on cultural affairs, the *Berliner Blatt* was specifically geared toward an intellectual elite, a concept that proved successful. Sixty percent of the readers interviewed in mid-1947 welcomed the new edition as "another organ of expression for Western democracy." Only 16 percent of a sample of readers felt the Berlin supplement represented an American standpoint while 52 percent labeled it as impartial.[35]

Soviet reactions to the Truman Doctrine and to the Marshall Plan in 1947 reassured U.S. policy makers that their decision to deploy more anti-Soviet propaganda had been the right one. In August 1947 Stalin established the international Communist Information Bureau (Cominform). Molotov presented a plan designed to integrate the economies of all East European countries. By the fall of 1947, the Cold War would be in full swing.

The leaders of the *Neue Zeitung*, above all Wallenberg and Hobbing, supported the intensified effort to counter communist propaganda. But they were not always willing to accept orders. Starting in the summer of 1946, the *Neue Zeitung* received an increasing number of memoranda from various military government offices recommending the reprinting of articles, editorials, and speeches on subjects ranging from denazification and atomic energy to Soviet occupation policy and the SPD/KPD union. Because of the ICD's pressures, Wallenberg became increasingly frustrated with his job at Schellingstraße 39. Coworkers described him as overworked and tired and in dire need of a vacation. Moreover, there was a serious shortage of personnel at the paper. Many staffers had left in May 1946 and were not replaced. Another 30 percent cut in personnel of the military government was planned for fall 1946, much to the horror of the editor in chief.[36]

35. "Information Control," Monthly Report of the Military Governor No. 21, OMGUS, March 1947, 20, DK 101.006, IfZ; "Public Operation Branch," OMGBY Weekly Detachment Report, No. 97, Week ending 20 March 1947, RG 260, OMGBY 13/142–2/9, BHStA; Henry P. Pilgert and Helga Dobbert, *Press, Radio, and Film in West Germany* (Bad Godesberg: Historical Division, Office of the Executive Secretary, Office of the U.S. High Commissioner for Germany, 1953), 58; Elmer Plischke and Henry P. Pilgert, *U.S. Information Programs in Berlin* (Historical Division, Office of the Executive Secretary, Office of the U.S High Commissioner for Germany, 1953), 12, DK 157.028, IfZ; biographical sheet in Enno Hobbing, *How to Act and Talk Like A College Graduate in Eleven Days* (Bethesda, Md.: Stone Trail Press, 1986), vi; "Report on Reactions of leading personalities in Berlin to the *Neue Zeitung* Berlin Edition," n. d. (approx. summer of 1947), RG 260, OMGUS 5/241–1/7, IfZ; Hans Wallenberg to Director, Office of Director of Information Control, OMGUS, "Berlin Supplement *Neue Zeitung*," 1 December 1946, RG 260, OMGUS/ISD 5/241–1/11, BArch; Hurwitz, *Stunde Null*, 353.

36. Douglas Waples, Lt. Col., Chief, Publications Control Branch, to Col. Kinard for Brigadier General McClure, "Mr. Toombs' Memoranda re Klostermann," 7 July 1946, OMGUS/ISD 5/269–1/7, IfZ; Edward T. Peeples to Hans Wallenberg, 10 July 1946, RG 260, OMGUS 5/241–1/7, IfZ; "Notes on Trip to Berlin," 16 and 17 July, 1946, RG 260, OMGBY 10/117–

The lack of manpower and supplies posed a major problem to Wallenberg. The shortage of paper and newsprint caused circulation to drop 27 percent, from 1,500,000 in March 1946 to 1,100,000 in November. Editors had to submit requests for cars, gasoline, and printing rollers. In Munich the staff had to "scrounge transportation for moving newsprint from the mill to the newspaper." Rusty, battered radiators were supposed to provide heat, but plant managers could not even obtain coal.[37]

The editor in chief believed these shortages reflected the lack of appreciation of his work among OMGUS officials. What right did the State or the War Department or the ICD have to send news and editorials if they could not even provide the paper or the gasoline necessary for the venture? Such fundamental dissatisfaction turned every petty dispute into a major debate. Shortly after his appointment in March 1946, Wallenberg offered his resignation. He would do this repeatedly as he became increasingly exasperated with the ICD's interference and the supply problems. Each time, McClure called him in to headquarters, stroked Wallenberg's ego, and convinced him to stay on the job a while longer.[38]

In 1947 these internal disputes coincided with a general rise of suspicion among Americans regarding émigrés. Individual *Neue Zeitung* staffers continuously complained about the fact that the American press corps looked down upon their paper. In March 1947 the army paper, *Stars and Stripes,* charged that the *Neue Zeitung* was simply printing propaganda from Washington. When Byrnes visited Munich in September 1946, Hans Wallenberg

---

2/5, BHStA; "*Die Neue Zeitung* Editorializes on the Venedey Case," 20 August 1946, RG 260, OMGUS 5/241–1/7, IfZ; "Jim," OMGUS/ICD, to Henry P. Leverich, Chief Area V, OIC, Department of State, "Trip to U.S. Zone," 15/17 April 1946, courtesy of Harold J. Hurwitz; General Lucius D. Clay, oral history interview by Richard D. McKinzie, 10; Nicholas Nabokoff to Ambassador Murphy, "Mr. Victor Hunt's and Mr. N. Nabokoff's visit to Munich," 1 October 1946, RG 84, Office POLAD, Berlin, classified general correspondence, 1946, dec. file 891, box 123, WNRC.

37. OMGBY Weekly Reports, Nos. 46–54, 22 March–13 May, 1946, RG 260, OMGBY 13/142–2/5, BHStA; OMGB Land Director, After Action Report of April, 1946, RG 260, OMGBY 13/147–2/21, BHStA; Public Operation Branch, Weekly Operations Report, No. 44, 30 October–5 November, 1946, RG 260, OMGUS 5/233–1/14, IfZ; John DeForrest, "Re. *Neue Zeitung*," 29 November 1946, RG 260, OMGUS/ISD 5/241–1/7, BArch; "Public Operation Branch," OMGBY Weekly Detachment Report, No. 78, week ending 7 November 1946, RG 260, OMGBY 13/142–2/8, BHStA.; F. N. Leonard, U.S. civilian, Chief, OMGBS/Information Control Branch, to J. L. Kaiser, OMGBS, 20 March 1947, RG 260, OMGBS 4/11–2/24, LAB; David E. Warne, Chief, Press Section, RO, memorandum to Lt. Col. R. B. McRae, Chief, Reorientation Branch, CAD, "Report on a Survey Trip to Germany, Austria, and Venezia Giulia," no date (trip was finished on November 25, 1946), RG 260, OMGUS 5/242–2/15, IfZ.

38. Max Kraus, interview, 6 July 1991; Hurwitz, *Stunde Null*, 264; Netzer, *Die Neue Zeitung*, 17.

barely succeeded in gaining access to him and was "humiliated in the process." Editor Heinz Norden was denied accommodations at the Berlin press camp. Such inconveniences, Wallenberg furiously wrote to the ICD, placed "editors, correspondents and photographers of this press at a crippling disadvantage as against their counterparts [foreign correspondents] working for private enterprise."[39]

These disputes between the editors of the *Neue Zeitung* and their American colleagues reflected the increasing doubts on the part of many American-born officers in the military government regarding the editors' aptitude for their mission. "Clay was basically antagonistic to employ Germans [émigrés] in his operation," Henry Kellermann from the Bureau of German Affairs in the State Department remembers. He felt they could not be very good representatives of the United States. In April 1947 Clay issued a secret order urging the removal of non-American-born soldiers from military government. And in 1948 the State Department itself launched an initiative to eliminate all foreign-born Americans from the military government.[40]

Part of this attitude can be explained with the prevalence of anti-Semitism in the United States in the 1930s and 1940s when Jews became the prime target in a predominantly Protestant culture. Many Americans perceived Jews either as a strange mixture of conspiratorial clannishness and mysterious medieval attitudes or as representatives of everything that was scary about modernity, banking, commerce, and journalism. In 1946, 55 percent of the American people felt that "Jews have too much power in the United States." Congressional debates echoed the public's concern. The U.S. Immigration Act of 1924 had already made it very hard for refugee Jews to enter the United States. Even the Displaced Persons Act, drafted in 1948 and designed to help victims who did not want to return to their home countries, favored ethnic Germans over Jewish immigrants.[41]

39. W. M. Pillsbury, Plans and Directives Branch, OMGBY/ICD, to Robert McClure and Arthur Eggleston, "Conversation between Colonel Kinard and Mr. Wallenberg on Subject of Radio News Item," 20 March 1947, RG 260, OMGUS 5/241–1/11, BArch; Arthur Eggleston to Gordon Textor, 27 May 1947, RG 260, OMGUS 5/241–1/11, IfZ; Hans Wallenberg to Director, OMGUS/ICD, 25 September 1946, RG 260, OMGUS 5/266–3/18, IfZ.

40. In the long run, these efforts were rather unsuccessful. Frank A. Keating, Deputy Military Governor, to Director, OMG Hesse, "Employment and Renewal of Contracts of Naturalized American Civilian Employees," 7 April 1947, RG 260, OMGUS, U.S. Occupation HQ, box 581, file AG 49, B43, WNRC (Frank Keating was appointed acting Deputy Military Governor in April 1947; I am indebted to Guy Stern for this reference); Delbert Clark, "Clay will retain German-Born Help," *New York Times*, 5 May 1947, p. 5; Bausch, *Kulturpolitik*, 179f.; Henry Kellermann and Max W. Kraus, interview, 16 May 1994; Jack M. Stuart, interview, 20 March 1994; letters to the author from Ernst Cramer, 9 March 1994, and W. Phillips Davison, 15 March 1994.

41. Frederic Cople Jaher, *A Scapegoat in the New Wilderness: The Origins and Rise of Anti-Semitism in America* (Cambridge, Mass.: Harvard University Press, 1994), 177–241, 246,

Simultaneously, in 1947 American society turned increasingly anticommunist after the inauguration of a new Republican Congress. Determined to crush the last remnants of the New Deal, a breed of conservative politicians, combined with both religious right-wingers and super-patriotic businessmen, found anticommunism a very attractive rallying point. While Republicans identified anticommunism with values and customs lying at the heart of their identity, orthodox clergymen often likened the conflict to the last battle between Satan and Christ. Most important, both conservatives and liberals truly feared Soviet political and ideological power in the international arena and its influences at home. At the crossroads of these two developments—the increasing anti-Semitism along with the rise of anticommunism—Jewish émigrés often became identified as Bolsheviks.[42]

In the unfolding Cold War this accumulation of perceived threats raised a fundamental question: were the exiles loyal to America? Could an intellectual Jew of European descent be a good representative of American life? In the spring of 1946 State Department researchers stated that three men, namely, Hans Wallenberg, Egon Jameson, and Arthur Steiner, ran the U.S. paper in Germany with a readership of ten million people. "None of these is a U.S. national," the report pointed out dryly, ignoring the fact that both Wallenberg and Steiner had U.S. citizenship.[43] Meanwhile, the Hearst Press denounced famous Jewish writer Alfred Kantorowicz, an émigré from New York and frequent contributor to the *Neue Zeitung*, as "one of Russia's top espionage agents" in the United States.[44]

In 1947 the writer Curt Riess, who had been working for the Office of Strategic Services, applied for a job at the *Neue Zeitung*. But the Counter Intelligence Corps declared him "not eligible for entry into occupied Zones" because he had befriended "leading communists." The Intelligence Branch of the ICD identified Hans Mayer, a freelance journalist who occasionally

247; Leonard Dinnerstein, *Uneasy at Home: Antisemitism and the American Jewish Experience* (New York: Columbia University Press, 1987), 178–217; Robert S. Wistrich, *Antisemitism: The Longest Hatred* (New York: Pantheon Books, 1991), 114–25; Richard Breitman and Alan M. Kraut, *American Refugee Policy and European Jewry, 1933–1945* (Bloomington, Ind.: Indiana University Press, 1987).

42. Michael N. Dobkowski, *The Tarnished Dream: The Basis of American Anti-Semitism* (Westport, Conn.: Greenwood Press, 1979), 171–208; Melvyn P. Leffler, *The Specter of Communism: The United States and the Origins of the Cold War, 1917–1953* (New York: Hill and Wang, 1994), 59–63.

43. "Jim," OMGUS/ICD, to Henry P. Leverich, Chief Area V, OIC, Department of State, "Trip to U.S. Zone," 15/17 April 1946, courtesy of Harold J. Hurwitz.

44. A. F. Hennings, Capt. Ass. Executive, USFET, to Director of Intelligence, OMGUS, "Investigation of Alfred Kantorowicz," 13 February 1947, RG 260, OMGUS 5/246–3/29, IfZ; Alfred Kantorowicz, curriculum vitae and statement, Berlin, 4 March 1947, RG 260, OMGUS 5/246–3/29, IfZ; Kantorowicz to Arthur Eggleston, 6 March 1947, ibid.

wrote book reviews for the *Neue Zeitung*, as "a member of a Communist organization in Switzerland . . . though he allegedly denies any connection with the KPD of Germany."[45]

Americans felt that the exiles themselves had not sufficiently internalized the values of a democracy sufficiently to provide a fit example to the Germans. They were too exposed to special "emotional influences" in German affairs.[46] "Only persons of American schooling and education who thoroughly believe in our American form of democracy, its Constitutional background and practices, should be our United States representatives in Germany," a group of U.S. businessmen touring the U.S. zone in May 1947 told the secretary of war. "If we hope to bring the principles of democracy to the Germans we must send persons who will be living examples of our thinking upon government at its best."[47]

This assessment dealt a blow to many émigrés, and their reactions once again confirmed their strong ties to Germany. They believed they were in a unique position to have absorbed the American spirit while still possessing a bond with their homeland. The *Neue Zeitung* emphasized that new democratic ideas had to come from emigrated intellectuals because the German intelligentsia had failed over and over again. "My Place Is In Germany," freelance writer and former émigré Alfred Kantorowicz exclaimed on 14 February 1947, stressing that his exodus to the United States was not fate but part of his struggle on behalf of Germany. The editors pointed to the "moral and political" benefits that every returned exile brought back to his original home.[48]

45. James O'Sheen, Lt. Col., Chief of Intelligence, OMG Hesse, to Chief of Intelligence, OMGBY, 6 March 1947; note by Anthony F. Kleitz, Lt. Col., Chief of Intelligence Branch, ICD, 19 March 1947, RG 260, OMGBY 15/101–3/26, BHStA.

46. Correspondence between Robert Murphy, Lucius D. Clay, Gordon E. Textor, Berlin, and Curt Riess, New York, November 1947–May 1948, RG 84, Office POLAD Berlin, classified general correspondence of POLAD, 1948, box 8, WNRC; "Geburtsland: Deutschland," *Neue Zeitung*, 26 May 1947, p. 1; Delbert Clark, "Clay will retain German-Born Help," *New York Times*, 5 May 1947, p. 5; Edward Peterson, *The Many Faces of Defeat: The German People's Experience in 1945* (New York: Peter Lang, 1990), 164.

47. L. M. Mac Donald, T. W. Smith, Jr., Henry E. Luhrs, "Report of Representatives from the Toy Manufacturers of the U.S.A., Inc., on their trip to Germany sent to the War and the State Dept.," June 1947, RG 107, Office of the Secretary of War, Assistant Secretary of War, correspondence Howard Peterson, dec. file 091 (Germany), box 7, NARA.

48. F. C. Weiskopf, "Die Schule des Exils," *Neue Zeitung*, 24 June 1946, *Feuilleton*; Karl O. Paetel, "Heimkehr," *Neue Zeitung*, 4 January 1947, *Feuilleton*; Manfred George, "Der große Ausverkauf," *Neue Zeitung*, 6 January 1947, *Feuilleton*; Carl Weiskopf, " 'Denk ich an Deutschland in der Nacht . . . ,'" *Neue Zeitung*, 7 February 1947, *Feuilleton*; Alfred Kantorowicz, "Mein Platz ist in Deutschland," *Neue Zeitung*, 14 February 1947, *Feuilleton*; Leopold Goldschmidt, "Innerpolitische Rundschau," *Neue Zeitung*, 22 August 1947, p. 5. For more on

In the midst of this debate, ICD chief McClure returned to the Pentagon to lead the Civil Affairs Division. Clay appointed Gordon E. Textor, a West Point graduate and a colonel in the Engineering Corps, as his successor. Impressing some of his staffers as "pompous" and stiff, Textor proved to be a much harsher chief than his predecessor. In August 1947, when Wallenberg turned in another resignation in order to protest some new intrusion, Textor immediately accepted it. Wallenberg, much to his dismay, was permitted to return home to the United States. Shortly thereafter, Leopold Goldschmidt, Arthur Steiner, and Erich Kästner turned in their resignations.[49]

Wallenberg's sudden departure was perhaps the most confusing aspect of his editorial career at the *Neue Zeitung*. The editor in chief was a staunch anticommunist and often criticized the SED to a degree that was far beyond his authority. Therefore, the decision to let the Jewish editor of the *Neue Zeitung* depart did not reflect an interpersonal conflict but a political move. At the same time, however, U.S. officials distrusted the newspaper because they believed that the editors were not sufficiently pro-American and anticommunist. In fact, shortly after Wallenberg's departure, on 28 October 1947, General Clay publicly proclaimed the beginning of the "Operation Talk Back," designed to attack "Communism and the police state before the German people."[50]

In 1946–1947, the *Neue Zeitung* became a hotly debated issue in the conflict between East and West. U.S. officials such as Byrnes and Clay were reluctant to break openly the Potsdam Agreement, which forbade inter-Allied press criticism. While it was natural for U.S. officials to talk tough to the Soviets and pursue their own policies regarding reparation, dismantling, and economic reconstruction, overt criticism of the Soviet military government would have meant the official recognition of a split in the great four-

exile literature in postwar Germany, see Gerhard Roloff, *Exil und Exilliteratur in der deutschen Presse, 1945–1949: Ein Beitrag zur Rezeptionsgeschichte* (Worms: Heintz, 1976); Jessica C. E. Gienow-Hecht, "Anti-Communism and Other Enemy Images in the U.S. Occupation of Germany, 1947–48," *Enemy Images in American History*, ed. Ragnhild Fiebig-von Hase and Ursula Lehmkuhl (Providence, R.I.: Berghahn Books, 1997), 281–300.

49. "Ein Rücktritt," *Tagesspiegel*, 6 August 1946; "Ob 1000 Redakteure fallen," *Berlin am Mittag*, 29 September 1947; Max W. Kraus, letter to the author, 8 March 1994; Max Kraus, interview, Washington, D.C., 6 July 1991; Hans Lehmann, interview; Jack M. Stuart, interview, 20 March 1994; Hurwitz, *Stunde Null*, 165, 231, 267, 321; Bausch, *Kulturpolitik*, 141, 173.

50. Backer, *Winds of History*, 202; Hurwitz, *Stunde Null*, 333ff.; Peter Wyden, interview.

power coalition. President Truman himself avoided such rhetoric in public until March 1947 when he announced his intention to provide Greece and Turkey with massive economic help. The editors of the *Neue Zeitung* discreetly compromised on this directive by following an anticommunist but not an anti-Soviet course. In their view, the inter-Allied tensions were primarily caused by East German communists who were simply disguised Nazis and wanted to avoid punishment for their crimes by building a separate state.

When inter-Allied conflicts intensified and the Soviets banned the *Neue Zeitung* from their zone, OMGUS and the State Department came to recognize the newspaper as a viable tool for inter-Allied policy and the promotion of American ideology in the Soviet zone. Simultaneously, American observers began to question the émigrés' aptitude for their job because they seemed too leftist, too emotional, and therefore inappropriate for service in the impending word war.

Wallenberg's departure from the plant in September 1947, then, marked the end of an era in the history of the *Neue Zeitung*. "He has brought this paper to international attention, he has turned it into a voice of America . . . sounding not as an instructor but out of a deep understanding for humanity," a farewell article in the *Neue Zeitung* read. "It made those who might have been bitter and resistant at the beginning, feel that this was not propaganda but the discreet spreading of truth" in order "to give the German people what they were lacking more than anything else: the hope for a future."[51] This formula had been the *Neue Zeitung*'s secret recipe for success. But as subsequent events showed, after Wallenberg's departure the paper would never again be what it once had been.

51. "Ein Wort des Abschieds," *Neue Zeitung*, 12 September 1947, p. 5.

Woman amid debris in postwar Germany.

*Courtesy Presse-und Informationsamt der Bundesregierung, Bonn.*

German children in postwar Berlin play on the rubble in front of the Brandenburg Gate.

*Courtesy Presse-und Informationsamt der Bundesregierung, Bonn.*

Lucius D. Clay, military governor of the U.S. zone.

*Courtesy Bundesarchiv Koblenz [Bild 14618514718].*

Robert D. Murphy, political advisor to the *Neue Zeitung* from the U.S. State Department.

*Courtesy Bundesarchiv Koblenz [Bild 1831R68237].*

Sergei Tjulpanov, head of Information Control Division in the Soviet zone.

*Courtesy Bundesarchiv Koblenz [Bild 1831V4595].*

Hans Habe, founder and first editor in chief of the *Neue Zeitung*.

*Courtesy Bundesarchiv Koblenz [Bild 146197134113A].*

Hans Wallenberg *(sitting at desk)*, editor in chief of the *Neue Zeitung* from 1946 to 1948, puts some finishing touches on a forthcoming issue, while Hans Lehmann *(left)* looks on. Behind Wallenberg are *(left to right)* Else Reventlow, Erich Kästner, Arthur Steiner, and Egon Jameson.

*Courtesy Beatrice del Bondio-Reventlow.*

Editorial staff at the *Neue Zeitung*, October 1945. Hans Wallenberg *(first row, second from left)* stands next to Hans Habe *(seated)*. Behind and between them is Max Kraus *(wearing glasses)*. Ernest Wynder is fourth from the right.

*Courtesy Kurt Wittler.*

Ernst Cramer, deputy editor in chief of the *Neue Zeitung* from 1948 to 1949.

*Courtesy Peter Wyden.*

Streetcar advertising the *Neue Zeitung*.

*Courtesy Institut für Zeitgeschichte, Koblenz, Sammlung Netzer [ED 352].*

# 6

## SABOTAGE AND HOUSECLEANING: U.S. COLD WAR INFORMATION POLITICS, 1947–1948

WALTER KOLBENHOFF WAS SHOCKED. FOR TWO YEARS, THE FORTY-YEAR-OLD novelist had been leading a comfortable and creative life as editor of the cultural section at the *Neue Zeitung* under Hans Wallenberg. His award-winning novel *Von unserm Fleisch und Blut* (Of our flesh and blood) had just been published by the prestigious publishing house Bermann-Fischer. Yet the newly appointed American-born editor in chief, Jack Fleischer, almost fired the author. "You have done extremely little work for the *Neue Zeitung,*" his new boss threatened Kolbenhoff in June 1948. To work for the official voice of the U.S. army, Fleischer expounded, had nothing to do with literary creativity, "which is what you might be interested in, and which you can, of course, perform during your leisure time."[1]

Hans Wallenberg's resignation in August 1947 marked the end of the émigrés' independence at the *Neue Zeitung* and triggered a dramatic—if short-lived—change. Clay hoped to forestall communist influence in Germany and appointed a professional U.S. journalist for the plant in Schellingstrasse 39, much to the horror of the German staffers. This change in policy officially shifted the *Neue Zeitung*'s role from that of a mediator between occupation forces and German civilians in the U.S. zone to that of a loudspeaker directed toward all German-speaking readers. Nonetheless, U.S. officials proved to be reluctant and awkward propagandists. They became increasingly censorious of the paper. They made quite an effort to expand the *Neue Zeitung* materially by increasing the circulation and exporting hundreds of thousands of copies to the East. They appointed a new editor in chief. But they hesitated to tell him what to print.

Grandson of an immigrant couple from Pomerania, thirty-three-year-old Jack Fleischer, a lean, quiet, bespectacled man, had grown up in Milwaukee. In 1940 he became a foreign correspondent for the United Press in Scandinavia and Berlin, and from 1945 to 1947 he worked for *Time* and *Life* In-

1. Jack Fleischer to Walter Kolbenhoff, 19 June 1948, Walter Kolbenhoff collection, DLS; Fleischer to Kolbenhoff, 16 August 1948, ibid.; Kolbenhoff, *Von unserm Fleisch und Blut.*

ternational in Germany and New York. In 1947, burdened by his responsibilities as a young husband and a father-to-be, the young journalist inquired about a job in military government. Clay welcomed the chance to exchange Wallenberg for Fleischer, who had frequently accompanied the general in his special train between Berlin and Stuttgart.[2]

From the start, Fleischer felt that the U.S. military government in Bavaria paid little attention to the official press. ICD chief Gordon Textor "had no background in journalism or anything like that," and offered little professional help. The head of the ICD in Bavaria, James Clark, a former advertising or newspaper man, "wasn't very active," Fleischer recalls; "he drank too much, and there was very little direction of [how] things were to be hand[l]ed."[3]

In an effort to exert more central control and avoid waste and inefficiency, Fleischer adopted an authoritarian course on Schellingstraße 39 and introduced sweeping organizational changes. By creating a copy desk he hoped to prevent overlapping articles in different sections.[4] The layout of the *Neue Zeitung*'s front page followed an American format with more short news articles (particularly on Americana) in order to give readers a survey of the latest news at first glance.

Fleischer altered patterns of hierarchy and cooperation at the plant. In lieu of Wallenberg's editorial "seminar-conferences" and biweekly coffee chats, he consulted only a select number of older departmental chiefs for guidance and advice in "blitz meetings." A kitchen cabinet, consisting primarily of American-born staffers, was responsible for editorial policy. A typical harbinger of the new climate at the plant was Eugene Jolas. Born in New Jersey as the son of a French family, Jolas and his parents had returned to the French-speaking part of Lorraine, then part of the German empire, where the boy had to attend German schools. In the 1920s he had served as the editor of *Transition,* a prominent publishing outlet for the Lost Generation expatriated to France. There, Jolas had expounded his admiration for James Joyce and the hallucination of the senses, proposing a "Proclamation" for the journal that climaxed with the statement that "the plain reader be damned." Jolas, whose biographical background no doubt deeply tinged his disdain for both postwar Germans and admirers of German *Kultur,* earned a reputation as one of the most wrathful and anti-German U.S. press

2. Jack M. Fleischer, Morrilton, Ark., letters to the author, 22 March 1993 and 24 March 1993; Jack M. Fleischer, interview, Little Rock, Ark., 27 April 1993.

3. Jack Fleischer, interview; W. P. Davison, letter to the author, 15 March 1994; Max Kraus, letter to the author, 8 March 1994.

4. Max Kraus, interview, and Jack M. Fleischer, interview; Hurwitz, *Stunde Null*, 263.

directors while a chief scrutiny officer at the American-sponsored wire service, DANA. Moreover, the ICD assigned an in-house officer from the Counter Intelligence Center to the *Neue Zeitung:* Thomas Schulz from North Dakota monitored the staffers' time of arrival in the morning in order to eliminate laziness and inefficiency.[5]

In the summer of 1948 Fleischer intensified his efforts to reduce labor and expenses when the paper's circulation dropped overnight from an estimated 1,550,000 to 880,000 copies per issue after the currency reform. Distribution for the Soviet zone ceased completely because all borders were closed to postal communications. However, most of the decline occurred in the industrial areas of the French and British zones where money was particularly scarce or was spent only on new consumer goods. With the advent of the currency reform in June 1948, the purchase of a newspaper became a financial decision. Originally, most people subscribed to the *Neue Zeitung* as their second paper in addition to their local newspaper. After the currency reform, many subscribers claimed they could not afford a second paper anymore, particularly since news in the *Neue Zeitung* was sometimes outdated due to the paper's often belated arrival, frequently more than twenty-four hours after publication. Moreover, as the newspapers became freer and more readily available, the licensed press was able to extend its number of pages and features and publish more local editions—an attraction that the *Neue Zeitung* could never match. And finally, the paper never carried classified advertising and display ads. An opinion poll at the end of 1948 revealed that financial constraints forced many readers to cancel their subscriptions to the paper. By November 1948 production had fallen below the 600,000 mark, a decrease of approximately 65 percent within six months. A sample survey of 1,900 readers in the following month showed that in the U.S. zone readership steadily declined to only 10 percent of the population.[6]

As another consequence of the reform, the plant lost most of its financial reserves for newsprint, paper, and transportation (the salaries for U.S. em-

5. Jack M. Fleischer, letter to the author, 29 July 1993; interviews with Jack M. Fleischer, Hans-Joachim Netzer, Hans Lehmann, and Olaf Meitzner; Schmitz, "DANA/DENA," 69ff., 94f.; Hurwitz, *Stunde Null*, 57, 265f.; Netzer, "Die *Neue Zeitung*," 17; Malcolm Cowley, *Exile's Return: A Literary Odyssey of the 1920s* (London: Penguin Books, 1976), 274–77.

6. OMGBY, Monthly Military Reports, June, July 1948, RG 260, OMGBY 13/142–1/6, BHStA; OMGBY/ISD, Monthly Report for Period ending 30 August 1948, RG 260, OMGBY 10/117–3/13, BHStA; Max Kraus, memorandum, 1 September 1948, courtesy of Max Kraus (Stiftung Haus der Geschichte der Bundesrepublik, Bonn); Bericht Nr. 1 des Deutschen Institutes zur Erforschung der öffentlichen Meinung, Heidelberg, "Was denken die Abonnenten der *NZ* über die *NZ*?" July 1948, RG 260, OMGUS 5/233–1/14, IfZ; Merrit, *Public Opinion in Occupied Germany*, 274f.

ployees were paid out of the U.S. War Department budget). Financial considerations forced the editor in chief to cut salaries and reduce the number of stringers. Fleischer even considered firing a number of German employees.[7]

However, his actions eroded the German staffers' loyalty to the *Neue Zeitung*. He failed to understand the peculiar atmosphere that had tied the editors together and allowed them to create such a successful newspaper. Instead, as his letter to Walter Kolbenhoff shows, their nonchalant work ethic and their lack of efficiency exasperated him.[8]

Fleischer's resolute tone corresponded with the changed political climate in Germany and the intense East-West information war. Clay's press announcement in October 1947 led to an informational program "to explain to the German people the basic concepts of democracy as opposed to the communistic system." The plan, known as "Operation Talk Back," aimed at inculcating the principles of democracy in the German people through the projection of American ideals and information material. Designed to erase any totalitarian influence in the German consciousness, it would warn the defeated people of the dangers and moral weaknesses of communism and inform them about U.S. foreign policy in order to prevent any Soviet distortion of the facts.[9] Like the BBC and RIAS, the *Neue Zeitung* was supposed to "tell the truth," but the propagandistic purpose would taint a powerful tool of communication.

In practice, "Operation Talk Back" had serious flaws. OMGUS took almost three months to establish a Political Information Branch, which would be responsible for the dissemination of anticommunist information. Yet the division's authority remained uncertain because the branch headquarters in Berlin did not have representatives in the state military governments, which were responsible for controlling the licensed and official press. Moreover, the division's head, Alfred Boerner, deputy chief of ICD plans and directives, was locked in a bitter personal struggle with Thomas Headen, deputy chief for "programs." This feud inhibited much of the coordination of the Political Information Branch.[10]

7. Jack M. Fleischer, interview; Cancellation of contract, Jack M. Fleischer to Else Reventlow, *Neue Zeitung* plant, 16 August 1948, Else Reventlow collection, FES.

8. Jack Fleischer to Walter Kolbenhoff, 19 June 1948 and 16 August 1948.

9. Monthly Report, No. 28, quoted in Gehring, *Amerikanische Literaturpolitik*, 74; Quarterly Report of the Military Governor, OMGUS/IC, No. 30, October–December 1947, p. 2, quoted in Hurwitz, *Stunde Null*, 333ff.

10. "Vigorous Information Program: Military Government Political Information Program," sent out by Deputy Military Governor, Berlin, 10 February 1948, RG 260, OMGBY 10/92–2/7, BHStA; Gordon E. Textor to General Daniel Noce, CAD, Department of the Army Special Staff, 17 February 1948, RG 165, Entry 463, box 399, dec. file 000.7, Sec. 1, NARA; Hurwitz, *Stunde Null*, 337.

These complications mirrored OMGUS's uneasiness with the campaign. U.S. officials such as Gordon Textor and Arthur Eggleston, chief of the Press Control Branch, realized that no propaganda campaign could comply with the Allied ban on open criticism of another occupation power. They feared that "Operation Talk Back" would tarnish their mission and convey the impression that they were adopting totalitarian techniques as well.[11]

Due to this dilemma, the few directives from the ICD to the *Neue Zeitung* often contradicted one another. On the one hand, U.S. officials supported the vigorous information program and made every effort to distribute the *Neue Zeitung*. They emphasized that the *Neue Zeitung* should vehemently attack any antidemocratic signs.[12] The ICD as well as the Civil Affairs Division of the War Department asked the *Neue Zeitung* to print stories muckraking social conditions in Soviet Russia. These included George Orwell's *Animal Farm*, Arthur Koestler's *Darkness at Noon*, and John Steinbeck's critical appraisal of a recent trip to Russia.[13] But simultaneously they assured each other repeatedly that "the problem is being approached in a truly scientific manner" and that "we have been very careful not to allow this program to degenerate into a mere daily 'slug fest' with the Soviets." Eggleston vehemently reminded the staff that "this must be an attack and critical examination of a particular political and economic way of thinking and acting and not an attack upon a government and people which happen to be the foremost exponents of this way of thinking and acting."[14] Paradoxically, as the vigorous information program developed, U.S. officials were increasingly unwilling to admit their ideological involvement. They were unable to solve the lasting dilemma facing "Operation Talk Back": how could one

11. Hurwitz, *Stunde Null*, 336.

12. Textor to Foss, "Objectives and Policies of the *Neue Zeitung*," 15 December 1948, RG 260, OMGUS 5/243–2/6, IfZ.

13. Proposal by Harold Hurwitz, Publications Editor, Political Information Branch, 25 August 1948; Harold Hurwitz, memorandum to Boris Shub, RIAS, "Use of Material in the Pamphlet 'Aus der Geheimchronik einer Diktatur' by Dr. Fritz Loewenthal," 26 August 1948, RG 260, OMGUS/ISD 5/266–1/32, BArch; C. R. Smith, Maj., AGD, Administrative Officer, cable to OMGUS, Arthur Eggleston, Gordon Textor, et al., 12 November 1947, RG 165, War Department, Civil Affairs Division, Entry 463, box 227, dec. file 000.7, Sec. XII, NARA; "Swiss Rights," Laurence P. Dalcher, Assisting Chief, Publications Control Branch, to Deputy Director, 6 November 1947, RG 260, OMGBY 10/118–1/11, BHStA.; W. B. Phillips, Chief, Political Information Branch, ICD, to Deputy Director for Policy, ICD, "Recommendation to obtain Steinbeck's *Russian Journal* for *Neue Zeitung*," 9 February 1948, RG 260, OMGUS/ISD 5/270–3/1, BArch.

14. Gordon E. Textor, ICD, to Daniel Noce, CAD, 17 February 1948; "Mission of Die *Neue Zeitung*," 13 December 1948, RG 260, OMGUS 5/243–2/6, IfZ; "Implementation by Press Control Branch," Arthur Eggleston to Gordon Textor, 27 October 1947, RG 260, OMGUS/ISD 5/246–3/29, BArch.

propagandize for a way of life and, at the same time, expose an enemy's propaganda methods?

The change of editorship and the impact of Clay's "Operation Talk Back" clearly influenced the content of the *Neue Zeitung* beginning in the fall of 1947. Less than two weeks after the military governor's announcement on 28 October 1947 the *Neue Zeitung* began printing forceful articles contrasting Soviet totalitarianism with Western democracy. It depicted the increasing gap between material and social conditions in the Eastern and the Western zones. It inspired an intellectual debate about the origins of Marxism.[15] And it extensively covered the Berlin blockade.

In tune with the ICD's order to expand antifascist reeducation to include anticommunism, the *Neue Zeitung* skillfully juxtaposed articles on the persistence of Nazism with those on the rise of communism. Headlines such as "The Rights of Man" and "Tolerance" emphasized the values of democracy. Salient code words, such as "New Nationalists at Work" or "The Rat Catchers," branded the nascent neo-Nazism in postwar Germany.[16]

At the same time, the *Neue Zeitung* used a very similar terminology for its portrayal of totalitarian methods in the Soviet zone. Headline terms like "deportation," "Gestapo," or "purges" appeared frequently in connection with conditions in the East. On 5 January 1948 the *Neue Zeitung* even likened Molotov's blatant accusations against the United States to Adolf Hitler's propaganda strategy and to his book *Mein Kampf*.[17] In short, the paper

15. "Status of Political Re-education Program (Anticommunism)," OMGUS, ISD, Political Information, Berlin, 5 December 1947, RG 260, OMGUS 5/242–2/28, IfZ; "Furcht vor der Wahrheit," *Neue Zeitung*, 15 December 1947, p. 5; "Späte Rechenschaft," *Neue Zeitung*, 5 January 1948, p. 5; "Wahrheit . . . ," *Neue Zeitung*, 1 April 1948, p. 5; "Stets das Gegenteil," *Neue Zeitung*, 25 April 1948, p. 5; "Selbstmord," ibid.; "Brot für Deutschland," *Neue Zeitung*, 2 May 1948, p. 7; "Auf einmal 'faschistisch,' " *Neue Zeitung*, 11 August 1948, p. 5; "Der Unterschied," *Neue Zeitung*, 21 September 1948, p. 5; " 'Die Ausgestoßenen,' " *Neue Zeitung*, 22 February 1948, p. 5; Spectator, "Weltpolitische Rundschau der 'NZ,' " *Neue Zeitung*, 18 July 1948, p. 7; "Eine Sowjetantwort," *Neue Zeitung*, 5 October 1948, p. 5; René König, "Geistesgeschichte der ost-westlichen Spaltung," *Neue Zeitung*, 9 October 1948, p. 5.

16. "Die Rechte des Menschen: Antworten auf eine Umfrage der UNESCO," *Neue Zeitung*, 25 January 1948, p. 5; 29 January 1948, p. 5; 1 February 1948, p. 5; "Freiheit in praxi," *Neue Zeitung*, 11 March 1948, p. 5; "Demokratie in Frage und Antwort," *Neue Zeitung*, 18 September 1948, p. 5; "Toleranz," *Neue Zeitung*, 21 October 1948, p. 5; "Neue Nationalisten am Werk," *Neue Zeitung*, 1 July 1948, p. 2; "Die Rattenfänger," ibid., p. 5.

17. "Gleichschaltung," *Neue Zeitung*, 14 November 1947, p. 5; "Kotikow gibt Verschleppungen zu," *Neue Zeitung*, 25 April 1948, p. 2; "K-5—die Gestapo der Ostzone," *Neue Zeitung*, 15 July 1948, p. 2; "Große Säuberungswelle in der SED," *Neue Zeitung*, 4 August 1948, p. 1; "Ein Volksbetrug," *Neue Zeitung*, 27 May 1948, p. 5; "Spectator, "Weltpolitische Rundschau," ibid.; "Die Tarnung," *Neue Zeitung*, 27 June 1948, p. 5; "Sowjets wollen Berlin versorgen," *Neue Zeitung*, 21 July 1948, p. 1; "Späte Rechenschaft," *Neue Zeitung*, 5 January 1948, p. 5.

implied that communism used the same propaganda, the same terror, the same purges, and the same lies as the Nazis had.

The *Neue Zeitung*'s portrayal of Soviet representatives turned increasingly polemical and cynical despite ICD orders not to attack individuals. As early as December 1947, after the closing of the second UN meeting in Lake Success, the paper bluntly concluded that the Soviet delegates had displayed an unwillingness to cooperate with the Western powers' campaign for equal rights and world peace. All of the subsequent articles covering Soviet politics reflected the paper's increasing disgust with Soviet leaders and soldiers, and they did not hesitate to predict a permanent division between the Allies as early as January 1948.[18]

The city of Berlin became a central topic in the columns of the *Neue Zeitung* in the summer of 1948. The currency reform of 21 June replaced the Reichsmark by the Deutsche Mark, thus monetarily uniting the three Western zones. When a few days later, the new currency was distributed in West Berlin as well, the Soviet military government issued its own currency, the Ostmark. Accusing the western Allies of deliberately breaking the Potsdam Agreement, the SMAD blocked all access between Bizonia and Berlin on 24 June. Western Allies responded to the blockade by prohibiting the export of any provisions from the West into the Russian sector. Subsequently, the Soviet military government demanded that the three Western powers leave the city. Berlin was located in the middle of their zone. Moreover, Soviet policy makers felt threatened by the Western Allied activities in Germany, by their negotiations over a transatlantic military alliance, as well as by the defeat of the Communists in Italy. Stalin wanted to push the Western allies out of Berlin. In response to the blockade, the United States and the United Kingdom began to airlift supplies to Berlin, an effort lasting until 12 May 1949.[19]

During the Berlin crisis, the local supplement to the *Neue Zeitung*, the *Berliner Blatt*, played an even more important role than the main edition published in Munich. It served as a "signpost" for the local Berlin press and for many politicians and intellectuals. Special issues explained major events such as the distribution of the new Deutsche Mark. Once the airlift had begun, the *Neue Zeitung* tirelessly urged the "island population" to endure.

18. "Der Vorhang fiel," *Neue Zeitung*, 5 December 1947, p. 5; "Wilde Anklagen im Kontrollrat," *Neue Zeitung*, 22 February 1948, p. 2; "Historischer Wendepunkt," *Neue Zeitung*, 25 January 1948, p. 5; "Sokolowski verläßt Kontrollratssitzung," *Neue Zeitung*, 21 March 1948, p. 1.

19. "Berlin erhält zwei Währungen," *Neue Zeitung*, 24 June 1948, p. 1; "Ein Brot kostet 400 Reichsmark," ibid.; "Werden sie vernünftig?" ibid., p. 5; Leffler, *Specter of Communism*, 82; Avi Shlaim, *The United States and the Berlin Blockade, 1948–1949: A Study in Crisis Decision-Making* (Berkeley: University of California Press, 1983).

"David and Goliath: 'Quickly, my shield!' "

*This cartoon by Helmut Beyer was published in the* Neue Zeitung *on 19 December 1947. With the giant Soviet Union blasting "Eastern Ideologies," David seeks to defend himself with "European Aid" proffered by the United States.*

Captions such as "Messages of Hope" and "Calm and Strength" reminded readers that the Western powers were in control of the situation. Humorous metaphors served to diminish the seriousness of the evolving crisis.[20]

The *Neue Zeitung*'s coverage of every major issue reflected its increasingly anticommunist stand. Articles on Americana focused almost exclusively on the generosity of the United States. Headlines such as "To My Ger-

20. "Kampf um Berlin verschärft sich," *Neue Zeitung*, 27 June 1948, p. 1; "Geduld gegen Gewalt," *Neue Zeitung*, 14 September 1948, p. 5; "Berlin dankt für die Luftbrücke," *Neue Zeitung*, 2 October 1948, p. 1; " 'NZ' heute mit Bilderseite 100 Tage Luftbrücke," *Neue Zeitung*, 2 October 1948, p. 1; Eugen Brehm, "Kein endgültiger Bruch zwischen Ost und West," *Neue Zeitung*, 19 December 1947, p. 5; "Botschaften der Hoffnung," *Neue Zeitung*, 22 December 1947, p. 11; "Ruhe und Stärke," *Neue Zeitung*, 24 July 1948, p. 5; Olaf Meitzner, interview; Hurwitz, *Stunde Null*, 353, 355.

man Friends" and "Americans about Germany" signaled the vivid attention that not only politicians but also U.S. voters paid to the occupied country.[21]

In imitation of Werner Sombart, many articles focused on the question "Why is there no socialism in the U.S.?" Politically, the American citizen, as the paper explained, was the complete antithesis of the European socialist. Americans' foremost concerns were not ideological but purely materialistic, focusing on cars, middle-class homes, washing machines, and many other wonderful things. Two consecutive reports in November 1948 meticulously recorded "How the Worker Lives in the U.S." and "How the Farmer Lives in the U.S." In the Soviet zone, these two occupational groups formed the core of the socialist movement. But in the United States these same groups were suspicious of high brow theories, ideologies, and governmental interference.[22]

Although the *Neue Zeitung* had staunchly supported high culture until mid-1947, it now championed popular taste and the commercialization of *Kultur.* Cultural affairs did not need a sponsor or state control, the paper now declared. State control was totalitarian. In a democracy, culture had to develop naturally and according tc popular taste. Either Germany would become a well-functioning democracy, making some concession to popular cultural taste and commercialization, the subtext went, or the country would be able to preserve its traditional *Kultur* only guarded by a powerful—perhaps totalitarian—political elite. But the two were incompatible.[23]

American middle-class values also clearly influenced the coverage of women, which changed dramatically after 1947, not only in the *Neue Zei-*

21. "Trumans Appell," *Neue Zeitung*, 27 October 1947, p. 5; " 'Sie sind nicht allein" *Neue Zeitung*, 22 December 1947, p. 4; Bernard M. Baruch, "Einige gute Worte für Onkel Sam," *Neue Zeitung*, 4 August 1948, p. 7; "Amerikaner wünschen feste Berlin-Politik," *Neue Zeitung*, 4 August 1948, p. 6; "Dorothy Thompson: 'An meine deutschen Freunde,' " *Neue Zeitung*, 19 October 1948, p. 3; "Amerika über Deutschland," ibid., p. 5; Stefan Weyl, "Was Amerika über Deutschland liest," *Neue Zeitung*, 9 November 1948, p. 5.

22. "Der 'kleine Mann' an der Jahreswende," *Neue Zeitung*, 29 December 1947, p. 5; "Amerikanische Alltagssorgen," *Neue Zeitung*, 8 February 1948, p. 6; "Brief eines Emigranten aus USA," *Neue Zeitung*, 22 April 1948, p. 6; "Der 'Car' im Leben der USA," *Neue Zeitung*, 11 September 1948, p. 4; Bernhard Taurer, "Wie lebt der Arbeiter in den USA," *Neue Zeitung*, 6 November 1948, p. 5; "Wie der Farmer in den USA lebt," *Neue Zeitung*, 13 November 1948, p. 5.; Bernhard Taurer, "Warum keine Arbeiterpartei in USA," *Neue Zeitung*, 21 August 1948, p. 5; "US-Bürger dulden keine Intoleranz," *Neue Zeitung*, 23 September 1948, p. 5.

23. "Ovationen für Mickymaus," *Neue Zeitung*, 3 November 1947, *Feuilleton*; Hans Naef, "Neue amerikanische Karikatur," *Neue Zeitung*, 22 February 1948, p. 4; Bruno E. Werner, "Der amerikanische Roman und die europäische Spätlese," *Neue Zeitung*, 8 February 1948, p. 4; Manfred George, "Probleme des amerikanischen Theaters," *Neue Zeitung*, 6 May 1948, p. 4; "Artur Holde, "Das amerikanische Musikpublikum," *Neue Zeitung*, 20 June 1948, p. 4.

*tung* but in the public discourse as well. During the public debates around the creation of the *Grundgesetz* (Basic Law), conservatives successfully advocated a natural law perspective according to which women assumed indisputable gender roles as wives and mothers. The discussion of female beauty and the role of a wife indicated that as social, political, and material conditions improved, women were no longer needed for political or professional activism. In fact, they prevented veterans, POWs, and aspiring young men from entering the public arena. Consequently, the portrayal of the modern ideal woman showed some familiar prewar traits: she was to be pretty, sensitive, moral, caring, wise, educated, curious, and a support to her husband.[24] This argument echoed a development in the United States, where thousands of American women returned to the home to make room in the public sphere for the returning GIs.

The coverage of youth and education under Jack Fleischer also revealed a new anticommunist and more pro-American tone in the columns of the *Neue Zeitung*. Two topics, the founding of the Free University of Berlin and the education of the very young in society, dominated the discussion of juvenile affairs in 1947–48. According to the *Neue Zeitung*, communist ideology required state intervention in educational matters and used schools and universities to indoctrinate future citizens. Therefore, the debate between students and administrators of the Humboldt University of Berlin, located in the Eastern sector, over the issue of political intervention in academia, became one of the most heatedly debated issues in the *Neue Zeitung*. At the University of Berlin, enrolled students now had to take mandatory lecture courses in philosophy and history taught by communist professors. Having covered the dispute at great length, in July 1948 the paper published an appeal from Berlin academics and supporters calling for the establishment of a Free University of Berlin so that academic research and instruction would not be destroyed. The enterprise started in October of the same year, funded in part by the *Neue Zeitung*.[25]

24. "Der Engel von Sibirien," *Neue Zeitung*, 7 March 1948, p. 5; Siegi Steiner, "Noch ein Brief zur Modefrage," letter to the editor, *Neue Zeitung*, 20 May 1948, p. 5; José Ortega y Gasset, "Über die Frauen," *Neue Zeitung*, 20 May 1948, p. 3, Walther Kiaulehn "Die Schönheitengalerie," *Neue Zeitung*, 1 July 1948, p. 3; Luise Rinser, "Angelsächsische Frauenromane," *Neue Zeitung*, 13 November 1948, p. 4; Moeller, *Protecting Motherhood,* 38–75.

25. Hildegard Brücher, "Von Erlangen bis Hannover," *Neue Zeitung*, 21 November 1947, p. 5; "Studenten bekunden Solidarität," *Neue Zeitung*, 6 May 1948, p. 2; "Für unabhängige Lehre und Forschung," *Neue Zeitung*, 24 July 1948, p. 4; "Für die Freiheit der Wissenschaft," *Neue Zeitung*, 16 October 1948, p. 4; "Intelligente Rebellen," *Neue Zeitung*, 2 November 1948, p. 5; James F. Tent, *The Free University of Berlin: A Political History* (Bloomington, Ind.: Indiana University Press, 1988).

At the same time, the *Neue Zeitung* now displayed far more faith in children's development in postwar Germany. Optimistic essays on elementary education, exchange programs, and an international upbringing disseminated an air of hope. Children's essays even served anticommunist propaganda. Asked by the *Neue Zeitung* what they would do if they were invisible, some children wrote that they dreamed about going to Siberia to liberate their fathers from forced labor. One student said he would like to lecture to Josef Stalin, while another asked the victorious powers to bomb Germany in the next war with dollars instead of shells.[26]

In sum, Jack Fleischer's editorship introduced an anti-Soviet twist along with a clearly American line of interpretation into virtually every major topic of interest. The new staff chose a tone that linked neo-Nazis with Soviets. They tied the United States closely to German *Kultur*, portraying U.S. society as the antithesis of the Soviet way of life. They advocated the commercialization of *Kultur* as a side effect of Germany's democratization. They praised the model of a pretty housewife living outside the public arena. They advocated anticommunist education along with a renewed faith in children as the key to a better and wiser society. They tried to fulfill the premises of the "Vigorous Information Program."

Yet Fleischer's editorial line reflected not only the split among the Allies but also the intellectual simplifications of the "Red Fascism" doctrine in the United States. Anticommunism, dating back to the nineteenth century, turned into a national battle cry after World War II when the Soviet Union remained the United States' only global challenger. The Soviet threat, many believed, consisted not only of military intervention but also of sneaky political subversion. To contain the Soviets abroad, Americans had to contain communism at home. In 1947 the House Un-American Activities Committee (HUAC) began to expose domestic communist influences in a series of hearings. During the next four years, approximately 3,000 government employees were charged with being communists or communist sympathizers and lost their jobs. Controversial speakers were banned from American universities while numerous stars disappeared from the movie screens. Teachers, professors, and public officials were required to sign loyalty oaths or risk losing their jobs. Citizens spied on their families, neighbors, and co-

26. Wilhelm Tieze, "Wir müssen ihnen helfen," *Neue Zeitung*, 15 December 1947, p. 4; I. L. Kandel, "Erziehung zum Frieden," *Neue Zeitung*, 12 January 1948, *Feuilleton*; Walter Kolbenhoff, " 'Wenn ich unsichtbar wäre,' " *Neue Zeitung*, 4 April 1948, p. 4; "Verlorene Generationen?" *Neue Zeitung*, 2 May 1948, p. 3; "Jugend der Welt tagt in München," *Neue Zeitung*, 13 June 1948, p. 2.

workers in order to safeguard "national security."[27] The pressure for a rigidly propagandistic anti-Moscow coverage in the *Neue Zeitung,* then, was partly rooted in the increasingly nasty politics of anticommunism across the Atlantic. Munich turned into a mirror of the evolving political disputes in Washington in 1947–1948.

Meanwhile, Soviet and American information officers embarked on a fierce paper war. U.S. officials developed complicated strategies to increase the circulation of the *Neue Zeitung*. They shipped hundreds of thousands of copies to the Soviet zone, thus reflecting the importance placed on the paper as the Cold War began.[28] By the end of October 1947, Textor proposed that the *Neue Zeitung* should target Eastern readers through two distribution channels, Munich and Berlin. The Berlin circulation would be increased from 150,000 to 250,000 copies per issue. Simultaneously, the Berlin publishing house Deutscher Verlag would place some 50,000 copies directly with dealers in the Soviet zone. Another 250,000 would be distributed along the zonal borders. An additional flow of copies from the Munich plant would supply distributors in the southern portion of the Soviet zone. Even the Soviet Military Administration in Germany in Berlin-Weissensee received a share of the *Neue Zeitung*—fifteen copies per issue.

This jungle of numbers and complicated export strategies to the Soviet zone together with the rather vague references to the content of the paper pointed to a new and strange rationale on the part of U.S. officials like Textor. They cared much more about export quantities to the East than about the quality of material for the West. In fact, less than half of the total circulation—1,078,800 copies—went into areas where the *Neue Zeitung* belonged according to its initial design, the U.S. zone.[29]

27. Günter Bischof, "The Politics of Anti-Communism in the Executive Branch During the Early Cold War: Truman, Eisenhower, and McCarthy(ism)," in *Anticommunism and McCarthyism in the United States, 1954: Essays on the Politics and Culture of the Cold War*, ed. André Kaenel (Paris: Edition Messene, 1995), 53–78; Mary Sperlin McAuliffe, *Crisis on the Left: Cold War Politics and American Liberals, 1947–1954* (Amherst, Mass.: University of Massachusetts Press, 1978); David M. Oshinsky, *A Conspiracy So Immense: The World of Joe McCarthy* (New York: Free Press, 1983); Robert Griffith, *The Politics of Fear: Joseph R. McCarthy and the Senate* (Lexington, Ky.: University Press of Kentucky, 1970); Leffler, *Specter of Communism*.

28. POB Quarterly Operations Report, 1 January–31 March 1948, RG 260, OMGB/ID 10/66–1/8, quoted in Bittorf, "*Neue Zeitung*," 35.

29. Gordon E. Textor to James A. Clark, 31 October 1947, RG 260, OMGUS/ISD 5/246–3/29, BArch; Fred B. Bleistein, Chief, Production Section, 23 April 1948, RG 260, OMGUS 5/260–1/20, IfZ; Semimonthly OMG Report for Period February 1–29, 1948, RG 260, OMGBY 13/142–1/6, BHStA; Jack Fleischer to Commanding General, ICD, Press Control Branch, "Distribution," 30 March 1948, RG 260, OMGUS 5/260–2/1, IfZ; OMGUS Historical Report, July 1947–June 1948, RG 260, OMGUS CO/559/3, BHStA; OMGUS/ISD, His-

This change of intention created an odd paradox. While the ICD bombarded inhabitants of the Soviet zone with copies of the official U.S. newspaper, those living in the American zone increasingly complained about the scarcity of Western newspapers. Deliveries were usually sold out within fifteen minutes. Western readers craved information but also paper for heating or bartering or wrapping rationed salted herring. Consequently, they often turned to Eastern publications, which the Soviets exported in great numbers to the West—50,000 copies of the *Tägliche Rundschau* to the city of Munich alone.[30]

The Soviet military government continued to resent the *Neue Zeitung*. Numerous refugees from the East flocked into the office of the Berlin bureau since it was the only Western address they knew, having previously read it in the paper. In return, Soviet officers occasionally arrested editors of the *Neue Zeitung* and accused them of planning an anti-Soviet conspiracy. Meanwhile, the Soviet-controlled press continued to spread rumors: that the *Neue Zeitung* employed Ku-Klux-Klan methods to arouse readers' scorn against the communists; that the paper's Berlin bureau was a spy nest; that it screened locals, sent them as special agents into the Soviet zone, and forced them to deliver falsified news back to Western publications.[31]

Soviet authorities attempting to thwart the paper's penetration of the

---

torical Report for POB, July–December 1948, "Die *Neue Zeitung*, comparison of editions from January 1948 to February 1949," RG 260, OMGBY 10/130–2/2, BHStA; *Die Neue Zeitung*, circulation list Nr. 22, 18 March 1948, RG 260, OMGUS 5/240–3/14, IfZ; circulation list Nr. 18, 4 March 1948, RG 260, OMGUS/ISD 5/240–3/14, BArch.

30. ICD Opinion Surveys, Report No. 77, 5 November 1947, courtesy of Harold J. Hurwitz; Extract from Weekly Intelligence Report, Section II Politics, 19 December 1947, Office of Liaison and Security, Sulzbach Rosenberg, OMGUS, RG 260, OMGBY 10/117–1/17, BHStA; OMGBY, ICD/POB, to Mr. Martindale, Intelligence Branch, "Distribution of Overt Periodicals," 21 January 1948, RG 260, OMGBY 10/84–2/32, BHStA; OMGUS/ICD, Opinion Surveys Report No. 118, 3 May 1948, RG 260, box 119, "Public Opinion—(U.S. Zone) Germany (Newspaper Readership)," OMGUS Reports, Nr. 372, BHStA; Werner Friedmann in *Neue Züricher Zeitung*, 9 October 1947, translation "Exchange of Newspapers between the German Zones," RG 84, Foreign Service Posts, Munich Consulate General, Miscellaneous Records, 1946–48, box 6, WNRC; Quarterly Historical Report, January–March 1948, OMGUS Historical Branch, RG 260, OMGUS, CO 557/1, BHStA.

31. "Spionagezentrale in der Buggestraße? Merkwürdige Zwangsinterviews durch eine amerikanische Dienststelle," *Berliner Zeitung*, 18 January 1948; "Das Hetzblatt der Amerikaner," *Neues Deutschland*, 30 February 1948; "Von der Phantasie bis zur Verleumdung: Journalistische Methoden der 'amerikanischen Zeitung für die deutsche Bevölkerung'," *Der Morgen*, 27 January 1949; "Offene Mordhetze," *Neues Deutschland*, 8 February 1949; "Ku-Klux-Klan in Berlin," *Vorwärts*, 8 February 1949; "Amerikanischer Agent geflüchtet," *Berliner Zeitung*, 2 March 1949; Peter Bönisch, interview; Müller, *Der Springer-Konzern*, 94; Harold J. Hurwitz, *Demokratie und Antikommunismus in Berlin nach 1945*, vol. 2, *Die Anfänge des Widerstands* (Cologne: Verlag Wissenschaft und Politik, 1990), 2:1228.

Eastern zone often threatened local dealers. In November 1948 East German police interfered with the paper's distribution in Weimar, Leipzig, Chemnitz, and Finsterwalde, seizing more than 3,000 copies in the township of Merseburg alone. Military officials blamed Thuringian distributors for not selling enough Soviet-licensed papers, emphasizing that the sale of Western papers was undemocratic. Under Soviet pressure, the city of Erfurt reduced its order from 2,000 to 1,000 while newsstands in Rostock, Brandenburg, and Luckenwalde refused delivery in advance. A Chemnitz distributor even sent back his whole order of one November 1947 edition because it was "not permitted for sale."[32]

After a severe protest from Textor to his Soviet counterpart Colonel Tjulpanov, the Soviet Information Control changed its strategy. Rather than openly confiscating copies of the *Neue Zeitung*, special commandos now searched post offices and mail trains at night, carting away entire packages of "undesirable" newspapers without informing the dealers. Soviet press officers threatened local distributors and salesmen with severe punishment, including years of imprisonment in forced labor camps, if they continued to sell the *Neue Zeitung*. After the confiscation of 1,200 copies in Grimma, one dealer grew so scared that he fled from the city leaving his entire family behind. In the state of Brandenburg, the police ordered a regionwide prohibition of the paper in May 1948. Simultaneously, SED functionaries reinforced their activities at the *Neue Zeitung* distributor in Berlin, Deutscher Verlag, encouraging workers to strike and request higher wages. Only on 1 June 1948, when Textor consequently banned all Soviet publications from the American zone, did the Soviets lift the restrictions in order to comply with U.S. demands.[33]

32. E. Strunk, Deutscher Verlag, Berlin, to Bert S. Fielden, Chief, Press Section, 14 November 1948, RG 260, OMGUS 5/241–1/11, BArch; "Reception of AMZON newspapers in the Soviet Zone," 2 February 1948, RG 260, OMGUS 5/246–3/29, IfZ; "Textor protestiert bei Tulpanow," *Tagesspiegel*, 5 December 1947.

33. Fred B. Bleistein to Deputy Director, OMGUS/ICD, "Distribution Difficulties in the Soviet Zone," 6 May 1948, RG 260, OMGUS 5/260–1/20, BArch; John H. DeForrest, POB, to Commanding General, OMGUS, "Distribution of *Neue Zeitung* in the east zone," 17 March 1948, RG 260, OMGUS 5/243–3/9, IfZ; Landeskriminalpolizei Brandenburg, Kriminalamt Eberswalde, to Zeitungsverlag Becker, Eberswalde, 12 May 1948, RG 260, OMGUS 5/260–1/21, IfZ; typewritten manuscript by Deutscher Verlag, "Vertriebserfahrungen der letzten drei Wochen in Ostzone und russischem Sektor," 13 May 1948, ibid.; Gordon Textor, letter to Colonel Tulpanov, 19 May 1948, RG 260, OMGUS 5/260–1/20, IfZ; Semimonthly Summary for Period from 16 through 29 February 1948, 5 March 1948, RG 260, OMGBS 5/39–1/19, LAB ; Gordon E. Textor to Colonel Tulpanov, 19 May 1948, RG 260, OMGUS 5/260–1/20, IfZ; Monthly OMG Report for Period 1–31 May 1948, RG 260, OMGBY 13/142–1/6, BHStA.

The next major clash over the paper's penetration of the Eastern zone followed the currency reform on 21 June 1948. The reform rendered the purchase of the *Neue Zeitung* almost impossible for Eastern readers because they did not have access to the new Deutsche Mark. The ICD then decided to sell the *Neue Zeitung* to East German readers in exchange for Ostmarks despite the loss of revenue. Soviet authorities reacted to this move by freezing payrolls and all liquid assets of the *Neue Zeitung* in the Eastern zone, including some 60,000 marks designed to cover the expenses of the Berlin bureau. In August 1948, SMAD Order No. 105 banned distributions of U.S.-authorized publications from the Soviet zone and eliminated the organized network of distributors for Western licensed publications. In East Berlin a communist-controlled central distribution firm now handled all newspaper distribution.[34]

The ICD had already decided to change its strategy. By the spring of 1948 U.S. officials had grown very worried about the waste of dollars and paper caused by Soviet confiscations. Consequently, the ICD decreased circulation in the Soviet zone from 280,000 to 81,800 copies between mid-April and mid-May 1948. Three months later, officials began to clandestinely send a "pony edition"—30,000 special photostatic copies of the Berlin edition in pocket form (7.5 x 11 inches)—into the Eastern zone. "I don't expect to get a mark back," Textor informed Clay at a staff meeting on 14 August 1948, "but it will be a means, we hope, of getting information into the iron curtain zone."[35]

In their efforts to thwart communist influence, ICD officers expanded their paper battle far beyond the Soviet and the U.S. zones to all areas "which traditionally have had considerable Communist tinge." Targets included the Saar and the Ruhr region, Kiel, Hamburg, Austria, and Switzerland.[36] This procedure caused harsh disputes among the three Western occu-

34. Jacob Kaiser to Robert Murphy, 30 August 1948, RG 84, Foreign Service Posts, POLAD Berlin, classified general correspondence of POLAD, 1944–49, box 8, WNRC; Tom Hutton, Chief of Branch, OMGUS, Information Control Branch, to Director, ICD, "Financial Crisis in Western-Licensed Press and Overt Newspaper, *Die Neue Zeitung*," 6 August 1948, RG 260, OMGUS/ISD 5/269–1/2, BArch; OMGUS Staff Meetings, 14 August 1948, RG 260, Fg 12/14, IfZ; Hurwitz, *Stunde Null*, 338.

35. Fred B. Bleistein to T. P. Headen, Deputy Director, ICD, "Distribution of the '*Neue Zeitung*' in Soviet Zone," 14 May 1948, RG 260, OMGUS 5/260–1/21, IfZ; OMGUS Staff Meetings, 14 August 1948, RG 260, Fg 12/14, IfZ; Secret Report, "Sovzone Edition of *Echo der Woche*," 11 July 1950, RG 466, US HICOG BE, Public Affairs Division, classified subject files, 1949–53, box 7, WNRC.

36. Textor to James A. Clark, 31 October 1947, RG 260, OMGUS/ISD 5/246–3/29, BArch; typewritten manuscript to T. P. Headen, OMGUS, ICD, Munich, 3 February 1948, RG 260, OMGUS 5/240–3/14, IfZ; Gordon Textor to Military Governor, "Proposal for Small Cir-

"Don't worry—this is just going to be a sign reading 'Communist Zone.' "

*This cartoon by Helmut Beyer was published in the* Neue Zeitung *on 11 September 1948. German readers would have immediately recognized that the man whom the painter tries to reassure is struck by the abbreviation for concentration camps, "K.Z."*

pation powers. British occupation authorities, for example, furiously pointed out that Hamburg lay in their zone and was home of the popular British army paper, *Die Welt*, the *Neue Zeitung*'s fiercest competitor.[37]

These efforts underlined that the *Neue Zeitung* was no longer designed to be a mere channel to the population of the U.S. zone. Instead, it would

culation of Die *Neue Zeitung* in Switzerland," 13 April 1948, RG 260, OMGUS 3/243–3/9, IfZ; Monthly Report of the Military Governor, 1–30 September 1948, OMGBY, RG 260, OMGBY 13/142–1/6, BHStA; OMGBY/ISD, Monthly Summary for Period ending 30 September 1948, RG 260, OMGBY CO-350/6, BHStA.

37. A. L. Pose, ISD, to D/Chief, ISD, 2 December 1948, FO 1056/212, PRO; Klaus Wust, interview, New York, 19 March 1993; Wilhelm Kaisen, Senate President of Bremen, letter to

be the American mouthpiece to all the inhabitants in the German-speaking world. But neither the ICD nor the Civil Affairs Division (CAD) of the Army Department provided the *Neue Zeitung* with regular guidance. Fearful that their own mission would be tarnished, U.S. officials struggled hard to define the "Vigorous Information Program" as a scientific endeavor but failed to clarify its objectives. Due to this reluctance, the "word war" quickly deteriorated into a "paper battle." Printed paper simply became a peacetime weapon that, if effectively deployed, would eventually make the enemy collapse. As future events would show, Fleischer had to pay dearly for his superiors' failure.

German readers disapproved of the paper's new editorial course. Immediately after Clay's public announcement of the program of anticommunism in late 1947, public opinion indicated a rising tide of anti-American attitudes in Germany that lingered until after the election of the German federal parliament. Much of this opposition was the result of Germany's impending restoration to nationhood. The more imminent sovereignty appeared, the less Germans were willing to listen to patronizing advice.

German editors of licensed regional newspapers announced their refusal to join the program because "it was bad enough for Germany to have the Allies settle their differences on her soil." The friction between East and West would only hasten the tragic division of Germany, one editor expostulated. Moreover, geographically Germany was much closer to Russia than to the United States. Therefore, the country had to find a way to get along with Moscow. "If some people believe that we should suddenly get out the old flag of anti-Communism, with everything belonging to it," wrote one Christian Democratic editor in late 1947, "then they should be reminded that once before 'anti-Communism' was used to give fools and criminals political power in Europe."[38]

Editors focused much of their criticism on the *Neue Zeitung*. The Berlin

---

OMGUS, 19 October 1948, RG 260, OMGUS 5/240–314, IfZ; Duncan MacBryde, Chief, OMGUS/ISD, Bremen Division, to Director, OMGUS/ISD, "Northwest Germany Edition of Die *Neue Zeitung*," 25 October 1948, RG 260, OMGUS 5/240–3/14, IfZ. For further study on the Hamburg press see Daniel A. Gossel, *Die Hamburger Presse nach dem Zweiten Weltkrieg: Neuanfang unter britischer Besatzungsherrschaft* (Hamburg: Verlag Verein für Hamburgische Geschichte, 1993), esp. 64–104, 116–40; Heinz-Dietrich Fischer, *Reeducations- und Pressepolitik unter britischem Besatzungstatus: Die Zonenzeitung* Die Welt, *1946–1950. Konzeption, Artikulation und Rezeption* (Düsseldorf: Droste, 1978); Karl-Heinz Harenberg, "Die Welt: Eine deutsche oder eine britische Zeitung?" (Ph. D. dissertation, Universität Hamburg, 1976).

38. Memorandum to OMGB/ICD, "Anti-Allied and Anti-Occupation Trend in the Bavarian Press," 24 February 1948, RG 260, OMGBY 10/125–1/20, BHStA; Marguerite Higgins, "Reluctance to Go Ahead With American Campaign To Counter Soviet Propaganda Is Noticeable In Attitude of Most Journals," *New York Herald Tribune*, 19 November 1947.

*Tagesspiegel* charged that the newspaper "has nullified what it would be, according to Eisenhower's words: an example for the German press, through objective news reporting, love of truth, and high journalistic professionalism." In the Bavarian *Fränkisches Mitteilungsblatt*, Thomas Dehler, Land chairman of the Free Democratic Party, demanded the cessation of the paper. The *Neue Zeitung* had grown old, he wrote. It mirrored the psychological problem of the occupation, it was too long. Why not kill the paper "by euthanasia" rather than subject it to a long, drawn-out illness? Germans were very eager to reenter the international arena as a democratic country, *Der Tag* added on 29 June 1949. "But we want to see this world with our own eyes"—not through the lenses of the U.S. army paper.[39]

Most readers shared the resentment of the licensed press against the vigorous information campaign, albeit for different reasons. Many increasingly resented the presence of U.S. troops in Germany. Drunkenness, immorality, black market activities, and even assaults on locals on the part of U.S. soldiers rendered Germans doubtful about American ways and institutions. Others shared the view of the businessman who exclaimed in a public opinion poll in 1948: "My God, now they are making a propaganda action just like during Hitlers [*sic*] times." For over two years, U.S. officers had tirelessly preached the ideal of objectivity; they now abused their own principles. They were no better than the Nazis in regard to their propaganda techniques.[40]

Many Germans disliked not so much the "ideological" message as America's readiness to spend money on propaganda rather than food, despite the widespread poverty in Germany. "My children have hunger [*sic*]," said a housewife. "The one who satisfies [*sic*] them gets me." Workers in particular often mentioned that their counterparts in the Soviet zone had more to eat: "The U.S. is injecting poison, trying to get the people to hate each other.

39. Donald Shea to Director of Intelligence, OMGUS, "Translation of an article written by Thomas Dehler," 25 March 1949, RG 260, OMGBY 13/130–1/3, BHStA; "Auch ein Glückwunsch," *Tagesspiegel*, 26 October 1948; Report, "Zum Fall '*Neue Zeitung*,' " 10 February 1949, RG 260, OMGBY 10/90–3/1, BHStA; "Die Zeitungen der Besatzungsmächte," *Der Tag*, 29 June 1949.

40. Manuscript of a speech given by Max Rheinstein before the Faculty Club and Alumni Association of the Law School at the University of Chicago, 14 February 1947, Alvin J. Rockwell Papers, OMGUS, Subject file 1944–1949, box 33, folder "Germany—General [1946–50], no. 1," HSTL; manuscript by James Warburg, n. p., n. d. (1946?), Dean Acheson papers, box 27, "Assistant Secretary and Undersecretary of State, 1941–1948," folder State Department—Under Secretary—correspondence, 1945–47, HSTL; William M. Lyons, Public Safety Officer, Military Government Liaison & Security Office, Landkreis Tölz, to Chief of Intelligence Section, OMGBY, "Supplementary Report," 24 November 1947, RG 260, OMGBY 10/84–3/5, BHStA.

I [don't] give a damn for the West, which is said to be in danger. I want to have a cup of coffee in the morning." Refugees reportedly felt that due to their own poverty they had "nothing in common with America. The Russian people is [*sic*] very poor too. Thus we are nearer to them."[41]

The bitterness over Clay's "Operation Talk Back" must be viewed in the context of West Germany's development in 1948. Encouraged by the ongoing discussion of the Basic Law, the formation of parliament, and the creation of a federal republic, West Germans began to cherish the restoration of their sovereignty. Opinion polls revealed that while in 1947 only 11 percent stated that U.S. supervision interfered with the freedom of the *Neue Zeitung*, one year later 22 percent were very critical of this arrangement and often found the paper "too American." In both polls, large numbers of those interviewed expressed serious doubts about the objectivity of the newspaper. No more than 51 percent found the paper "impartial" while 22 percent called it "one-sided."[42]

A number of American observers shared the Germans' complaints. Journalists such as Walter Lippmann and Marguerite Higgins castigated the propaganda campaign on the grounds that it completely ignored the German experience. While Soviet propaganda played on the Germans' hunger, Edwin Hartrich wrote in the *New York Herald Tribune*, "too many military government and Army officers in making statements or speeches to Germans indulge in rhapsodies of 'democracy' as if it could be eaten, worn or spent." Even a few officers in military government dared to criticize the "Vigorous Information Program." "Let us avoid any suggestion of superior wisdom or racial superiority in this program," the Bavarian press chief, James Clark, advised Textor in December 1947. "Ours is a big country and a powerful one—but neither is it utopia, nor do we have all the answers."[43] However, such good intentions did more to discredit their authors than to revise the "Operation Talk Back," as later events would show.

This criticism combined with the worsening inter-Allied relations caused

41. William M. Lyons, Public Safety Officer, Military Government Liaison & Security Office, Landkreis Tölz, to Chief of Intelligence Section, OMGBY, "Supplementary Report," 24 November 1947, RG 260, OMGBY 10/84–3/5, BHStA.

42. Hurwitz, *Stunde Null*, 266; Anna J. Merritt and Richard L. Merritt, *Public Opinion in Occupied Germany: The OMGUS Surveys, 1945–1949* (Urbana, Ill.: University of Illinois Press, 1970), 274f.

43. Monthly Summary for Period Ending 31 August 1948, OMGBY/ISD, RG 260, OMGBY 10/117–3/13, BHStA; Edwin Hartrich, "American Propaganda in Germany: Anti-Communist Campaign Is Hampered by Lack of Paper, Caution of Germans and Awkwardness of Men in Charge," *New York Herald Tribune* (Paris edition), 26 November 1947; ICD Report from James Clark to Gordon Textor, "What can be done in Germany?" 15 December 1947, RG 260, OMGBY 10/124–1/24, BHStA.

a surge of anticommunist measures within military government circles. Until mid-1948, U.S. officials openly approved Fleischer's efforts "to show the benefits of democracy" and to "attack the *idea* of communism." But after a nine-month period of laissez-faire, observers within the ICD and the Political Adviser's Office suddenly began to scold the *Neue Zeitung* for its lack of anticommunist zeal.[44] Their complaints coincided with the beginning of the Berlin blockade, which turned the paper battle into a propaganda war. It made clear to ICD officials that the conflict with their Soviet colleagues was not merely a dispute over zonal jurisdiction but over weltanschauungen. Pressed by the necessity to take a firm anticommunist stand, they could no longer focus their efforts on export strategies but were forced to examine critically the *Neue Zeitung*'s content.

On Thursday, 15 July 1948 Textor sent an unclassified teletype to Fleischer, stating that he was "more than a little concerned over the lack of direct support given by *Die Neue Zeitung* to the problem of projecting information supporting US policy . . . and actions in Germany." To Fleischer, the charge came as a considerable jolt. He retorted that between May and mid-July 1948 his staff had printed some sixty-two editorials supporting U.S. policy and discussing matters of general American interest. More importantly, "your TWX was [the] first communication I received from you on editorial policy of *Neue Zeitung* in [the] nine months [since] I have been editor in chief."[45]

Harsh criticism concerning the paper's weak American coverage continued throughout the summer and fall of 1948. In August 1948 Robert McClure, now a member of the Civil Affairs Division in the Army Department, disciplined the *Neue Zeitung* for its negative coverage of U.S. movies. Even superficial Hollywood productions still contained a genuine American atmosphere that would further Germany's reorientation. "This is not freedom of the press," McClure thundered, "it is sabotage."[46]

Sabotage—this word ran through more than one report circulating in the Political Adviser's Office in the second half of 1948. Secret documents discredited numerous staffers in the official media as near-communists. Anonymous investigators found that a large part of the RIAS (Radio in the Ameri-

44. Semi-monthly Report, OMGBY, 1–16 November 1947, RG 260, OMGBY 13/142–1/5, BHStA; "American Interest and Military Government," RG 260, OMGUS 5/243–2/6, IfZ; Hurwitz, *Stunde Null*, 265.

45. Jack M. Fleischer to Lucius D. Clay, Berlin, 18 October 1948, and Jack M. Fleischer, teletype to Gordon Textor, 21 July 1948, both courtesy of Jack M. Fleischer.

46. Robert A. McClure, Brigadier General, Chief, New York Field Office, CAD, Department of the Army, to Gordon E. Textor, 23 August 1948, RG 260, OMGUS/ISD 5/243–2/6, BArch.

can Sector) broadcasting station in Berlin, for example, was a hotbed of communism, filled with American and German personnel who were "pink or worse."[47]

The successive developments in the *Neue Zeitung* mirrored events across the Atlantic where much of the "Red Scare" was grounded in the belief that Washington's foreign difficulties sprang from communist subversion abroad. In occupied Germany, instead of inducing a reexamination of the "Vigorous Information Program," the internal criticism sparked a wave of anticommunist paranoia throughout the military government. According to T. B. Wenner, assistant in Robert Murphy's office, the entire ICD was not above suspicion due to "extreme liberalism if not 'pinkism' in responsible places" and "a wishy-washy attitude" in the implementation of the new U.S. information program. If the division wanted to retain full operational control, Wenner concluded, it had to "clean house" and "more aggressively tackle the job of representing the U.S. case to Germans."[48]

Textor tried to counter these charges by encouraging his division to pursue a more aggressive course. In addition, all those who had worked for the ICD through the period of inter-Allied harmony found themselves now suddenly exposed to severe criticism. The scapegoat of the "housecleaning" would not be the entire ICD but the *Neue Zeitung*.[49]

While Textor embarked on an active purge in his division, internal disputes divided Fleischer and a group of German nationalists at the *Neue Zeitung*. Fleischer's consolidation of the plant struck many of his German subordinates as impractical, ignorant, and ideologically tainted. They perceived the change as an unwelcome "Americanization" of the *Neue Zeitung* and saw themselves downgraded from independent journalists to mere interpreters of the American message to Germany.[50] This development, many thought, ran counter to the reawakened political life in postwar Germany and the promise of the country's impending sovereignty under an independent parliament.

On the German side, political alliances split the editorial office into two

47. Tom Wenner, memorandum to Ambassador, "RIAS," 12 March 1948, RG 84, Foreign Service Posts, POLAD Berlin, Top Secret Correspondence of Robert Murphy, 1948, box 1, WNRC.

48. T. B. Wenner, Secret Estimation, no date, RG 84, Foreign Service Posts, POLAD Berlin, Top Secret Correspondence of Robert Murphy, 1948, box 1, WNRC.

49. "Subject: Dr. Franz Roh," 21 April 1948, RG 260, OMGBY/ID 10/9–3/3, BHStA; Robert Murphy to J. W. Riddleberger, Thomas B. Wenner, Charles W. Thomas, 13 March 1948, RG 84, Foreign Service Posts, POLAD, Berlin, Top Secret Correspondence of Robert Murphy, 1948, box 1, WNRC.

50. Hurwitz, *Stunde Null*, 266.

camps. Werner Kolbenhoff, Alfred Andersch, Else Reventlow, and other *Feuilleton* staff members held socialist or social democratic ideals. Another group agreed with the views of foreign editor Hans Lehmann, who advocated Germany's speedy reconstruction, national independence, and integration with the West. While reluctant to print articles on denazification, he welcomed pushing anti-Soviet and anticommunist themes.

For the first two years, a general loyalty to the émigré editors in chief had overshadowed this factionalism. Many believed Habe and Wallenberg would always protect the editors against reproaches from the ICD. In 1946 some of the socialist staffers, including Andersch and Kolbenhoff, founded the magazine called *Der Ruf*. Much to the horror of the ICD, the magazine became an enthusiastic champion of socialist concepts tinged with German nationalism in a pan-European context. It quoted the *Neue Zeitung* verbatim, it reprinted contributions from the paper's staff members, and it received valuable advice from Hans Wallenberg concerning how far *Ruf* editors could go with their criticism of the U.S. military government.[51]

To most German editors, the new American staffers, such as Fleischer, Eugene Jolas, and Thomas Schulz, did not represent protectors but rather strangers who controlled the *Neue Zeitung*'s employees around the clock. "Their obvious occupation consisted of studying all manuscripts line by line to see if they corresponded with the current policy from Washington." In fact, they seemed to be qualified primarily because of their loyalty to the American line. It was, as editor Hans-Joachim Netzer observed, "as if the dependence upon possible guidance from the headquarters . . . had replaced the journalistic institution." What Fleischer and his U.S. staff perceived as indispensable features of American journalism, appeared as censorship to their German staffers. The new American staff regarded some of their rebellious subordinates as a bunch of arrogant intellectuals who, in turn, saw their U.S. superiors as resenting all Germans.[52]

Fleischer's staunchest opponents were the young, nationalistic reporters behind Hans Lehmann. Lehmann had been working as a journalist during the Third Reich, an activity for which the CIC had demanded his removal from the *Neue Zeitung*. Fleischer "did not like him at all . . . [and] didn't

51. Jérôme Vaillant, *Der Ruf: Unabhängige Blätter der jungen Generation, 1945–1949* (Munich: K. G. Saur, 1978), xii, 53, 72ff., 106f., 108, 119f., 130, 135, 140, 146, 190f.; Reinhardt, *Alfred Andersch*, 133ff., 146f.; Kolbenhoff, *Schellingstraße 48*, 22f., 185f., 232–36; Burkhardt, "Feuilleton und Kunstbeilage der *Neuen Zeitung*," 9f.; "Violations and Actions" in "Cumulative Annual History Report of Publication Control Branch, ICD, 1 July 1946–30 June 1947," OMGBY/ICD Munich, 16 July 1947, RG 260, OMGBY 10/117–3/13, BHStA.

52. Hurwitz, *Stunde Null*, 264f.; Netzer, "Die *Neue Zeitung*," 16f.; Hans-Joachim Netzer, interview.

trust the man." To him, Lehmann's writings often smacked of Nazi ideology because they prematurely advocated Germany's full restoration to nationhood in a European context. Privately, the editor in chief suspected that Lehmann used the rising tide against communism in order to hide his own past.[53]

Lehmann's views gained the support of several young and very self-conscious German journalists at the plant. Twenty-one-year-old Peter Bönisch, son of a Russian mother and a German father and a parachutist during the war, had begun his journalistic career in the Berlin bureau of the *Neue Zeitung*. In 1947, after Soviet officers had almost kidnapped him, the tall, handsome, tousle-haired reporter moved to the Munich office. "In his speech and mentality Peter was like the old-time Berlin cabbies, half ego and half *Schnauze* [loudmouth]," his chief editor in Berlin, Peter Weidenreich, remembered decades later. Weidenreich spent an entire year teaching the younger Peter that authority was worth nothing and "that news sources were liars until proven otherwise," even the saintly General Clay.[54]

Twenty-five-year-old Carl Hermann Ebbinghaus, son of a famous philosopher and grandson of an even more famous psychologist, had seen the end of the war as a tank soldier imprisoned in a British POW camp near Hannover. It was only sheer luck that he survived the war at all. As a soldier stationed in Belgium in 1942, he had kept a diary in which he had consistently called Hitler "that pig." The book was found, and Ebbinghaus was court-martialed. But the German judge produced a psychiatric opinion that found Ebbinghaus insane due to a past unhappy love affair and thus protected him from the gallows. At the *Neue Zeitung*, Ebbinghaus soon rose to prominence under Hans Wallenberg due to his editorial skills. He also became a close friend of Hans Habe's daughter, Alke Schlag. Orders and manuscripts often landed on his desk first before the chief read them. With Fleischer's rule, however, Ebbinghaus' exceptional position came to an end.[55]

The fourth man in the anti-Fleischer camp was Enno Hobbing, the German émigré from Berlin. A graduate of Harvard in 1940, Hobbing served as a prisoner interrogator in the European theater before replacing Peter Weidenreich as the *Neue Zeitung*'s chief of the Berlin bureau during the summer of 1946. On 3 April 1948 the *Berliner Blatt* was separated from the Munich plant in order to function on its own in case of a crisis. It now con-

53. Hans Lehmann and Jack M. Fleischer, interviews; Jack M. Fleischer, in Bayerischer Rundfunk broadcasting, "Die *Neue Zeitung*"; Hans Lehmann, "Eine europäische Bilanz (VI)," *Neue Zeitung*, 11 April 1948, p. 5; Hans Lehmann, "Eine europäische Bilanz (VIII)," *Neue Zeitung*, 18 April 1948, p. 5.

54. Wyden, *Wall*, 208; Peter Bönisch, interview.

55. Carl Hermann Ebbinghaus, interview.

sisted of twelve pages for the city and two eight-page issues for the Russian zone. Circulation jumped from 175,000 to a total of 385,000, 241,000 copies of which went into the Soviet zone—a powerful publication for the young émigré.[56]

In the absence of adequate guidance as to Clay's propaganda campaign, Hobbing, an independent and very strong-minded man, enjoyed a completely free hand to design editorial policy. Shortly after the beginning of the blockade, in June 1948, Hobbing published an article, entitled "The Answer of the World," triggered by a public appeal from the mayor of Berlin, Ernst Reuter, who urged the Western allies to support the city: "With the surrender of Berlin, the Western powers would really abandon the entire European continent," Hobbing confidently stated. "[Berlin] is the issue of the entire free world." He had no guarantee that his article accurately reflected U.S. intentions, and his superiors severely reproached his action. But Hobbing, proclaiming that State Department directives were "either completely unreal or crassly obvious," boasted that only he could understand the difficult situation in Berlin.[57]

Most noteworthy, although Hobbing's single-minded actions often evoked strong criticism, Gordon Textor, head of the ICD, liked the chief of the Berlin bureau. He knew that much of the Berlin press campaign in the unfolding Cold War depended on this man.[58] As head of a division thought to be tainted by communism, Textor was grateful for any sign of radical anticommunism among the staffers of the *Neue Zeitung*. As a consequence, when Fleischer and Hobbing eventually clashed, Textor backed up Hobbing, the émigré, rather than Fleischer, the experienced U.S. journalist and head of the *Neue Zeitung*. American officials were convinced that the outcome of the Berlin crisis would determine the shape of Germany as well as that of Soviet-American relations. If West Berlin were integrated into the Eastern zone, the Soviets might be able to bait Germany into the communist

56. OMGUS Staff Meetings, 10 April 1948, RG 260, Fg 12/13, IfZ; Krieger, *Lucius D. Clay*, 345–50.

57. Hurwitz, *Stunde Null*, 355; "Berlin appelliert an die Welt," *Neue Zeitung*, 27 June 1948, p. 2; "Sie sind gewarnt!" ibid., p. 5; Charles W. Thayer, "Report on European Trip December–January 1948–1949," (diary entry from 12 January 1949), p. 49a, Charles W. Thayer papers, box 11, HSTL; Netzer, "*Neue Zeitung*," 17; Enno R. Hobbing to Mike Fodor, 9 August 1948, RG 260, OMGUS/ISD 5/243–2/6, BArch; Enno Hobbing to Boerner, "Difficulties in Dealing with IPO," 19 August 1948, RG 260, OMGUS 5/243–2/6, IfZ; Enno Hobbing, memoranda to Boerner, 23 and 26 August 1948, ibid.

58. D. C. Mulloney, Chief, Overt Management Branch, "Comments of Overt re Memo, subject Bookkeeping Procedure for *Die Neue Zeitung* addressed by Mr. Hobbing to Mr. Boerner," no date, RG 260, OMGUS 5/243–2/6, IfZ; Gordon E. Textor, memorandum to Enno Hobbing, 9 September 1948, RG 260, OMGUS 5/260–2/1, IfZ.

sphere of influence, thereby stalling the country's integration into a Western alliance. The anticommunist manipulation of public opinion in Berlin was much more important to Textor than the resolution of an internal struggle at the *Neue Zeitung.*

In contrast, the German leftist editors at the *Neue Zeitung* in Munich, such as Else Reventlow and Walter Kolbenhoff, remonstrated against "a string of German and American intrigues" that began to penetrate the office after Wallenberg had resigned. The rise of anticommunism had made strange bedfellows, Reventlow noted in her correspondence, for example, Lehmann, Ebbinghaus, and Bönisch who supported a decisively pro-German nationalist course, and Enno Hobbing who failed to grasp that Berlin did not represent the West. "For Hobbing, there was and is . . . only one problem and one fight—the fight against Bolshevism," Reventlow concluded. "But for us in the West, during the past year, nationalism has become the state's enemy no. 1—Bolshevism is not present at every intersection as it is in Berlin."[59]

The intensifying tensions between Fleischer and "the nationalists" culminated in a putsch in the late summer of 1948. On Saturday, 21 August, Fleischer became seriously ill with pneumonia. Confined to bed for several weeks, he did not return to the plant until 10 October. This incident was crucial because September 1948 marked one of the great crisis moments of the early Cold War in Berlin. On 7 September the military governors of the four sectors ceased their meetings. During the following three weeks, the Soviets and the Allies exchanged a number of protest notes accusing each other of having stalled the negotiations. Finally, the United Nations Security Council prepared a resolution condemning the blockade, but the Soviet representative vetoed it.[60] When Jack Fleischer returned to his editorial office, the international political climate had changed dramatically.

The chronology of events at the Munich plant during Fleischer's absence remains obscure, but the result was a "housecleaning" at the *Neue Zeitung* that included almost the entire American and German-American staff. During Fleischer's absence, Enno Hobbing temporarily assumed control in Munich, promoting Lehmann and Bönisch to, as Fleischer put it, "unjustified positions of importance." Finally, on 13 October 1948, Hobbing informed Max Kraus (managing editor), Tom Schulz (administrative assistant), and

59. Else Reventlow, Munich, to Rolf Reventlow, Algiers, 13 December 1948, courtesy of Beatrice del Bondio-Reventlow, Munich; Else Reventlow, Munich, to Hans Wallenberg, New York, 1 and 30 January 1949, Else Reventlow collection, FES.

60. Gerhardt, *Krisenmanagement der Vereinigten Staaten*, 111–28, 354; Hans Herzfeld, *Berlin in der Weltpolitik, 1945–1970* (Berlin: Walter de Gruyter, 1973), 263.

Egon Jameson (chief of the correspondents) that he would recommend their dismissals to Textor.[61]

Clay and Textor agreed with these measures. Clay wanted a newspaper that would fulfill the requirements of the "Vigorous Information Program." Textor was preoccupied with ridding his division of the stigma of communism. Hobbing seemed to be a staunch anticommunist, Fleischer did not. Instead, he had antagonized Hobbing and, in the eyes of Textor, had not printed enough anticommunist articles. Consequently, Textor reacted quickly to Hobbing's demand. On 13 October 1948 the information division's chief notified the editor in chief that he, Fleischer, would be "purged." Despite Clay's close acquaintance with Fleischer, three days later the general appointed Kendall Foss as the new head of the *Neue Zeitung*. Foss was a good friend of Enno Hobbing.[62]

Fleischer was stunned—and hurt. In a bitter letter to General Clay, the editor in chief expressed his year-long frustration as the head of the *Neue Zeitung*. "Where is my successor and where is the new staff?" With the dismissal of the last three U.S. employees at the plant, there was not a single American left, Fleischer complained. "I cannot vouchsafe for the staff either concerning ability or political reliability," he warned Foss in November 1948. Fleischer remained on the job until 15 November in order to introduce Kendall Foss to the procedures at the plant; afterward, he was appointed chief of Public Information for the Office of Military Government in Bavaria.[63]

Many of those staff members who did not support the palace revolt shared his feelings. They may not have liked Fleischer, but they also resented the continual, drastic political changes within the paper and decided to leave. "I do not work for a propaganda instrument," said Robert Lembke. "The *Neue Zeitung* was not apt for individual thoughts," added Else Reventlow. Even Max Kraus chose to leave because if "members of the Ger-

61. Jack M. Fleischer to Lucius D. Clay, Berlin, 18 October 1948, courtesy of Jack M. Fleischer; Jack M. Fleischer to Bruce Buttles, POB, Munich, 4 January 1949, courtesy of Jack M. Fleischer.

62. Jack M. Fleischer, letter to the author, 5 December 1993. Hans Lehmann tells a different story. Due to his quarrels with Fleischer, he himself decided to resign in the fall of 1948, but ICD delegate Marcel W. Fodor explicitly asked him to stay. Lehmann suggested that Fleischer should go on a vacation, then fall sick, and never return to the plant, "which is what they did." Hans Lehmann, interview.

63. Jack M. Fleischer, Berlin, to Lucius D. Clay, 18 October 1948, courtesy of Jack M. Fleischer; Jack M. Fleischer, memo to Kendall Foss, Munich, 10 November 1948, courtesy of Jack M. Fleischer; Semi-Annual Historical Report covering period 1 July–31 December 1948, OMGBY/POB, 1 March 1949, RG 260, OMGBY 10/130–2/2, BHStA; Jack M. Fleischer, letter to the author, 5 December 1993; Jack M. Fleischer, interview.

man editorial staff can intrigue successfully against the editor in chief, then I didn't want to have anything to do with it."[64]

Although these despairing journalists came from different political camps, their decisions originated from the same frustration. They did not resent the new anticommunist rule in the *Neue Zeitung*. Instead, they despised the new U.S. policy that, as they saw it, sacrificed anti-Nazi reeducation for the sake of anticommunist propaganda. They did not understand U.S. goals in Germany anymore.

The *Neue Zeitung*, then, is a good example of the American military government's reluctance to intellectually direct its information program in Germany even after 1947. As soon as the émigrés had been removed from their influential positions and as soon as official policy came to overshadow the process of cultural transmission, the operation began to crumble. Fleischer's appointment in October 1947 and Clay's announcement three weeks later together with the ICD's aggressive export policy for the paper marked its change from a by-product of information control into a powerful U.S. propaganda tool in the fight against communism.

Yet, although Fleischer's editorial policy seemed to agree with U.S. diplomacy in Germany, his bosses turned out to be very unhappy with the venture. Fearing the impact of communism in Germany, they ignored his efforts but never found a better alternative. When questioned about the paper's objectives, officials often displayed a stunning ignorance. In October 1948 a graduate student from the University of California asked for information on the *Neue Zeitung*, but the Civil Affairs Division in the Department of Defense was not "able to find an authoritative statement of the paper's official policy." "There exists no stack of directives," Colonel Bernard B. McMahon, deputy chief of the department's reorientation branch, who had once supervised the paper's foundation when he headed the ICD in Bavaria, informed the curious student. "Aside from Gen. Eisenhower's statement of aims, the policy, quite Topsy-like, just grew."[65] Unwittingly, McMahon

64. Lembke quoted in Bayerischer Rundfunk broadcasting, "Die *Neue Zeitung*"; Else Reventlow, Munich, to Leopold Goldschmidt, Frankfurt a.M., 9 January 1949, Else Reventlow collection, box 21, FES; Max W. Kraus, interview, 6 July 1991; Semi-Annual Historical Report, 1 July–31 December 1948, OMGBY/ISD, 24 February 1949, RG 260, OMGBY 10/130–2/2, BHStA.

65. William W. Wertz, Jr., Berkeley, Calif., to Commanding Officer, Military Government Training School, Carlisle Barracks, Pa., 19 October 1948, RG 165, War Department, CAD, Entry 463, box 400, dec. file 000.76, Sec. 2, NARA; B. B. McMahon, Colonel, Infantry, Deputy Chief, Reorientation Branch, letter to Captain William W. Wertz, Jr., ibid.

stumbled on a problem that had haunted the development of the *Neue Zeitung* ever since Clay announced "Operation Talk Back." U.S. officials wanted to counter Soviet propaganda, but they did not want to be involved in the campaign; they did not want to be propagandists.

Nonetheless, the reactions to Clay's Vigorous Information Program and the editorial and ideological changes in the columns of the *Neue Zeitung* in 1947–1948 were essentially negative. The German public as well as the licensed press condemned the program outright. They resented the outbreak of inter-Allied conflicts on German territory and likened the campaign to Nazi indoctrination. Significantly, their concerns were initially echoed by many influential American journalists and observers in the military government.

Such criticism, however, led to a profound confusion in the minds of top officials, including Robert Murphy. As key actors in the Allied confrontation over reparations, interzonal travel, and communication, they were keenly aware of the negative effects of such disapproval. They began to identify communists in their own ranks. Very soon the ICD itself, now renamed Information Services Division (ISD) and one of the foremost tools in the anticommunist information program,[66] was charged with indoctrinating communism. The foremost targets were Jack Fleischer and the *Neue Zeitung*.

66. On 6 August 1948, the Information Control Division was renamed Information Services Division. The ISD was supposed to plan and supervise the U.S. propaganda campaign more effectively than the ICD while paying particular attention to public taste, interests, and opinion. Gunther Gerhardt, *Das Krisenmanagement der Vereinigten Staaten während der Berliner Blockade (1948/1949): Intentionen, Strategien und Wirkungen* (Berlin: Duncker & Humblot, 1984), 190.

# 7

# WHICH WAY BLOW THE WINDS? U.S. PROPAGANDA AND THE STRUGGLE FOR IDENTITY, 1949–1955

Tell me, which way blows the wind
Here at the *Neue Zeitung?*
Tell me where in the hell wir sind [we are]
Here at the *Neue Zeitung?*

. . . . . . . . . . . . . . . .

Shades of Wallenberg, guide my views
To accord with the last directive!
Is it the Nazis or is it the Jews?
Or is Clay just being protective?

. . . . . . . . . . . . . . . .

First it's the dream of a pagan god—
Valhalla mit viel [*with much*] ambrosia!
Then, overnight, at an OMGUS nod,
The paper goes strictly kosher!

O sad today is Germania's state
Since her enemies have annexed her,
But sadder the *Neue Zeitung*'s fate
Torn between Foss and Textor!

Tell me, friends, are we going to stop
Treating the press like Prussians?
We'd better—or else just close up shop
And give it up to the Russians.

—"Watchman, What of the Night?"
anonymous, 1948–1949.
Typewritten manuscript,
courtesy Jack M. Fleischer.

JACK FLEISCHER'S RESIGNATION FROM THE *NEUE ZEITUNG* DEMONSTRATED the dilemma inherent in the "Vigorous Information Program." The strategy to transform the antifascist reeducation program into an anticommunist crusade stirred up a profound confusion among American observers: what was the foremost threat in Germany in 1948? What were the objectives of the U.S. reeducation policy three years after the end of the war? What should the *Neue Zeitung* tell its readers? Fifty years later, it is very hard to grasp the challenges facing U.S. officials in Germany.

Scholars, such as Edward Peterson, Rand C. Lewis, and Hansjörg Gehring, contend that in 1947–1948 the American anticommunist campaign overshadowed its fight against fascism. In fighting communism, U.S. officials relaxed the emphasis on the anti-Nazi reeducation program. Many observers in military government were aware of this change but accepted it as a necessary measure to integrate West Germany into a Western orbit.[1]

The case of the *Neue Zeitung* suggests a less clear-cut change. U.S. officials could not "neatly" switch from antifascism to anticommunism. Both were always linked to their concerns about the direction of German nationalism if the country should regain autonomy.[2] Fleischer's successor, Kendall Foss, was known as a fierce anticommunist but would be fired due to charges of nationalism, anti-Americanism—and even pro-Soviet attitudes.

Kendall Foss was a thoughtful man. Born in 1904 in New Rochelle, New York, Foss had attended Harvard University from 1923 to 1927. Tall, with lengthy thick hair and deep worried eyes, the forty-five-year-old was a pious Quaker, a former Rhodes scholar, and a correspondent of the *New York Post* in Berlin. He adored German *Kultur* and had even adopted two German orphans. Foss intended to stay in Germany as long as he could and to become the most knowledgeable correspondent on the country. In the eyes of General Clay, Foss's anticommunist activities in Berlin established him as a perfect promoter of U.S. policy in Germany. As the first U.S. mediator between the general and a number of German students and professors from

1. Peterson, *The Many Faces of Defeat*, 55f.; Rand C. Lewis, *A Nazi Legacy: Right-Wing Extremism in Postwar Germany* (New York: Praeger, 1991), 36; Gehring, *Amerikanische Literaturpolitik*, 78, 108; Hans Borchers and Klaus W. Vowe, *Die zarte Pflanze Demokratie: Amerikanische Re-education in Deutschland im Spiegel ausgewählter politischer und literarischer Zeitschriften, 1945–1949* (Tübingen: Narr, 1979), 65.

2. See also Füssl, *Die Umerziehung der Deutschen*, 25–26.

Humboldt University in the Soviet sector, Foss had helped establish the Free University of Berlin.[3]

Editor in chief at the *Neue Zeitung* since November 1948, Foss quickly gained a reputation among his staff as a conciliatory and cooperative man who wanted to turn the paper into a forum of German-American understanding.[4] He revived Habe's layout technique and printed numerous articles on German *Kultur* and history as well as philosophy and thus boosted circulation by approximately 25 percent to 800,000.

While Kendall Foss agreed with U.S. policy makers that nationalism was a dangerous sentiment among Germans, he attempted to use the *Neue Zeitung* to encourage patriotism, which he distinguished from nationalism. He based his editorial course on the Quakers' idea of compromise and discussion. Few articles of his expressed an outright pro-Western opinion; most conveyed arguments in favor of Germany's reunification. Democracy and reunification, Foss believed, would come about not by military force but by a form of Darwinian evolution. The fittest political system would survive.[5]

The editorial course Foss chose, however, did not coincide with the currents of U.S. occupation policy in Germany. As Bruce Kuklick, John Backer, and others have pointed out, after the Moscow Conference in 1947 U.S. officials saw that their version of a free and democratic Germany could be realized only in an independent West Germany. Not surprisingly, information officials watched the new editor in chief with increasing suspicion. Foss had been in office for less than a fortnight when reports critical of the *Neue Zeitung*'s "new nationalist tone" began circulating. Investigators such as Thomas P. Headen, now deputy director of the Information Services Division (ISD), accused Foss of "vicious, slanted and inaccurate attack[s]"

3. Operations Branch, Security Group, ID, General Staff, U.S. Army, Report on Kendall Foss, 8 February 1949, RG 260, OMGUS/AG 1949/3/1, IfZ; Carl Hermann Ebbinghaus, Jack M. Fleischer, interviews; Smith, *Lucius D. Clay*, 375; Tent, *Mission on the Rhine*, 291–299; Tent, *The Free University of Berlin*, 94–97, 104–109, 170–75; Herbet, *Die "Neue Zeitung,"* 164.

4. Netzer, "*Neue Zeitung*," 17.

5. Peter Schmid, "Zwischen Idealismus und Terror," *Neue Zeitung*, 16 November 1948, p. 4; Spectator, "Weltpolitische Rundschau der 'NZ'," *Neue Zeitung*, 30 November 1948, p. 5; "Am Problem vorbei," *Neue Zeitung*, 16 December 1948, p. 7; " 'Reichsausweise,' " *Neue Zeitung*, 25 November 1948, p. 5; "Doch ein Auftakt," *Neue Zeitung*, 2 December 1948, p. 5; Kendall Foss, "Nacht der Entscheidung," *Neue Zeitung*, 24 December 1948, p. 1; "Berlin wählte trotz Terror die Freiheit," *Neue Zeitung*, 7 December 1948, p. 1; Franz Rupp, "Im Westen sieht alles anders aus," *Neue Zeitung*, 11 January 1949, p. 2; "Illusionisten am Werk," *Neue Zeitung*, 25 January 1949, p. 5; Charles W. Thayer, report to George V. Allen, Assistant Secretary, "European Trip: December–January 1948–1949," Charles W. Thayer Papers, box 11, HSTL.

"But Marianne—one day he will have to learn how to walk."

*This cartoon by Helmut Beyer, published in the* Neue Zeitung *on 18 November 1948, depicts the struggle for control of the Ruhr area. The French Marianne indicating the buggy marked "Internationalization" represents France's desire to keep the area under international control; meanwhile, English and American forces contend that the area should "Return to German Administration," the slogan printed on the infant's shirt.*

against the military government, written in a style that was "not in accordance with even third-rate American journalistic practices." Worst of all, Foss hired a number of journalists who had been active in the press after 1933, including an aide of Joseph Goebbels.[6]

The ISD's suspicion regarding the resurgence of Nazism was not un-

6. Undated report, RG 260, OMGUS 5/260–2/6, BArch; Thomas P. Headen, Deputy Director, ISD, to Colonel Gordon Textor, 5 January 1949, RG 260, OMGUS/ISD 5/260–3/5, BArch; Memorandum of the Council of Employees, 29 November 1948, Max Kraus collection, No. 92/09/105.1.14, SHBRD; Hans Lehmann, "Mitteilung an die Dena und DPD vom

founded. Denazification had proven a far more difficult task than was initially assumed. U.S. teams trying to identify former Nazi members never had the time to examine thousands of Nazi records. In March 1946 U.S. occupation officials turned the program over to German authorities, who subsequently passed various amnesties. Moreover, throughout all three Western occupation zones, U.S. observers noted a sudden revival of a "fascist spirit" in 1948. According to several opinion polls, numerous Germans believed that National Socialism had been a good idea badly carried out.[7]

During the months leading to the creation of the Federal Republic and the restoration of German sovereignty, U.S. policy makers grew increasingly worried that their "democratic experiment" in Germany might not work out. No one could predict how a West German state would orient itself and, more important, if it would remain in the Western camp. U.S. observers feared that free elections would increase German nationalism, alienate German policy makers from the Western allies, and render the country vulnerable to Soviet offers of reunification. German politicians from all parties highlighted the issues of unification and nationalism. To many Germans, the Berlin blockade was a constant reminder of their crippled national identity. With families torn apart and businesses floundering, voters were easily convinced that unification should be a priority of the new West German state.[8]

Very soon ISD observers detected evidence supporting their worst fears about the *Neue Zeitung*. In a single issue, analysts reported, the paper had published several pieces "designed to arouse nationalistic passion." One essay, written "in dime-novel style," told the story of a poor German who wanted to sell one of his eyeballs to a blind American farmer for $10,000 to better his financial circumstances. "There is little point to this sob-sister story," complained the analyst of the ISD. German readers "will be outraged by the thought that overfed, money-mad Americans are now using dollars to buy the very eyeballs of poor, starving Germans with beautiful blue eyes."[9]

4. Februar 1949," Akten der Bayerischen Staatskanzlei, Stk 112928, BHStA; Hans Lehmann, interview; Kuklick, *Division of Germany*; John H. Backer, *The Decision to Divide Germany: American Foreign Policy in Transition* (Durham, N.C.: Duke University Press, 1978).

7. Lewis, *A Nazi Legacy*, 28–38; Robert Lewison, "Education For What?" in *This Is Germany*, ed. Arthur Settel (New York: Sloane, 1950), 89–115.

8. Clara Menck, "The Problem of Reorientation," in *The Struggle for Democracy in Germany*, ed. Gabriel A. Almond (Chapel Hill, N.C.: University of North Carolina Press, 1949), 281–307; "Germany," Department of State Policy Statement, 26 August 1948, in *Foreign Relations of the United States 1948*, vol. 2, *Germany and Austria* (Washington, D.C.: United States Government Printing Office, 1973), 1305–308; Hermann Graml, "Die Außenpolitik," in Benz, *Bundesrepublik Deutschland*, 1: 349–55.

9. Report "*Neue Zeitung*, New Year's issue 121/122, 31 December 1948, first edition,"

Worst of all, ISD investigators complained, the *Neue Zeitung* had published a series of articles on the views of "The Man In the Street" in which Germans criticized the occupying powers as a result of their injustice, "myopia and obtuseness." Of those interviewed, 13 percent condemned the "moralistic gravy" the United States poured over the country's reconstruction, 28 percent said that democracy in Germany had become a farce, and 10 percent even went so far as to say that the military government exploited ideological buzzwords such as "democracy" for the sake of an "East-West tug-of-war" on the backs of the Germans. "Will the praise now bestowed upon us in England and America save us from the revenge of the Soviets?" one reader sarcastically asked. "Or will we be used merely for providing 'rearguard' action and then be permitted, with sympathy and regret, to disappear in[to] concentration camps[?]"[10]

Significantly, observers who accused the *Neue Zeitung* of echoing these "anti-American," nationalist tendencies, simultaneously charged the paper with being procommunist—"the main evils in German thinking." A confidential thirteen-page political analysis for the period between 25 November and 28 December 1948 accused the editors of bluntly disregarding current orders and long-range policies of the State and the War departments. "It would appear almost as if American supervising personnel are being tricked by various German staff members into carrying articles, *which while pro-American on the surface, are actually pro-Nazi or pro-communist*" (italics mine).[11]

The merger of communism and nationalism in the minds of many U.S. officials was grounded in the fear that any offers from Soviet occupation authorities would attract German nationalists. As Rolf Steininger has shown, Stalin wanted a "weak Germany with strong political forces looking to both the West and the Soviet Union" in order to achieve a political balance. To U.S. officials, however, such an alliance would impede the fruits of democratic reeducation and the efforts to rebuild West Germany, integrate France

n. p., n. d., RG 260, OMGUS 5/243–2/6, IfZ; Report, 6 January 1949, RG 260, OMGUS 5/260–2/1, IfZ.

10. Observer, "Innenpolitische Rundschau," *Neue Zeitung*, 27 November 1948, p. 7; 11 December 1948, p. 11; 18 December 1948, p. 11; Confidential Report, n. d., RG 260, OMGUS/AG 1949/3/1, IfZ.

11. Report " 'Observer', *Neue Zeitung* columnist," n. p., n. d., RG 260, OMGUS/ODI 7/31–3/6, BArch; Marcel W. Fodor, Political Information Branch, "Complaint against the serialization of 'Stalin's Friend' published in *Neue Zeitung*," 11 January 1949, RG 260, OMGUS 5/243–2/6, IfZ; Confidential Report, n.d., RG 260, OMGUS/AG 1949/3/1, ibid.; also in RG 165, Entry 463, box 506, dec. no. 000.76, Sec. 1, NARA.

and Germany, and consummate the North Atlantic Treaty.[12] Any attempt on the part of the *Neue Zeitung* to seek a compromise among the Allies rather than to antagonize the Soviets, appeared to lend support to a nationalist-communist conspiracy under the umbrella of reunification.

U.S. officials reacted dramatically to the *Neue Zeitung*'s portrayal of German affairs. In the columns of the newspaper, the ISD investigator charged, Hitler and Ribbentrop were portrayed as "blundering anglophobes." Reichsmarschall Hermann Göring came across as "a man of good will and a hero who left nothing untried to avert the catastrophe." And Otto Strasser, Hitler's one-time follower, was presented as the hope of a dawning German empire after her quick rearmament. At the same time, the report detected a communist conspiracy visible in the installment series "I Was Stalin's Friend," which portrayed the Soviet leader as a brave, clever "superman," the kind that Germans adored. The appeal of this conspiracy, as the investigator pointed out, was obvious in a number of letters to the editor that praised the series with phrases such as "I am becoming a friend of Stalin . . . [because] Stalin took from the rich and gave to the poor." The paper was clearly driven by anti-American tendencies. It ridiculed former U.S. presidents and exaggerated minor conflicts between the British and American forces.[13] Such coverage, U.S. officials argued, endangered all their political and economic accomplishments of the past four years.

In order to regain control over the *Neue Zeitung*, Textor appointed a new operations manager for the plant. Bruce Buttles was a former *Christian Science Monitor* reporter who had no editorial experience and did not speak German. He clashed with Foss almost from his first day at the plant. While Buttles demanded an intelligence check of every staff member above the level of clerk, Foss requested such a screening only for key personnel. This conflict split the entire staff at the plant, including the remaining six or seven Americans.[14]

12. Rolf Steininger, *The German Question: The Stalin Note of 1952 and the Problem of Reunification* (New York: Columbia University Press, 1990), 11, 20, 115; Leffler, *Preponderance of Power*, 319.

13. Nikolai Korganow, "Ich war Stalins Freund," *Neue Zeitung*, 21 November 1948, p. 1; 30 November 1948, p. 1; 2 December 1948, p. 5; 4 December 1948, p. 7; 7 December 1948, p. 5; 9 December 1948, p. 7; 11 December 1948, p. 11; 16 December 1948, p. 7; 18 December 1948, p. 9; 21 December 1948, p. 5; 28 December 1948, p. 5; 4 January 1949, p. 5; 8 January 1949, p. 7; 11 January 1949, p. 5; 13 January 1949, p. 7; Fodor, "Complaint against the serialization of 'Stalin's Friend,' " Confidential Report, n. d., RG 260, OMGUS/AG 1949/3/1, ibid.; Thomas P. Headen, Deputy Director, ISD, to Colonel Gordon Textor, 5 January 1949, RG 260, OMGUS/ISD, 5/260–3/5, BArch.

14. Hurwitz, *Stunde Null*, 267; Bittorf, "*Neue Zeitung*," 32; Foss, memorandum to Textor, "Attached Memorandum from Mr. Buttles on Political Clearance," 11 December 1948,

Foss's efforts to protect his staff from repeated security screenings raised suspicion about his personal integrity. Screening was an important procedure for most ISD officers because it represented the only standardized way to ensure the loyalty and political "cleanliness" of a German employee. Misgivings about Foss multiplied when the personnel office of the ISD ascertained that the editor in chief intended to stay in Germany and liked to mix with the German aristocracy—the group that reportedly most resented the occupation forces. Suspicions about Foss climaxed in February 1949 when a detailed intelligence investigation revealed that Foss had been a member of various "communist" or "communist infiltrated" organizations. Some of his staff, Buttles later related to the press, simultaneously worked for the official Red Army paper *Tägliche Rundschau*. Worst of all, investigators discovered that Foss had visited Russia, worked as a correspondent there, and had "expressed anticapitalistic ideas."[15] Foss's background presented additional evidence confirming that U.S. officials' fears that German nationalism was the most dangerous hindrance to the establishment of a Western alliance were not unfounded.

In early 1949 the quarrels around Foss turned from an internal affair into a public scandal, known as *Der Fall Neue Zeitung* (The Case of the *Neue Zeitung*). In January, Clay denounced the militaristic, nationalistic, and anti-Semitic tendencies in a number of licensed magazines and newspapers. In response, the Aschaffenburg newspaper, *Main-Echo*, charged that the U.S. military government even employed former Nazi propaganda reporters in the *Neue Zeitung*.[16] Other German newspapers, too, discerned an appeal to German nationalism in the paper. But they identified it as a plot by military government officers who wanted to prepare German readers for the country's rearmament and integration in the Western alliance. A biting cartoon in the 1949 New Year's edition of the humorous Munich magazine *Simpl* showed Germany as a baby sitting on a chamber pot while studying the *Neue Zeitung*. The caption under the picture read sarcastically: "Well, I guess I'll give up diapers altogether and get into uniform right away."

---

RG 260, OMGUS 5/265–1/11, IfZ; Secret Report, "Die *Neue Zeitung*," n. d., RG 260, OMGUS 10/89–2/2, BHStA; "Für Ostgeld," *Telegraf*, 11 February 1949; "House Organ," *Time*, 21 February 1949, Secret Report, "Die *Neue Zeitung*," n. d., RG 260, OMGUS 10/89–2/2, BHStA.

15. Secret Report, "Die *Neue Zeitung*," n. d., RG 260, OMGUS 10/89–2/2, BHStA; Operations Branch, Security Group, ID, General Staff, U.S. Army, Report on Kendall Foss, 8 February 1949, RG 260, OMGUS/AG 1949/3/1, IfZ; "Für die Russen gearbeitet?", *Allgemeine Zeitung*, 11 February 1949.

16. "Hier irrte General Clay nicht," *Main-Echo*, 22 January 1949; Report to Colonel Textor, "General Clay's Press Conference on 26 January," 27 January 1949, RG 260, OMGUS 5/260–3/5, IfZ.

"Well, I guess I'll give up diapers and get into uniform right away."

*This cartoon, author unknown, was published first in the Munich* Simpl *and reprinted then in* Der Spiegel *on 5 February 1949. In depicting Germany as the baby reading the* Neue Zeitung, *this cartoon alludes to charges of nationalism against this newspaper.*

In the eyes of many American correspondents, in contrast, the military government had given the paper over to German neo-Nazis. Already at the end of November 1948, *Time* magazine published a lengthy essay criticizing the *Neue Zeitung* not only because it was written by Germans in German with no regard to U.S. newspaper practices, but also because it freely criticized the mistakes of U.S. officials. Under the headline "Old Times Again In Bavaria," the British *Daily Mail* correspondent Brian Connell warned his readers that the Nazis were "coming back." Headlines such as "U.S. Army

Paper is Under Attack As Employing Nazi Journalists," dominated the international press.[17]

The wave of sensational reports culminated in a three-column article entitled "*Neue Zeitung* Turns Nationalist," published in the Paris edition of the *New York Herald Tribune* on 27 January 1949. In this essay, editor Edwin Hartrich blatantly accused the paper of anti-Allied, pro-Germanic undertones, focusing mostly on foreign affairs editor Hans Lehmann. Lehmann, he claimed, had been a Nazi editor of noble descent who attempted to advertise his own nationalist course in the paper.[18] In order to quell the uproar, on 29 January Clay and Textor publicly announced an investigation of the editorial policies of the *Neue Zeitung*. Intelligence officers in Bavaria checked NSDAP files to see if they contained information on some fifteen German employees. Four days after the *Tribune* article, the ISD fired Hans Lehmann.[19]

Again, with the end of the occupation period approaching, this investigation reflected U.S. officials' increasing nervousness about Germany's susceptibility to nationalism and Soviet offers of reunification. There was no time left to discuss the pitfalls of democracy, the mistakes of the American occupation army, or the disadvantages of a divided Germany. The readers of the *Neue Zeitung* would soon go to the polls and they had to be pointed in the right political direction. Not only Germany but the entire Western sphere was at stake.

17. OMGBY/ISD, "Monthly Report for January 1949," RG 260, OMGBY 10/112–2/21, BHStA; " 'Die *Neue Zeitung*' nicht mehr neu," *Frankfurter Rundschau*, 25 January 1949; "Vorwürfe gegen die *Neue Zeitung*," *Tagesspiegel*, 30 January 1949; "U.S. Army Paper is Under Attack As Employing Nazi Journalists," *New York Times*, 25 January 1949; "Clay Investigates Policy of U.S. Newspaper Accused by Germans of Employing Nazis," *New York Times*, 29 January 1949; McMahon to Textor, 3 February 1949, ibid.; Textor to OMGUS/ISD, ibid.; "Uncle Sam, Publisher," *Time*, 29 November 1948; Brian Connell, "Old Times Again in Bavaria," *Daily Mail* (Paris edition), 4 December 1948.

18. Edwin Hartrich, "*Neue Zeitung* Turns Nationalist," *New York Herald Tribune* (Paris edition), 27 January 1949.

19. Thomas P. Headen to Colonel Gordon Textor, "Comments on attached article from the *Neue Zeitung*," 26 January 1949, RG 260, OMGUS/ISD 5/260–3/5, BArch; Secret Report, "Die *Neue Zeitung*," n. d., RG 260, OMGUS 10/89–2/2, BHStA; Jack Raymond, "Clay Investigates Policy of U.S. Newspaper," *The New York Times*, 29 January 1949; "Clays Erklärung über die *Neue Zeitung*," *Neue Zeitung*, 1 February 1949, p. 2; Ernest J. Cramer, memo to Mr. Isenstead, Chief, Research Branch, Intelligence Division, OMGB, 28 January 1949, RG 260, OMGBY 10/89–2/2, BHStA; "Dr. Lehmann entlassen" *Die Abendzeitung*, 2 February 1949; "Zeitung Foreign Editor Fired for Nazi Ties," *The Stars and Stripes*, 2 February 1949; translations in RG 260, OMBGY 10/89–2/2, BHStA; RG 260, OMGUS, 5/243–2/6, IfZ; Donald T. Shea, Intelligence Division, to Director of Intelligence, OMGUS, "Hans Lehmann," 4 February 1949, RG 260, OMGUS/ODI 7/21–3/1, BArch.

What followed was a blatant attempt to reel the paper back into line. On 3 February Textor summoned Foss to Berlin, severely reprimanded him, and ordered him to choose between his immediate resignation or "bringing the paper into line with current directives and guidances." Choosing the latter, Foss received a detailed list of editorial orders from Textor. Despite orders to keep silent, the devastated editor in chief informed his staff in an emergency conference about ICD's list of orders. No longer would the *Neue Zeitung* serve as a forum for German opinion. Instead, it would be the OMGUS house organ and present U.S. viewpoints, politics, and affairs; and it would be checked regularly by ISD headquarters.[20]

The staff members were outraged. "We were disappointed in our love, we were disappointed friends," recalls Peter Bönisch today. "We could not imagine that our friends, the Americans, would play such dirty tricks." When Foss ended his speech, Bönisch and Carl Hermann Ebbinghaus got up and left the room. "You know what we are going to do now?" Bönisch told Ebbinghaus. "We will slam the door here so tightly that no one can open it anymore." The two men wrote up a statement they sent out by teletype to the major newswire services. The *Neue Zeitung*, astonished readers read the next day in their newspapers, "is no longer a newspaper but an information sheet." The OMGUS directive, the two editors concluded, resembled an anti-German campaign. Privately, many of the other people on staff voiced similar concerns.[21]

During the weeks following Bönisch and Ebbinghaus's news release, the press in all four zones widely covered the conflicts in Schellingstraße 39. Headlines such as "*Neue Zeitung* Not for the Germans Anymore," or "Major Conflicts at the *Neue Zeitung*" filled the newspapers. Both Ebbinghaus and Bönisch were fired, and nine other editors turned in their resignation. Under threat of arrest, Bönisch, Ebbinghaus, and Hildegard Brücher were later forced to repudiate the statement.[22]

20. Textor to Foss, "Reiteration of Instructions with Respect to the Editorial Policy and Conduct of Die *Neue Zeitung* Editorial Operations," 3 February 1949, RG 165, Entry 463, box 503, dec. file 000.76, Sec. 1, NARA; Textor to Chief, CAD, Department of the Army, "Editorial Policy of *Die Neue Zeitung*," 9 March 1949, RG 165, Entry 463, box 503, dec. file 000.76, Sec. 1, NARA.

21. Peter Bönisch, interview; Copy of statement by P. H. Bönisch and C. H. Ebbinghaus, RG 260, OMGUS 5/243–2/6, IfZ; Note from the editors of the foreign policy section to the board of the *Neue Zeitung*, 28 March 1949, Hans-Joachim Netzer collection, ED 352/1, IfZ; translation of DENA story of 31 March 1949, dated 1 April 1949, RG 260, OMGUS 5/236–1/17, IfZ.

22. "*Neue Zeitung* nicht für die Deutschen," *Tägliche Rundschau*, 8 February 1949; "Große Differenzen bei der *Neuen Zeitung*," *Frankenpost*, 8 February 1949; "Rücktritte in der '*Neuen Zeitung*,' " *Süddeutsche Zeitung*, 8 February 1949; "Die Affaire *Neue Zeitung*," *Die*

Meanwhile in Washington, D.C., Hartrich's article in the *New York Herald Tribune* sparked a number of queries from senators and congressmen to the Civil Affairs Division (CAD) in the Department of Defense. Americans reading about the crisis in their local papers called their representatives' offices complaining about U.S. information policy in Germany. The American Legion in Kansas, for example, was loudly protesting the "publication of Nazi propaganda paper *Die Neue Zeitung*"; one citizen wrote to his congressman, "What gives?"[23]

Lacking data on both the paper and the overall information program, officials in the Department of Defense did not know how to respond. Above all, they did not want to assume any responsibility for the *Neue Zeitung*. Having no idea what to recommend, except to confirm internally that the charges of nationalism were "well founded," the Civil Affairs Division finally informed the state representatives that "*Die Neue Zeitung* is not, and never has been, a Nazi propaganda paper."[24]

The uproar in the international press rang the bell for the last round of the *Neue Zeitung*. On 9 February 1949, when it became clear that ISD chief Gordon Textor was unable to solve the problem, Clay imposed a directorate of three Americans over Kendall Foss.[25] They were John Elliot, Marcel Fodor, and Jack Stuart. John Elliot, originally a writer for the *New York Herald Tribune*, had been chief of the Political Activities Branch in the Civil Affairs Division of OMGUS in Frankfurt.[26] Marcel W. Fodor, born in Hun-

*Abendzeitung*, 8 February 1949; "Rücktritt deutscher Redakteure," AP, 8 February 1949, copy, RG 260, OMGUS 5/243–2/6, IfZ; interview with Carl Hermann Ebbinghaus; "Die Affäre der '*Neuen Zeitung*'," *Die Abendzeitung*, 8 February 1949; "Die Presse in der amerikanischen Zone Deutschlands," *Neue Zürcher Zeitung*, 15 February 1949; "NZ Redakteure können bleiben," DENA manuscript, 18 February 1949, Max Kraus collection, 92/09/105.1.14, SHBRD; "Hildegard Hamm-Brücher," *Internationales Biographisches Archiv/Munzinger Archiv* (Ravensburg: Archiv für publizistische Arbeit, Munzinger Archiv, 1949ff) 1/95; Peter Bönisch and Carl Herrmann Ebbinghaus, interviews.

23. Charles H. Cloud, Paul Miller, Chairman of the Americanism Committee, American Legion, Winfield, Kansas, to Congressman Herbert Mayer, n. d., transcript dated 4 February 1949, RG 165, Entry 463, box 503, dec. file 000.76, Sec. 1, NARA; Textor to Zachariah Sjister, The American Jewish Committee, Paris, 7 February 1949, RG 260, OMGUS 5/260–2/1, Bl. 15, IfZ; letter from Andrew F. Schoeppel to Kenneth C. Royall, Secretary, Department of the Army, 8 February 1949, RG 165, Entry 463, box 506, dec. file 000.76, Sec. 1, NARA.

24. CAD to OMGUS/ISD, cable, 3 February 1949, RG 165, Entry 463, box 503, dec. file 000.76, Sec. 1, NARA; G. L. Eberle, Chief, CAD, letter to Charles E. Saltzman, Assistant Secretary of State, 15 February 1949, ibid.; Eberle, "Reported Nazi Propaganda Publication in US Zone Germany," 18 March 1949, ibid.; Reorientation Branch to Senator Andrew F. Schoeppel, 17 March 1949, ibid.

25. Textor to Chief, CAD, Department of the Army, "Editorial Policy of *Die Neue Zeitung*," 9 March 1949, RG 165, Entry 463, box 503, dec. file 000.76, Sec. 1, NARA.

26. John Elliot, OMGUS/CAD, to Howard Elkinton, Carl Schurz Memorial Foundation, Inc., Philadelphia, 8 September 1948, RG 165, Entry 463, box 404, 014 Germany, Sec. 3,

gary, had fled from Budapest and Vienna to Chicago before the war and served as European correspondent for the *Chicago Daily News* and the *Washington Post.* Jack M. Stuart, a graduate of Georgetown University who joined the newspaper business in Philadelphia, New York, and Washington, completed the triumvirate. After the war, Stuart, a member of the Psychological Warfare Division, had set up the licensed DENA news agency in Bad Nauheim.[27] Ernst Cramer, an émigré from Augsburg and Foss's deputy since December 1948, supposedly functioned as a liaison between the directorate and the German staff. He remembers, however, that the directors spent a lot of time arguing while he himself ran the paper.[28]

A fierce anti-communist perspective united these men. Marcel Fodor had begun to work with Enno Hobbing in the Berlin office in the fall of 1948, where the two became very good friends. "Never was such a chance to expose the inhumanity of the Ruskis as at present," Fodor wrote from Berlin to the journalist Dorothy Thompson, on 1 October 1948. "I believe we should pay back the Soviets' blunder with their own coins."[29]

With only a few months left until the first federal elections, the board was under great pressure to make up for Foss's forum style and to disseminate "U.S. ideas" as quickly and thoroughly as possible. Under the new supervision, the newspaper turned into a more pro-American mouthpiece of the U.S. military government. Its tone was an exhilarated version of the *Neue Zeitung* under Jack Fleischer and, thus, a sharp departure from the forum style of Habe, Wallenberg, and Foss. Philosophical discussions on politics ceased completely. Now the Germans were told what was right and wrong and what their future was to be. The only enemies of German democracy, authors pointed out repeatedly, were communism and neo-Nazism. Over

NARA; Marcel W. Fodor, Washington, D.C., letter to Dorothy Thompson, 9 January 1948, Series No. I, box 10, Dorothy Thompson Collection, Syracuse University Library, hereafter cited as SUL; Ernst Cramer, interview, 1 December 1994. According to Ernst Cramer, Elliot was soon replaced by Ray Stover, a former reporter of a small newspaper in Texas.

27. Dorothy Thompson and Rose Wilder Lane, *Dorothy Thompson and Rose Wilder Lane: Forty Years of Friendship. Letters, 1921–1960*, ed. William Holtz (Columbia, Mo.: University of Missouri Press, 1991), 5, 14, 19, 21, 23, 26, 63f., 105, 195; Marcel W. Fodor, letters to Dorothy Thompson, 3 November 1947, 9 December 1947, 11 December 1947, 15 December 1947, 22 December 1947, 27 December 1947, 6 January 1948, 9 January 1948, 14 January 1948, 25 February 1948, 25 April 1948, Series No. I, box 10, Dorothy Thompson collection, SUL; Jack M. Stuart, interview, New York, 12 July 1993; Jack M. Stuart, letter to the author, 24 March 1993.

28. Ernst Cramer, interview, Berlin, 16 December 1991. For an organizational chart of the *Neue Zeitung* staff during the triumvirate, see Herbet, *Die Neue Zeitung*, 176.

29. Marcel W. Fodor, Berlin, to Dorothy Thompson, 1 October 1948, Series No. I, box 10, Dorothy Thompson collection, SUL; letter from Marcel W. Fodor, Berlin, to Dorothy Thompson, 27 June 1948, ibid.

and over again, articles emphasized that the country could be restored to nationhood only with the support of the United States, even if the price was permanent partition and a Western defense union against the Soviet Union.[30] Virtually every major field of interest—including the coverage of television, advertising, politics, philosophy, and history—reflected the effort to propagandize a Western way of life, defended by the United States of America.[31]

Curiously, even individual U.S. observers deplored the change of the paper after Foss on the grounds that it no longer paid sufficient attention to German affairs and concerns. By eliminating most émigrés from the operation, one U.S. reader wrote in the *New York Herald Tribune*, OMGUS had forfeited those people who were best equipped to understand and mold the German mind. "The case of the *Neue Zeitung* proves how disastrous the results of this un-American practice are."[32]

In the end, the board was dissolved less than two weeks after the German Parliamentary Council ratified the Basic Law in May 1949, thus formally inaugurating the Federal Republic. After the middle of 1949, the paper was published at three different locations under three different editors in chief in order to speed up the coverage and distribution of news and to make the sale more attractive for newsdealers. Now the *Neue Zeitung* competed not only against the new free German press but also against itself. Internally, the

30. George Hilt, "Seien wir auf der Hut," *Neue Zeitung*, 18 January 1949, p. 5; Walter R. Firnhaber, Wiesbaden, "Die Feinde der Demokratie," letter to the editor, *Neue Zeitung*, 22 January 1949, p. 11; "Verteidigungspläne," *Neue Zeitung*, 27 January 1949, p. 7; "Notwendige Abwehr," *Neue Zeitung*, 3 February 1949, p. 7; George Hilt, "Grenzen der Demokratie," *Neue Zeitung*, 12 February 1949, p. 11; "Verteidigungsbilanz," *Neue Zeitung*, 17 March 1949, p. 7; "Ein Vertrauensbeweis," *Neue Zeitung*, 2 April 1949, p. 11; "Unter falscher Fahne," *Neue Zeitung*, 21 April 1949, p. 7.

31. "Das amerikanische Panorama," *Neue Zeitung*, 26 February 1949, p. 4; Erika Neuhäuser, "Das Experiment 'Neue Welt'," *Neue Zeitung*, 12 March 1949, p. 4; André Maurois, "Onkel Sam ist nicht krank," *Neue Zeitung*, 12 March 1949, p. 5; "Werbung durch den Kulturfilm," *Neue Zeitung*, 12 April 1949, p. 4; "Fernsehen macht rasche Fortschritte," *Neue Zeitung*, 16 April 1949, p. 14; Henry Steele Commager, "Eine Analyse des amerikanischen Charakters," *Neue Zeitung*, 23 April 1949, p. 9; Herbert Seggelke, "Telefilm: Ein neuer Weg," *Neue Zeitung*, 25 May 1949, p. 4.

32. W. Moll, Information Specialist, to OMGUS/ISD/PIB, "*Neue Zeitung*," 14 February 1949, RG 260, OMGUS 5/245–2/6, IfZ; Col. Peter P. Rhodes, "Missions and Functions of the Intelligence Division, OMGB," December 1948, RG 260, OMGBY 10/73–2/33, BHStA; F. Lawrence Babcock, Policy & Programming Branch, to All Branch and Section Chiefs, All Land Directors, ISD, "Programming of ISD Overt Activities, Definition of Targets," 16 February 1949, RG 260, OMGUS 5/243–2/6, IfZ; Curt L. Heymann, Munich, to Thomas P. Headen, Berlin, 18 February 1949, RG 260, OMGUS/ISD 5/245–2/6, BArch; E. W. Gerald, letter to the editor, "German-Americans," to *New York Herald Tribune* (European edition), 2 February 1949.

three editions rivaled and often even contradicted each other. Circulation fell dramatically. By 2 June the total press run was a mere 351,000 copies per issue.[33] In contrast, the *Tägliche Rundschau* swamped Berlin, its suburbs, and part of the West with 700,000 copies.[34]

It would be wrong to attribute the paper's diminished popularity exclusively to the resignation of the émigré editors in chief or the palace revolt earlier that year. In May 1949 press censorship ended. Many former newspapers began publishing again and struggled to regain their share of the press pie. Some sold their papers for 75 percent of the price of the *Neue Zeitung*. Soon the market was saturated with many types of publications while consumers had little money to spend. What little they had, they preferred to spend on German papers.[35]

This would have been the ideal moment either to turn the *Neue Zeitung* over to a German publisher or to end the venture altogether. General Clay left Germany on 15 May, while the Department of Defense transferred OMGUS's occupation control to the State Department's High Commission, headed by the civilian John McCloy. However, the ISD returned to its earlier strategy: it kept the paper but failed to develop a coherent policy. U.S. officials continued to be concerned about Germany's future political orientation and did not want to forgo one of their few precious means to influence the German mind.[36]

33. Textor, memorandum to all ISD Personnel, 1 June 1949, RG 260, OMGUS 5/236–1/17, IfZ; also in RG 260, OMGUS 5/242–2/7, IfZ; Crowell to Office of the Operations Coordinator, "Weekly report for Colonel Textor," 11 February 1949, RG 260, OMGUS/ISD 5/264–1/13, BArch; Crowell to Textor, 29 April 1949, Weekly Report *Die Neue Zeitung*, RG 260, OMGUS 5/264–1/13, IfZ; Crowell to Textor, Weekly Report, 4 June 1949, ibid.; Calculation January–May 1949, RG 260, OMGUS 5/260–2/1, Bl. 15, IfZ; Hurwitz, *Stunde Null*, 267; Netzer, *Neue Zeitung*, 18.

34. Crowell to Textor, Weekly Report *Die Neue Zeitung*, 13 May 1949, RG 260, OMGUS/ISD 5/264–1/13, BArch; OMGBS/ISD to Col. Babcock, Director OMGBS, "Circulation Losses of West-Licensed Newspaper Since Imposition of Russian Blockade," 17 June 1949, RG 260, OMGBS 4/11–2/10, BArch.

35. Calculation January–May 1949, RG 260, OMGUS 5/260–2/1, Bl. 15, IfZ; Report of the Military Governor in the U.S. Zone, No. 50, "Information Control," OMGUS, 1 August–20 September 1949, DK 101.006, IfZ. For a more extensive account of the *Neue Zeitung*'s sales campaign, see Jessica C. E. Gienow, "Cultural Transmission and the U.S. Occupation in Germany: The *Neue Zeitung*, 1945–1955" (Ph.D. dissertation, University of Virginia, Charlottesville, Va., 1995), 340–49; " 'Steuern für die Konkurrenz': Bayerns Journalisten gegen die *Neue Zeitung*," in *Der Morgen*, 20 July 1949; "In eigener Sache," *Neue Zeitung*, 23 July 1949; "Brauchen wir Besatzungszeitungen?" *Der Tag*, 24 July 1949; "Der Fall *Neue Zeitung*," *Der Morgen*, 25 August 1949; Walther Schmidt, "*Neue Zeitung* Critic," letter to the editor, *New York Herald Tribune*, 24 August 1949.

36. John T. Lawrence, US civilian, to OMGB, Intelligence Division, "Essential Elements of Information," 11 February 1949, RG 260, OMGBY 10/66–2/73, BHStA; Hermann-Josef

Their fears were well founded. The results of the first elections for the German Bundestag, held in August 1949, were troubling. The CDU's narrow victory (31 percent) over the rather orthodox Social Democrats (29.2 percent) and the liberal F.D.P. (11.9 percent) was a far cry from U.S. expectations. Officials had hoped for a more decisive victory by the Christian Democrats, who advocated a capitalist market economy, a Christian weltanschauung, integration into the West, and a parliamentary democracy. Moreover, the new German chancellor, Konrad Adenauer, had no "real sympathy for public government, nor for democracy in practice as we understand it." His SPD opponent, Kurt Schumacher, came across as "a rabid nationalist" and "a dictator who rules his party with an iron hand." U.S. officials like George F. Kennan believed that unless Germany's energy and power could be tamed, the world might relive the disaster of the past two decades. Anti-Americanism ran high among West Germans. "They don't like us," observed Ludwell Denny from *The News* in the fall of 1949. As he saw it, the Germans' attitude revealed both arrogance and blackmail. "We are boss now," German officials said according to Denny; "if you try to interfere with us we will make a deal with Stalin."[37]

U.S. officials believed they had to retain their powerful print medium to influence German public opinion, even if they were not quite certain how to use it. Article One of the Occupation Statute of 8 April 1949 had provided West Germans with self-determination including full legislative, executive, and judicial power on the state and the federal level. But the statute also allowed the Western powers to intervene in the event totalitarian forces threatened German democracy. Two of McCloy's explicit tasks were to monitor and advise the state institutions and to prevent the return of antidemocratic forces. In an effort to support the High Commissioner, officials in the State Department, such as Henry Kellermann, director of the Office of Public Affairs in the department's Bureau of German Affairs, advocated taking over the *Neue Zeitung* "lock, stock, and barrel" despite its loss of influence.[38]

---

Rupieper, *Die Wurzeln der westdeutschen Nachkriegsdemokratie: Der amerikanische Beitrag, 1945–1952* (Opladen: Westdeutscher Verlag, 1993), 38, passim; Thomas Schwartz, *America's Germany: John J. McCloy and the Federal Republic of Germany* (Cambridge, Mass.: Harvard University Press, 1991).

37. Helga Grebing, "Die Parteien" in Benz, *Bundesrepublik Deutschland*, 1: 128–46; Hans-Peter Schwarz, *Vom Reich zur Bundesrepublik: Deutschland im Widerstreit der außenpolitischen Konzeptionen in den Jahren der Besatzungsherrschaft, 1945–1949* (Neuwied: Luchterhand, 1966), 440–564; Konrad Adenauer, *Erinnerungen, 1945–1953* (Stuttgart: Deutsche Verlags-Anstalt, 1965), 164–67, 182–92, 213–17, 233; Leffler, *Preponderance of Power*, 319; Rupieper, *Wurzeln der Nachkriegsdemokratie*, 81; Ludwell Denny, "By and Large, the Germans Dislike Us," *The News*, 11 October 1949.

38. Rupieper, *Wurzeln der Nachkriegsdemokratie*, 38f.; Henry Kellermann, interview.

Curiously enough, HICOG officials displayed the same confusion as their predecessors. To be sure, the International Press and Publications Division of the State Department viewed the *Neue Zeitung* as an immediate concern. Meticulous confidential reports and "Propaganda Programs" regularly pointed to the *Neue Zeitung* as one of the foremost anticommunist tools the United States had in Germany. A continuous vetting process controlled the loyalty of the German personnel. Occasionally, McCloy met with one of the editors in chief while State Department members visiting Munich regularly stopped by in Schellingstraße 39.[39]

But at the same time, HICOG officials complained about the lack of coordination and organization of those divisions charged with information strategy. The Information Services officers, as one observer from the Public Affairs Division noted, occupied themselves with operational problems and spent little time on propaganda. No one received the daily policy guidance cables from Washington in time; most of the time they did not arrive at all. Most former editors cannot recall any strict or regular guidance on the part of their American supervisors. Robert L. Lochner, chief of the Frankfurt section, remembers one single—though important—instance in four years where HICOG commissioners told him exactly what to write. On 4 November 1950 Lochner published an essay entitled "The United States and the German Contribution to European Security" in which he pleaded for the remilitarization of Germany "for the repulse of communist aggression."[40] Whenever the Public Affairs Division complained about stories printed in the *Neue Zeitung* ranging from erotic material to international politics, the various editors in chief flippantly excused or dismissed their criticism. In the

39. David E. Mark, HICOG, Political Affairs, "Propaganda Program & Time Tables," 7 April 1950, RG 466, U.S. HICOG BE, Political Affairs Division, Security-Segregated General Records, 1949–53, box 2, PEPCO, WNRC; Memorandum to U.S. Commander Berlin, "Psychological Warfare Team," 3 July 1951, RG 466, US HICOG BE, Public Affairs Division, classified subject files, 1949–53, box 7, WNRC; "Program Objectives of Public Affairs Division, Berlin Element: Target Groups & Media," 12 March 1952, RG 84, US HICOG BE 2535/35, LAB; Bavaria Land Commission Intelligence, "Records Pertaining to Loyalty Checks on German Personnel," 1949–51, RG 466, US HICOG, 2 boxes, WNRC; Historical Analysis of the McCloy Era, Journal 18 July 1949, RG 466, HICOG, John J. McCloy Papers, box 1-4, WNRC; list of guests at cocktail party on 12 October 1949; Journal 29 December 1950, ibid.; Documentation 2 October 1951, ibid.; Journal 15 July 1952, ibid.

40. Robert Haeger, "No More Conquerors," in Settel, *This Is Germany*, 1–22; Kenneth T. Downs, Chief, Public Affairs Division, HICOG, Berlin Element, to General Taylor, "Interim Report on Plans for Unified Propaganda Effort," 2 December 1949, RG 466, U.S. HICOG BE, Public Affairs Division, classified subject files, 1945–53, box 3, WNRC; "Die Vereinigten Staaten und der deutsche Beitrag zur europäischen Sicherheit," *Neue Zeitung*, 4 November 1950, p. 5; Robert L. Lochner, interview, Berlin, 10 April 1992.

fall of 1949 Henry Kellermann and Robert Murphy even hired Hans Wallenberg as editor in chief of the Munich edition, the man who had so often clashed with his bosses.[41]

U.S. officials continued to have mixed reactions to the paper, ranging from total approval to charges of subversion. Some, such as Henry Kellermann, urged stricter centralization, monitoring, and evaluation. Others suggested extending information efforts from official publications to indigenous media. Still others, including Ralph Nicholson, head of the Office of Public Affairs in HICOG, were convinced that "all these activities [publishing operations] are a waste of money" and "that the day for overt publications etc. is long past."[42] And on the far right end of the spectrum, Senator Joseph McCarthy attacked the paper. Appearing before his committee on 5 May 1953, Julius Epstein, a New York writer, accused Hans Wallenberg of membership in a communist organization while working for the *Neue Zeitung*. The case was dismissed, but McCarthy continued to assail the paper.[43]

The various editions of the *Neue Zeitung* continued to be published for

41. Kenneth T. Downs, HICOG BE, to General Taylor, Chief, Public Affairs Division, BE, "*Neue Zeitung* Article on 'Open-Door Policy' for May 26," 14 February 1950, RG 260, OMGBS, 4/11–2/24, LAB; Fodor, memorandum to Downs, 15 February 1950, ibid.; "Gegen jugendgefährdendes Schrifttum," *Der Tag*, 7 March 1950; "Hans Wallenberg wieder an der 'Neuen Zeitung'," *Neue Zeitung*, 28 October 1949, p. 1.

42. Kellermann, memorandum to Thomas E. Goldstein, "ISD Activity Reports," 2 March 1950, RG 59, 1950–54, box 2434, dec. file 511.62/3–250, NARA; E. W. Lower, Marcel W. Fodor, "Historical Division Monograph Draft 'US Information and Propaganda Programs in Berlin, 1949/1952,' " 23 April 1953, RG 84, US HICOG BE, 2535/18, LAB; "International Press and Publications Division," RG 59, Records of the Assistant Secretary of State for Public Affairs, 1945–50, Subject File, box 9, NARA; "Public Affairs Division Mission and Functions," n. d., RG 466, U.S. HICOG BE, Public Affairs Division, classified subject files, 1945–1953, box 6, WNRC; Albert Carter, C. Henderson, "Some Present Problems of Importance in the Information Field," 5 January 1952, RG 84, US HICOG BE 2535/12, LAB; Chief of British ICD to Deputy High Commissioner, 14 April 1950, FO 1056/160, PRO.

43. "Statement by Hans Wallenberg," 7 May 1953, Max Kraus collection, 92/09/105–5–14; "Statement by Ernest J. Cramer," 7 May 1953, ibid.; Hans Wallenberg to Max Kraus, Wheaton Hills, Md., 17 July 1953, ibid.; "Kaghan verteidigt Wallenberg vor dem McCarthy-Ausschuß," *Neue Zeitung*, 6 May 1953, p. 2; "HICOG zu den Vorwürfen gegen Wallenberg," *Chronik der Arbeit*, 8 May 1953; "Epstein zu seinen Äußerungen über Hans Wallenberg," *Neue Zeitung*, 11 May 1953, p. 2; "Shepard Stone weist Angriffe gegen Kaghan und Wallenberg zurück," *Neue Zeitung*, 12 May 1953, p. 6; "Bitterer Lorbeer," *Der Spiegel* 40, 30 September 1953, 14; U.S. Congress, House, Subcommittee of the Committee of Appropriations, *Hearings on Supplemental Appropriation Bill, 1954*, 83rd Congress, 1st Session on H. R. 6200, 1953, pt. 1, 26–32, 35f., 65–68, 73, 122; "*New York Times* zu den Krediten für die deutsche Presse," *Amerika Dienst*, 29 April 1953, MF 1424 (*Neue Zeitung*), Bundespresse- und Informationsamt, Bonn (hereafter cited as BPIA); Gienow-Hecht, "Anti-Communism and Other Enemy Images," 294–96.

four more years. In October 1951 the two West German editorial offices were consolidated into one that was located in Frankfurt while the *Feuilleton* remained in Munich. Both offices ceased publication in September 1953. Contemporary witnesses differ on the reasons; German observers cited financial considerations.[44] Henry Kellermann, in contrast, insists that the shut-down coincided with the termination of the Occupation Statute under which the military government had operated. The Berlin edition appeared until 31 January 1955, shortly before the High Commission left Germany. Last minute efforts to transfer the paper into German hands failed. So did plans to continue publication subsidized by U.S. tax money. Although Kellermann recalls that "Congress was lavish" in regard to U.S. cultural programs in Germany and the *Neue Zeitung* still made profits, officials in the State Department and Theodor Streibert, director of the U.S. Information Agency in Washington, believed that "the publication of a newspaper by the U.S. did not seem to be compatible with the status of the Federal Republic as a sovereign country."[45]

In the absence of independent reliable mediators who were culturally equipped to interpret and moderate the rising anti-Americanism in Germany, U.S. officials were uncertain about what to do. The continuous activities of neo-Nazi subgroups and the narrow victory of the Christian Democrats seemed to testify to the instability of German democracy. American policy makers feared not so much that Germany was apt to go communist as that a nationalist reaction would feed on a dogmatic anti-Americanism. With unification and national identity as two of the key themes in the German public in 1949, voters seemed susceptible to offers and concessions from the East. A German government might lean on the Soviet Union to achieve its independence from the West, the ideological differences notwith-

44. Hans-Joachim Netzer, Munich, letters to Steltzer, 12 July 1951 and 24 July 1951, Hans-Joachim Netzer collection, ED 352/1, IfZ; "Memo über die Unterhaltung mit Herrn Friedrich am 2. November 1951," ibid.; "Aufzeichnung," 26 April 1951, ibid.; Wallenberg, Frankfurt, letters to Manfred George, New York, 20 March 1952 and 17 November 1952, Archiv Manfred George, DLS; Office of US HICOG BE, Information Branch, "Berliner *Neue Zeitung* bleibt bestehen: Frankfurter Ausgabe eingestellt," 10 September 1953, Zeitungen und Zeitschriften dtsch., *Neue Zeitung*—Finanzierung, Ullstein Aktiengesellschaft, Archiv, Berlin (hereafter cited as UAAB).

45. Henry Kellermann, interview, 7 February 1992; "Wer hat Interesse?" *Der Spiegel* 5, 26 January 1955, 23; Friedrich Luft, Berlin, to Peter de Mendelssohn, Peter de Mendelsohn collection, courtesy of Anita Naef, Munich. For a more general contemporary account of U.S. postwar cultural policy toward Germany, see Henry K. Kellermann, *Cultural Relations as an Instrument of U.S. Foreign Policy: The Educational Exchange Program between the United States and Germany, 1945–1954* (Washington, D.C.: Dept. of State Publication 8931, U.S. Government Printing Office, 1978).

standing.[46] From this perspective, the Soviet Union emerged as the largest threat not only to the Federal Republic but to the entire Western system.

Nevertheless, U.S. information strategists never came to terms with their role as propagandists. Observers and readers refusing to understand the shift in U.S. perceptions were automatically branded as anti-American, communist, or neo-Nazi. Yet while the accusations lingered on well into the HICOG period, U.S. officials continued to fail to develop a coherent policy for the paper. Despite occasional outbursts of activity—such as the housecleaning in 1948 and the appointment of the board in 1949—they did not exert lasting control over the paper. Though they wanted the results propaganda might achieve, they were reluctant to take on the role of propagandists.

46. Henry A. Kissinger, Harvard University, "Analysis of Germany," 14 July 1952, Harry S. Truman papers, SMOF: Psychological Strategy Board Files, 1 box, file 091 Germany, file # 1, HSTL.

# EPILOGUE

ON A BREEZY SPRING DAY IN APRIL 1990 AN UNUSUAL GROUP OF VISITORS trickled into Harvey's Chelsea Restaurant at 108 West 18th Street in Manhattan. Bursting through the front door, they asked with thick German accents where the party was going on. They were aged men, seventy and older, their shoulders stooped, their hair thin. They had come from far away, as far as Pacific Palisades and East Berlin. They exchanged hugs, greetings, and boyish jokes, quietly noting who had died since their previous meeting a few years earlier. They told wild stories from places and people long past, ringing with furor, laughter, and hope. They were the former "Psy-War Boys."

For over forty years, the men and women who had worked in psychological warfare and at the *Neue Zeitung* remained in contact, organizing regular meetings every few years in Germany and the United States. To many, their efforts at the *Neue Zeitung* remained the achievement they were most proud of throughout their lives. Each time they sought to remember the spirit of hope and optimism that had guided their operation in postwar Europe. And sometimes they may have wondered: had it mattered? Had they really made a difference?[1]

Cultural and information activities always suffer from a lack of proof of effectiveness. Contemporary cultural programs officers who have faced recent budget cuts in the U.S. Information Agency find it difficult to measure accurately the importance of their work.[2] In the same vein, it is difficult to estimate exactly the *Neue Zeitung*'s influence on Germany's democratization. One cannot measure a newspaper's impact the same way that one can measure the impact of arms, trade agreements, and nuclear weapons. Words are not material goods; their influence is beyond mathematical calculation.

On first sight the story of the *Neue Zeitung* seems to be a reprise of the developments in the Office of Strategic Services (OSS) between 1943 and

1. "Als Robert Lembke noch Sportredakteur war . . . ," *Abendzeitung*, 30 October 1984; " 'Psych Boys' Recall Their War of Words," *Washington Post*, 18 November 1984, A23; Douglas Martin, "Together Again, These Sly Foes of Nazi Resolve," *New York Times*, 14 April 1990; Heym, *Nachruf*, 838–41; Marianne de Francisis, Baden-Baden, to Ernst Cramer, Berlin, 3 January 1993, courtesy of Ernst Cramer; Peter Adler, Rudolf Piechowiak, "Sie nannten sich die Psy-War-Boys: 'Krieg der Worte' gegen Hitler," television broadcasting, Carsten-Krüger Film- und Fernsehproduktion, ZDF, Germany, 1990.

2. Wolfgang Brandt, Program Section, and Lisa Washburn, director of the Regional English Language Office, interview by author, Amerika Haus Berlin, 26 September 1996.

1947. As Barry Katz and others have shown, German leftist émigrés in the OSS pushed their own political program without reference to some vague "American Dream." U.S. officials eventually got their bearings and began to limit the émigrés' maneuvering room.[3]

The case of the *Neue Zeitung*, however, illustrates the complexity of the postwar situation as well as the long-term impact of cultural endeavors. Jewish exiles in the military government had a far greater impact on Germany's future than their colleagues in the OSS in Washington, D.C. An examination of the careers of its staffers, once they left the newspaper, and the memories that lingered in the minds of former readers underscore this point.

The profiles of the *Neue Zeitung*'s employees reflect a multifaceted political outlook, which in no way resembled the rather uniformly leftist intellectual agenda of the German-born members of the OSS. Perhaps because of this diversity, the paper's impact on postwar Germany proved more enduring than the activities of the forerunner of the CIA. Some of the émigrés had written staunch anticommunist articles when the U.S. military government still formally adhered to the doctrine of inter-Allied harmony. Others defended a rather socialist agenda, and some even emigrated to Eastern Europe. The majority continued to work in the public sphere and the international arena.[4]

Berlin editor in chief Peter Weidenreich returned to the United States and changed his name to Peter Wyden. He pursued a journalistic career at various U.S. publications, including the *Saturday Evening Post* and *Newsweek*. Since the 1960s he has published several best-selling books, including *Wall: The Untold Story of Divided Berlin*. His son, Ron, is a Democratic Senator from Oregon who recently gained fame with his antitobacco campaign. Max Kraus, after his return to the United States, became a public affairs officer in the U.S. Information Agency's Foreign Service, a position he held for almost forty years. He was stationed in Phnom Penh, Paris, Geneva, Milan, and Leopoldville. Enno Hobbing, Weidenreich's self-assured successor in Berlin, worked as a correspondent for *Time* in Germany, Iran, Paris, and

3. Barry Katz, *Foreign Intelligence: Research and Analysis in the Office of Strategic Services, 1942–1945* (Cambridge, Mass.: Harvard University Press, 1989); Alfons Söllner, ed., *Zur Archäologie der Demokratie in Deutschland*, 2 vols. (Frankfurt a.M.: Europäische Verlagsanstalt, 1982); Jürgen Heideking and Christof Mauch, eds., *Geheimdienstkrieg gegen Deutschland: Subversion, Propaganda, und politische Planungen des amerikanischen Geheimdienstes im Zweiten Weltkrieg* (Göttingen: Vandenhoeck & Ruprecht, 1993); Friedrich Baerwald, "Zur politischen Tätigkeit deutscher Emigranten im Council for a Democratic Germany," *Vierteljahreshefte für Zeitgeschichte* 28 (1980): 372–83.

4. Kurt Pinthus, "Die Schaffenden des Geistes: Was Amerikas Literatur, Bühne und Film der Immigration verdanken," *Aufbau*, 1 April 1955.

Washington between 1949 and 1952. After the CIA hired him in 1953, Hobbing went to Central America where he became deeply involved in the Guatemalan Putsch. He returned to *Life* magazine in 1955 and subsequently served as staff director of the Council of the Americas, a public affairs coordinating body of U.S. corporate investors in Latin America, chaired by David Rockefeller. Hobbing died in 1995.[5]

Significantly, a number of émigrés eventually decided to return to Germany permanently where they often exerted a strong political influence. Stefan Heym spent only a brief time in the United States, where he published a novel entitled *The Crusaders*. Interpreting the invasion of Normandy as a crusade of carpetbaggers for free enterprise, the book was an indictment of the entire American warfare effort on the Western front.[6] In 1952 Heym returned his military decorations to the U.S. government and emigrated to the German Democratic Republic (GDR). Writing most of his books in English and publishing them in the West, he became a best-selling author and, eventually, the GDR government's foremost enfant terrible. Having contributed significantly to the fall of the Berlin Wall, the eighty-one-year-old writer successfully ran in 1994 as an independent district candidate of the PDS, successor to the GDR's Socialist Unity party. After the federal elections, because of his age, he became "chairman by seniority" of the German parliament.

Hans Wallenberg, the premature anticommunist editor in chief, and Ernst Cramer, the late deputy chief of the Munich edition, both joined *Die Welt* in the 1950s, once the official army paper of the British military government in Germany. In September 1953 the British authorities sold the paper to the young publisher Axel Springer, one of the most fervent advocates of the American presence in Germany. Wallenberg held various influential jobs at the publishing house and eventually became Springer's personal adviser. Ernst Cramer rose to prominence as the publisher of the Sunday edition, *Welt am Sonntag*, residing in an office near the Berlin Wall from which he could see the Eastern sector of the city. In October 1994 he

5. Biographical Note "Peter Wyden," courtesy of Peter Wyden; Strauss and Röder, *International Biographical Dictionary*, 1: 838; Peter Wyden, interview; Wyden, *Day One: Before Hiroshima and After* (New York: Simon & Schuster, 1984); Wyden, *Wall*; Wyden, *Stella*; Max W. Kraus, *They All Come To Geneva and Other Tales of a Public Diplomat* (Cabin John, Md.: Seven Locks Press, 1988); Stephen C. Schlesinger and Stephen Kinzer, *Bitter Fruit: The Untold Story of the American Coup in Guatemala* (Garden City, N.Y.: Doubleday, 1982), 155–56, 206–7, 228; Hobbing, *College Graduate*, vi.

6. Stefan Heym, *Nachruf*, 385, 389ff., 489, 492, 534; Heym, *The Crusaders* (Boston: Little, Brown, 1948); Habe, *Im Jahre Null*, 32, 130; Hay, "Literarische Positionen," 213f.

received an honorary doctorate from the Bar-Ilan University in Ramat Gan for his continuous efforts in the German-Israeli dialogue.[7]

Hans Habe, after his return to the United States, began to publicly air his disillusion with U.S. foreign policy. He lectured at the Jewish Club in Los Angeles on the frustration of German-American Jews who had tried to help reconstruct postwar Germany. In 1947 Habe wrote a series of articles in the New York *Aufbau* (entitled "America's Failure in Germany") in which he blasted U.S. policy makers for their ignorance of social and economic conditions in Europe. His novel, *Off Limits*, portrayed the ignorance, corruption, and demoralization of the American army in the U.S. zone. Having failed at another journalistic career in Munich (which culminated in a scandal featuring headlines such as "Out Of Germany With the Scoundrel!"), Habe eventually settled in Ascona, Switzerland, as a writer and a freelance journalist. In 1977 he received the Jerusalem medal from the mayor of the city "in recognition of his service for the state of Israel." Apart from a number of rather mediocre books, his writings never again approached the quality of his articles in the *Neue Zeitung*.[8]

The careers of the German employees, too, suggest a very complex and lasting political influence. Young reporter Egon Bahr from Berlin became a key leader of the SPD and the cofounder of the *Ostverträge*. He was until recently professor at the Institut für Friedensforschung und Sicherheitspolitik (Institute for Peace Research and Security Policy) at the University of Hamburg. Hildegard Brücher (later Hamm-Brücher), the *Neue Zeitung*'s editor for natural sciences, rose to prominence in the liberal F.D.P. and ran as a candidate for the federal presidency in 1994. Reporter Peter Bönisch continued his career as a journalist and then became CDU-Chancellor Hel-

7. Strauss and Röder, *International Biographical Dictionary*, 1: 790–91; "Profilierter Publizist und rühriger Organisator: Gespräch mit Hans Wallenberg," *Allgemeine unabhängige jüdische Wochenzeitung*, 24 December 1971, 11; Hans Steinitz, "Hans Wallenberg gestorben," newspaper clip in "Wallenberg," MA 1500/62, IfZ; Müller, *Der Springer-Konzern*, 127–83, 201, 228, 249, 252; "Kanzler Kohl dankt Ernst Cramer für Engagement," *Welt am Sonntag*, 30 October 1994; "Dankrede aus Anlaß der Verleihung der Ehrendoktorwürde der Bar-Ilan Universität," 30 October 1994, Centrum Judaicum, Berlin, courtesy of Ernst Cramer.

8. Süddeutscher Rundfunk, Redaktion Radio-Essay, "The German Jewish Club of 1933, Los Angeles: Ein vergessenes Kapitel der Emigration, rekonstruiert von Marta Mierendorf," broadcasted 10 January 1966, 9–10 P.M., UKW II, MS 200/F41, IfZ; " 'Europa hat eine Zukunft,' " *Telegraf*, 9 February 1947; "Verfrühte Demokratie?" *Badische Zeitung*, 4 Oktober, 1946; Hans Habe, "Amerikas Niederlage in Deutschland," *Aufbau*, 21 March 1947, pp. 1, 6; Habe, "Unsere Niederlage in Deutschland," ibid., 28 March 1947, p. 3; 4 April 1947, p. 7; Habe, "Die Niederlage in Deutschland," ibid., 11 April 1947, p. 1; Habe, "Bilanz der Erfahrungen," ibid., 18 April 1947, p. 3; Hans Habe, *Off Limits: A Novel Of Occupied Germany* (London: Harrap, 1956); Henry Nannen, "Hinaus aus Deutschland mit dem Schuft," *Stern* 22, 1 June 1952, p. 6; "Jerusalem-Medaille für Hans Habe," *Der Bund* 113, 16 May 1972.

mut Kohl's public relations adviser. Elisabeth Noelle (later Noelle-Neumann) founded in 1947 the Institut für Meinungsforschung in Allensbach, the German counterpart of the Gallup poll, still the most prominent barometer of public opinion research.[9]

Many staffers subsequently pursued successful journalistic careers. According to Hans Habe, the *Neue Zeitung* trained sixteen future editors in chief and roughly thirty additional editors who assumed leading positions in the German media. Walther Kohl, once an apprentice in Schellingstrasse 39, became a correspondent at the United Nations before he joined the Voice of America broadcasting station. His former colleague, Wolf Schneider, eventually headed the Gruner + Jahr School of Journalism in Hamburg. Olaf Meitzner made a career at the broadcasting station Hessischer Rundfunk. Hans Lehmann became an editor for the magazine *Revue* in Munich, and later on earned a living as freelance writer.[10] Not surprisingly, the layout of some national newspapers in the FRG, such as the *Frankfurter Allgemeine Zeitung* reveal a striking similarity with the example of the *Neue Zeitung*. While this does not indicate that German newspapers directly followed the model of the *Neue Zeitung*, it does hint at a shared system of customs, tastes, and beliefs.

Other staffers subsequently wrote fiction as their major profession. Erich Kästner produced a number of fine children's novels, poems, plays, and cabaret pieces before he died in 1976. Walter Kolbenhoff continued to write short stories, broadcasting plays, and novels. Carl Hermann Ebbinghaus earned his living by writing criminal stories. Finally, some members of the *Neue Zeitung* staff turned away from the news and writing business entirely. Emigré Kurt Wittler, for example, founded an air conditioning business in California while Karl Löwenstein became an international dealer for auto parts. Ernest Wynder staggered the scientific community in 1948 with his research proving a link between smoking and breast cancer. Today he is head of the American Health Foundation in New York.[11]

9. "Elisabeth Noelle-Neumann," *Internationales Biographisches Archiv* 25/92, K 003144-11 No-ME 1–4; Christoph Bertram, "Gut oder Böse," *Die Zeit* 38, 16 September 1994, p. 4; "Egon Bahr," *Internationales Biographisches Archiv* 5/91, P 010340-12 Ba-ME 1–4; Egon Bahr, Bonn, letter to the author, 29 March 1995; Salentin, *Hildegard Hamm-Brücher*, 54–151. Noelle-Neumann's past in the Third Reich sparked a heated debate in the mid-1990s when the communication scholar Christopher Simson, from American University, argued that her entire research was tainted by her training in the Third Reich. "Gestörte Kommunikation," *Der Spiegel* 36 (1997): 32–33.

10. Mosberg, *Reeducation*, 118; Hans Lehmann, editor in chief, *Revue*, Munich, to Ernest Langendorf, Bonn, 21 May 1952, RG 59, 1950–54, dec. file 511.622/4-3052, NARA.

11. Walter Kolbenhoff, Carl Hermann Ebbinghaus, Ernst Wynder, Karl Löwenstein, and Kurt Wittler, interviews; Lou Joseph, telephone interview by author, Des Plaines, Ill., 18 April 1995; Kolbenhoff, *Schellingstraße 48*, 2; Enderle, *Erich Kästner*, 92–133; Gerhard Hay, "Nachwort," in Kolbenhoff, *Von unserm Fleisch und Blut*, 216, 226–28.

* * *

Long after the *Neue Zeitung* went out of existence, the German public retained fond memories of it. When Congress voted against its continuation, subscribers reportedly flooded the Bureau of German Affairs with complaints. "Which paper am I going to read now?" asked an anonymous reader from the Soviet sector in Berlin. "Keep the *Neue Zeitung*," urged a professor from the West.[12]

Numerous German dailies wrote long "obituaries" honoring the paper and its role as cultural and political mediator. The United States needed interpreters like the *Neue Zeitung*, marveled U.S. correspondent Norbert Muhlen in the last issue of the paper. And the highbrow *Neue Zürcher Zeitung* added: "The death of this voice really will not serve anyone except the Soviet ruling powers in the East." A number of German politicians supported this view. "Why do they give away an invaluable potential of *good will*?" queried a delegate from a state parliament, "although the annual cost for the continuance of this paper never exceeded the sales price for a single tank?" Rumor had it that the German chancellor, Konrad Adenauer, even called up the paper's last editor in chief in Berlin, exclaiming: "But Mr. Fodor! Why didn't somebody tell me [that the *Neue Zeitung* was going out of business]? I would have bought it!"[13]

Over the decades, the *Neue Zeitung* has continued to attract the attention of readers, journalists, and scholars alike. Every few years a student of communication studies, German literature, or history sits down to research some aspect of the U.S. paper. On almost every tenth anniversary, German magazines, newspapers, and broadcasting stations publish another "obituary" for the *Neue Zeitung*. In 1993 the Dresdner Bank recorded a selection of Erich Kästner's *Neue Zeitung* essays on compact disc. On the occasion of the paper's fiftieth anniversary in November 1995, the Bayerischer Rundfunk broadcasted another radio feature.[14]

12. Collections of articles in Zeitung und Zeitschriften, dtsch, "Neue Zeitung," UAAB.

13. W. E. Süskind, "Statt einer Todesanzeige," *Süddeutsche Zeitung*, 28 January 1955; "Die *Neue Zeitung* begann mit der Umerziehung," *Hersbrucker Zeitung*, 13 October 1955; Norbert Muhlen, "Zwischen New York und Berlin," *Neue Zeitung*, 30 January 1955, p. 9; Netzer, "Neue Zeitung," 24; W. K. Papenhoff, *Neue Zeitung*, Parlamentsbüro Bonn, to Krüger, 12 May 1952, Sign. 681–144, B 145/873, BArch; Konrad Adenauer, letter to Hans Wallenberg (draft), n. d. (September 1953), Sign. 681–144 II, B 145/1748, BArch; Jack M. Stuart, interview by author. The rumor quoted above has been confirmed by a prominent member of the Berlin edition in a conversation with this author in 1993.

14. "Es gibt nichts Gutes, außer: Man tut es Chansons und Prosa von Erich Kästner," compact disc recorded by Brückenhaus audio productions, Dresden, 1993; Bittorf, "Die Insel in

In the summer of 1992 I ran an advertisement in several German newspapers, asking for people who had read the *Neue Zeitung* to identify themselves and share their reminiscences with me. The response was astonishing. Four decades later, individuals representing a diverse range of careers still vividly remembered this publication as "exemplary," "inspiring," or even "brilliant." People wrote long letters praising the *Feuilleton*. "The names Erich Kästner, Alfred Andersch had . . . an almost suggestive impact on myself," recounts the historian Rolf Schörken, who was a student when he read the paper.

Many emphasized how much the editorials in the *Neue Zeitung* had influenced their political weltanschauung. "This was the first democratic newspaper I read in my life," marveled Georg Hensel, a former POW and then a journalist. "I tried to learn from it." Some readers acknowledged that they developed a more global cultural and political worldview and an international awareness. They began to tolerate different points of view; they learned not to simply accept political developments but to ask for reasons and criticize. They also testified that they became very critical of communism and developed a more diversified picture of American culture and diplomacy. The United States was "not a 'hostile' country," realized Willy Prölß, at the time a commercial apprentice and from 1972 to 1996 mayor of Nuremberg. Instead, both Germany and America had simply very different cultures. "We were so insecure in our opinion," some remembered. In that situation, the U.S. army paper "was the opening of a door."[15]

Naturally, these responses do not have any statistical value. All these readers were rather young when they read the paper. The passage of time,

der Schellingstraße"; Sabine Rollberg, "Rückblick auf die Neue Zeitung," videotaped television broadcast, WDR, Germany, 1985, courtesy of Max Kraus; Hans-Joachim Netzer, Baden-Baden, letter to the author, 3 September 1995; Jessica Gienow, "Wer jetzt Luftschlösser baut, gehört übers Knie gelegt," *Frankfurter Allgemeine Zeitung* 242 (18 October 1995): 45.

15. The references quoted represent a selection from this poll. Questionnaires completed by Wilfried Wiegand, Niedenau, 9 August 1992 (today, Wiegand is chief of the cultural section of the *Frankfurter Allgemeine Zeitung*); Hans-Wolfgang Pfeiffer, Frankfurt, 20 August 1992 (today, Pfeiffer is chairman of management at the same paper); Alfred Koch, Munich, 13 August 1992 (at the time a school boy; Koch currently owns an advertising company); Franz Thoma, Munich, 4 September 1992 (for many years, Thoma ran the business section of the *Süddeutsche Zeitung*); Willy Prölß, Nuremberg, 5 October 1992; Klaus Asche, Hamburg, 6 January 1993 (Asche was for many years CEO of the Holsten brewery); Professor Dietrich Hoffmann, Göttingen, 19 September 1992; Rolf Schörken, Düsseldorf, 18 August 1992 (a historian); Hermann Glaser, Rosstal, 23 September 1992 (a historian); Georg Hensel, Darmstadt, 18 August 1992; Beate Balleisen, Triftern, August 1992 (at the time a teacher in an elementary school, then a journalist); Wilhelmine Knoller, Eicherloh, 31 August 1992 (at the time a salesperson in a grocery store); Wolfgang Ziehen, Giessen, 12 August 1992; Joseph Göbel (at the time a resident doctor), Berlin, 5 September 1992.

the change of the political climate during the last four decades, and their own ideological weltanschauung in the 1990s no doubt deeply influenced their recollections. Nevertheless, the remarkable fact is that individual Germans still remember this newspaper as something very meaningful in their lives. Some still hold on to copies of the *Neue Zeitung*.

In sum, the aftereffects of the *Neue Zeitung* were considerable. It exerted an enduring personal influence on staffers who subsequently played important roles in German and American political and cultural life. It also had an enormous impact on readers who remember it fondly after many decades. "If anyone should ever write an intellectual history [of postwar Germany]," one journalist wrote in 1955, "one may not forget the important . . . and superb role which the *Neue Zeitung* played in it."[16]

16. "Nachruf an eine Zeitung," clip, 1955, Personenkatalog Hans Habe, IfZ.

# CONCLUSION

SEVENTY-FIVE-THOUSAND SPECTATORS IN DOWNTOWN BERLIN WATCHED AS soldiers from Britain, France, and the United States marched to the Brandenburg Gate on 18 June 1994. Military bands played marches, parachutists fell from the sky, cannons boomed in salute, and helicopters flew in formation in a good-bye celebration to the city they had come to occupy almost fifty years earlier. A single DC-3 gliding through the clouds greeted Berliners as a symbol of all the planes that had participated in the airlift of 1948–1949.

American and German newspapers hailed the celebration as another sign of the end of the Cold War. They pointed to the success of the occupation and the powerful victory of a democratic society over a communist system. "There can be few examples of a mission so peacefully and successfully concluded," Berlin's mayor, Eberhard Diepgen, said in his farewell address.[1]

Diepgen's address as well as the entire event did not lack a certain irony. The original objective of the Allied presence in Berlin and elsewhere was not simply to fend off Soviet attacks on Germany but to erase totalitarianism in Germany and to reeducate the local population. The soldiers defeated Hitler, but they were not responsible for Germany's democratization. Perhaps an army of Allied teachers, journalists, advertisers, and professors should have marched on the streets of Berlin as an ideological farewell, instead of thousands of soldiers.

Under the influence of the Cold War, scholars such as Harold Zink, John Gimbel, and many others have, for over four decades, interpreted the U.S. occupation in Germany primarily as a political, economic, and military event shaped by leaders like Lucius D. Clay, James Byrnes, and George Marshall. Those who addressed cultural and educational aspects, such as James Tent and Harold Hurwitz, usually construed these as a by-product of the policy-making process.[2]

Most scholars of occupation history have deemed the American reeduca-

1. Stephen Kinzer, "Allied Soldiers March to Say Farewell to Berlin," *The New York Times*, 19 June 1994, p. 12; Joachim Nawrocki, "Goodbye! Au revoir! ПРОЩАЙ!" *Die Zeit* 35 (26 August 1994), 11.

2. Harold Zink, *The United States in Germany, 1944–1955* (Princeton, N.J.: Van Nostrand, 1957); Gimbel, *The American Occupation*; Tent, *Mission on the Rhine;* Hurwitz, *Die Stunde Null.*

tion program in Germany at least partly a political and social failure. A number of historians, including Edward Peterson and David Montgomery, have blamed U.S. policy makers for their lack of interest in Germany's democratization or for their willingness to accede to German demands.[3] Lutz Niethammer and Jutta Lange-Quassowski, among many others, have also criticized U.S. policy makers for their lack of effort in trying to depose former Nazis.[4] Others, such as John Gimbel, have portrayed occupation policy as a continuous conflict between various departments that often undermined the program's overall efficiency.[5] And almost all agree that in the unfolding Cold War, U.S. officials quietly abandoned antifascist reeducation for the sake of integrating West Germany into a Western European community and a transatlantic alliance.

These studies often ignore or downplay the inherent dilemma of cultural and information programs. Reeducation was never abandoned but intensified as an essentially antifascist campaign. It is true that U.S. policy makers wished to tie Germany into the Western orbit and even absolved a number of prominent Nazis. But they were reluctant to abandon reeducation and

3. John D. Montgomery, *Forced to Be Free: The Artificial Revolution in Germany and Japan* (Chicago: The University of Chicago Press, 1957); Peterson, *The Many Faces of Defeat*; Gulgowski, *The American Military Government of United States*; Clemens Vollnhals, *Evangelische Kirche und Entnazifizierung: Die Last der deutschen Vergangenheit* (Munich: Oldenbourg, 1989); Frei and Schmitz, *Journalismus im Dritten Reich*; Kurt Koszyk, *Kontinuität oder Neubeginn? Massenkommunikation in Deutschland, 1945–1949* (Siegen: Universität-Gesamthochschule Siegen, 1981); Eberhard Schmidt, *Die verhinderte Neuordnung, 1945–1952: Zur Auseinandersetzung um die Demokratisierung der Wirtschaft in den westlichen Besatzungszonen und in der Bundesrepublik Deutschland* (Frankfurt a.M.: Europäische Verlagsanstalt, 1970).

4. Niethammer, *Entnazifizierung in Bayern*; Klaus-Dietmar Henke, "Die Trennung vom Nationalsozialismus," in *Politische Säuberung in Europa: Die Abrechnung mit Faschismus und Kollaboration nach dem Zweiten Weltkrieg*, ed. Henke and Hans Woller (Munich: Deutscher Taschenbuchverlag, 1991), 21–83; Lange-Quassowski, *Neuordnung oder Restauration?*; Michael H. Kater, "Problems of Political Reeducation in West-Germany, 1945–1960," *Simon Wiesenthal Center Annual* (1987): 99–123; Gerhart Kostuch and Franz Kröger, *Germany Seen Through British and American Eyes* (Frankfurt a.M.: Moritz Diesterweg, 1969); Hermann-Josef Rupieper, "Bringing Democracy to the Frauleins: Frauen als Zielgruppe der amerikanischen Demokratisierungspolitik in Deutschland, 1945–1952," *Geschichte und Gesellschaft* 17 (1991): 61–91; Jutta-B. Lange-Quassowski, "Amerikanische Westintegrationspolitik, Reeducation, und deutsche Schulpolitik," in *Umerziehung und Wiederaufbau: Die Bildungspolitik der Besatzungsmächte in Deutschland und Österreich*, ed. Manfred Heinemann (Frankfurt a.M.: Klett-Cotta, 1981), 53–67; Henry Kellermann, "Von Re-education zu Re-orientation: Das amerikanische Re-orientierungsprogramm im Nachkriegsdeutschland," ibid., 86–102; Nicholas Pronay and Keith Wilson, eds., *The Political Re-education of Germany and Her Allies After World War II* (London: Croom Helm, 1985).

5. Gimbel, *The American Occupation in Germany.*

keenly aware of the loss of credibility that anti-Soviet propaganda might incur. Such a change would not only disrupt Allied harmony but also inspire Germans to liken their occupiers to National Socialists who had deployed similar propaganda tactics.

The editors of the *Neue Zeitung* solved this dilemma by identifying communist methods as Nazi techniques and German *Kultur* as compatible with U.S. democracy. In this respect, the story of the *Neue Zeitung* presents a window into U.S. cultural reeducation efforts and frustrations in Germany. It details the individual messages and ideas information officers tried to convey to the German populace and demonstrates how and why these concepts changed over time. It identifies the reactions of local readers to these ideas and shows the ensuing disagreements among individual members in OMGUS, readers, and licensed editors over the content of reeducation and democratization.

In her study of German postwar film, Heide Fehrenbach finds that local German interest groups wished to revive a cultural integrity that Hitler had denied them and that they felt was a prerequisite for the country's national sovereignty.[6] Here, the crucial role of the editors of the *Neue Zeitung* emerges because they had a foot in both U.S. popular culture and German highbrow *Kultur*. Moreover, after Hitler's rise to power, most of the German and even some of the emigré editors of the *Neue Zeitung* had experienced the "gray area" as *Mitläufer* between party alliance and resistance. Though their individual experiences differed tremendously, they shared a common if reluctant understanding of Germans who had silently complied with the Third Reich. As Joachim Radkau has shown, nineteenth-century bourgeois conservative culture dominated much of the German emigration to the United States. This concept of *Kultur* assigned the mediation and representation of values and norms to individual intellectual leaders. Fascism and exile fostered the émigrés' inclination to assume the roles of cultural middlemen after their return to Germany.[7] The émigrés at the *Neue Zeitung* believed that reeducation could not consist simply of familiarizing Germans with American culture and showing them the advantages of democracy. Instead, they encouraged local readers to broaden their closed notion of *Kultur* and accept other concepts and ideas. They packaged American culture

6. Heide Fehrenbach, *Cinema in Democratizing Germany: Reconstructing National Identity after Hitler* (Chapel Hill, N.C.: University of North Carolina Press, 1995), 6, 102, 164f., 254–56.

7. Joachim Radkau, *Die deutsche Emigration in den USA: Ihr Einfluß auf die amerikanische Europapolitik, 1933–1945* (Düsseldorf: Bertelsmann, 1971), 35, 116, 125; Lutz Winckler, "Mythen der Exilforschung," in *Exilforschung: Ein Internationales Jahrbuch*, vol. 13, *Kulturtransfer im Exil*, ed. Claus-Dieter Krohn et al. (Munich: edition text + kritik, 1995), 75f.

and ideas in the context of German highbrow culture, *Bildung*, and gender conceptions, and emphasized core democratic values, such as tolerance and individualism, by appealing to very traditional German interpretations of *Kultur*, such as elitist art. This approach specifically targeted the educated and more conservative upper and middle classes that had since the nineteenth century been most impregnable to modern developments and, particularly, to the American way of life.[8]

The story of the *Neue Zeitung* challenges Rebecca Boehling's claim that the advocates in charge of reeducation operated predominantly in subordinate positions where they had little influence.[9] In a sea of diplomatic and economic turbulence, the *Neue Zeitung* provided an island where nonfraternization between Germans and Americans was abandoned. An independent vision informed much of what the editors wrote. Sometimes their writings agreed with political priorities of top officials, and sometimes they did not. The public response, as well as the later careers of the staffers, proved the success of their carrot-and-stick methods and their long-term impact on postwar Germany.

The very independence granted the editors naturally tempered the rules that usually governed the procedures within military government and also made room for dissent. The lack of consensus on the mandate of the *Neue Zeitung* created a conflict, first between the staff and their American superiors, then among the staffers themselves, a conflict that must be projected against the fundamental contradictions and seeming inconsistencies characterizing the entire U.S. reeducation program. On the most basic level, there was a contradiction in the very idea of introducing democracy to a nation that lacked a firm, long-standing democratic tradition and that, in fact, had spent thirteen years squelching any remnants of democratic behavior. Thus, there was bias on one side and resistance on the other. Furthermore, despite all lip service, the Allies tried to impose democracy from the top down by employing nondemocratic means. Finally, and most important, U.S. policy did not follow a prescribed course of action but reacted to developments in Germany and Europe that were often beyond U.S. control, such as the walkout of the Soviets from the Kommandatura.

The case study of the *Neue Zeitung* provides a typical example of this

8. For a similar assessment of this give-and-take attitude in the areas of school reform and institutional transfer, see Roth, "Zur Problematik der Reeducation in Bayern," 121–125; Winfried Müller, *Schulpolitik in Bayern im Spannungsfeld von Kultusbürokratie und Besatzungsmacht, 1945–1949* (Munich: Oldenbourg, 1995); Wade Jacoby, "The Politics of Institutional Transfer: Two Postwar Reconstructions in Germany, 1945–1995" (Ph.D. dissertation, Massachusetts Institute of Technology, Cambridge, Mass., 1996).

9. Boehling, *A Question of Priorities*, 33, 44–45, 70–71, 123–25, 154–55, 269.

reactive policy. In his study of postwar German youth and education, Karl-Heinz Füssl has argued that in comparison to Soviet reeducation policy, American-born officials intentionally steered a rather subtle and restrictive course. This may have been true during the "vacuum" period of 1945–1947, when the ICD pursued what might be considered as a competitive effort to the *Neue Zeitung,* the creation of an independent indigenous press that would remain in place. But in 1948 American reorientation techniques moved closer to Soviet policy: the relative independence of the editors abruptly ended once the *Neue Zeitung* itself became a controversial issue in the conflict between East and West. Soviet officers interpreted the paper's critical portrayal of communist politics in the Eastern zone as a breach of the Potsdam Agreement, despite the fact that until at least the summer of 1947, the paper attributed the inter-Allied tensions to the divisive force of East German communists and not to the Soviet military government. The continuous disputes about the paper's content, the Soviets' ban of the *Neue Zeitung* in January 1946, and the unfolding Cold War led top officials in the military government to recognize the *Neue Zeitung* as a viable tool in the "Vigorous Information Program" in Germany. Consequently, information control officials broadened the reeducation program from an antitotalitarian to an anticommunist orientation.

During the past two decades or so, scholars such as Kenneth Thompson, Inis Claude, Michael Hunt, and others have increasingly criticized attempts of U.S. officials to impose American ideology, culture, and products on foreign (particularly vanquished) countries. Driven by a sense of superiority, racism, moralism, and a mission, they argue, Americans substituted the export of market goods for an international cultural dialogue. Looking at postwar conditions in Germany, Ralph Willett concluded in 1989 that U.S. efforts to tie Germany into a Western orbit succeeded best on the material level.[10]

This study takes a different view. It may very well be true that U.S. policy makers in the State and War departments had their own selfish motives when pondering what picture of the United States should be presented in

10. Kellermann, letter to author, 10 July 1995; Karl-Heinz Füssl, *Die Umerziehung der Deutschen,* 23–34; Inis L. Claude, Jr., "American Values and Multinational Institutions," in *Institutions for Projecting American Values Abroad*, ed. Kenneth W. Thompson, (Lanham, Md.: University Press of America, 1983), 9–1 to 9–9; Emmet B. Ford, Jr., "Diplomacy and the Transmission of Values," ibid., 11–1 to 11–8; Kenneth W. Thompson, ed., *Moral Dimensions of American Foreign Policy: Ethics in Foreign Policy Service* (New Brunswick: Transaction Books, 1984); Michael Hunt, *Ideology and U.S. Foreign Policy* (New Haven: Yale University Press, 1987); Gurevich, *Cultural Expansion*; Ralph Willett, *The Americanization of Germany, 1945–1949* (London: Routledge, 1989), 21f., 27.

postwar Germany. But they displayed indifference regarding the implementation of their cultural policy there. Until 1949, the Civil Affairs Division tended to reject any responsibility for the *Neue Zeitung*, even though the paper was presumably a prime instrument of reeducation. Moreover, press guidelines from the State and the War departments to the ICD/ISD (and the *Neue Zeitung*) often came late or were lost. If they trickled down to their point of destination, U.S. information strategists in Germany quietly dismissed them without informing their bosses in Washington, D.C. In the summer of 1995, I sent a copy of my manuscript to Henry Kellermann, the former representative of the Office of Public Affairs in the State Department's Bureau of German Affairs. Much to his surprise, fifty years after the fact, Henry Kellermann discovered the inefficiency of his detailed directives.[11] As the case study of the *Neue Zeitung* shows, U.S. reeducation and cultural transmission in Germany depended largely on the profiles and personalities of people who operated on the midlevel of the military government.

Meanwhile, OMGUS officials were deeply split in their assessment of the newspaper. When reading the many criticisms regarding the *Neue Zeitung*, one might get the impression that U.S. officials must have expected something very specific from the paper. They were articulate in saying what kind of paper they did not want. But they never clearly said what they did want apart from vague allusions such as "a democratic newspaper" or "an official organ of OMGUS." Consequently, the *Neue Zeitung*, like a chameleon, continually changed its color. As such, it represents a quite accurate example of the often confused, reluctant, and incoherent course of U.S. policy in postwar Germany. In 1945 the *Neue Zeitung* was no more than an accidental by-product of information policy and a model of sound democratic journalism. In 1946 it was supposed to be a vital tool of denazification but also a reminder of Soviet-American friendship. Less than one year later, the *Neue Zeitung* emerged as an anticommunist propaganda tool. And in 1949 it was ordered to combine anticommunist, antinationalist, and pro-American viewpoints.

It is open to speculation why U.S. officials were such reluctant propagandists. The principle of freedom of the press certainly played a powerful role, as did their inexperience with indoctrination. Perhaps they not only hesitated to adopt propaganda techniques but were also unable to do so. Propaganda typically feeds on a utopian vision. But as Stefan Possony has pointed out, Americans presumably had already developed the most favorable society in the world. Therefore, their propaganda was incomplete: it lacked the

11. Henry Kellermann, letters to the author, 16 May 1995 and 10 July 1995.

visionary quality necessary to develop a positive—let alone utopian—line of indoctrination. Instead it tended to be mostly negative, dismissing other societies while praising its own.[12]

My findings modify recent arguments presented by scholars of "postcultural imperialism," such as Reinhold Wagnleitner, Richard Kuisel, and others, who question the scenario of an uncontested "Americanization" of Western Europe. Wagnleitner emphasizes the decisively "European" bent of America's influence in Austria. Kuisel's and Fehrenbach's analyses of local reactions stress the high degree of self-consciousness and even resistance on the part of the "recipients" of U.S. culture. The *Neue Zeitung*'s example demonstrates the Germanic tinge of the United States' cultural program. It also proves that German-born editors as well as their readers were unwilling to simply absorb American culture but insisted on developing their own identity built on their pre-1933 cultural history.

"Cultural transmission" has recently become a powerful buzzword among students of both cultural and diplomatic history, above all, because it refutes the argument of the critics of "cultural imperialism." Hermann-Josef Rupieper has analyzed the intense interaction between U.S. officials and local citizens, emphasizing the flexibility of the former and the self-consciousness of the latter. Maritta Hein-Kremer's detailed examination of the Amerika Häuser stresses the partnership-like quality of the U.S. library program in Germany long before 1949.[13] Richard Pells recently argued that after World War II, a cross-cultural process of mutual fertilization—enforced by mass communication, cultural exchange, and international economic and political cooperation—led to the emergence of a global Western culture. And as Reinhold Wagnleitner and Richard Kuisel have shown, whatever elements of U.S. popular culture arrived on European shores in the form of movies, music, and consumer products altered their meaning

12. Stefan T. Possony, "Propaganda or Reason?" manuscript, Georgetown University, Washington, D.C., n.d. [1952?], Harry S. Truman Papers, SMOF: Psychological Strategy Board Files, 1 box, file 091, Germany—file 1, HSTL.

13. Rupieper, *Wurzeln der westdeutschen Nachkriegsdemokratie*; Maritta Hein-Kremer, *Die amerikanische Kulturoffensive: Gründung und Entwicklung der amerikanischen Information Center in Westdeutschland und West-Berlin, 1945–1955* (Cologne: Böhlau, 1996), 549; Jessica C. E. Gienow-Hecht, "U.S. Cultural Policy towards the Federal Republic of Germany, 1949–1968," in *The United States and Germany in the Era of the Cold War*, ed. Detlev Junker (Cambridge, Mass.: Cambridge University Press, forthcoming); Manuela Aguilar, *Cultural Diplomacy and Foreign Policy: German-American Relations, 1955–1968* (New York: Peter Lang, 1997); Hermann-Josef Rupieper, " 'To Solidify the Bond of Friendship between our Nation and Germany:' Die amerikanische Katholische Kirche in Nachkriegsdeutschland," in *Deutschland und der Westen: Festschrift für Klaus Schwabe zum 65. Geburtstag,* ed. Guido Müller (Stuttgart: Franz Steiner Verlag, 1998), 220–26.

dramatically under the influence of French, German, and Austrian elites, hopes, and ideals.[14]

But what happens in the process of cultural transmission? How does one culture absorb or transform another? And what is the significance of that process? This study has tried to shift the emphasis from the original messages to the transmitters. The selection of agents who transmit political or cultural values to the foreign arena represents the most vital factor in the process (and success) of cultural transmission.[15] The appeal of these values depends on the people who "transport" them abroad. In the case of the *Neue Zeitung*, the émigrés proved to be uniquely equipped to convey American values to a German audience. Emigrés like the editors of the *Neue Zeitung* could be found throughout the military government, often at the crossroads between U.S. officials and German citizens. Fritz E. Oppenheimer, a Jewish lawyer from Berlin who had emigrated to the United States in 1938, served as Clay's legal adviser in 1945–1946. Felix Gilbert, a historian born in Baden-Baden, served as research analyst of the Office of Strategic Services in the State Department in Washington, London, Paris, and Germany. Heinz (later Henry) A. Kissinger, a student from Fürth who had emigrated in 1938, worked for the U.S. news service in Europe before he became resident officer for the district of Krefeld in 1946.[16] Yet rarely did these exiles work

14. Reinhold Wagnleitner, *Coca-Colanization and the Cold War*; Kuisel, *Seducing the French;* Fehrenbach, *Cinema in Democratizing Germany*, 6, 102, 164f., Laura E. Cooper and Cooper B. Lee, "The Pendulum of Cultural Imperialism: Popular Music Interchanges Between the United States and Britain, 1943–1967," *Journal of Popular Culture* 27 (Winter 1993): 61–78; Jongsuk Chay, ed., *Cultural and International Relations* (New York: Praeger, 1990); James Petras, "Cultural Imperialism in the Late 20th Century," *Journal of Contemporary Asia* 23 (1993): 139–48; Yuji Takahashi, "The Resistance of the Asian Masses and Their Culture," *Perspectives of New Music* 30 (Summer 1992): 90–100.

15. It remains to be seen if the same could be said for other private initiatives in the transatlantic cultural exchange. Gary E. Kraske, *Missionaries of the Book: The American Library Profession and the Origins of Cultural Diplomacy* (London: Greenwood Press, 1985); Margaret Blanchard, *Exporting the First Amendment: The Press-Government Crusade of 1945–1952* (New York: Longman, 1986), 3, 40, 68ff., 108, 402.

16. Strauss and Röder, *International Biographical Dictionary*, vol. 1, 365f., 542; ibid., vol. 2, pt. 1, 376f. For more on "remigrés," see Claus-Dieter Krohn, Erwin Rotermund, Lutz Winckler, and Wulf Koepke, eds., *Exil und Remigration* (Munich: edition text + kritik, 1991); Reinhard K. Zachau has recently analyzed Habe's and Heym's individual roles, though mostly based on the paper itself and the two men's personal memories. Reinard K. Zachau, "Hans Habe als Herausgeber der *Neuen Zeitung*," in *Deutsch-jüdisches Exil: Das Ende der Assimilation? Identitätsproblem deutscher Juden in der Emigration*, ed. Wolfgang Benz and Marion Neiss (Berlin: Metropol Verlag, 1994), 151–64; Zachau, " 'Gute Europäer in Amerikas Uniform': Hans Habe und Stefan Heym in der Psychological Warfare," in *Der Zweite Weltkrieg und die Exilanten: Eine literarische Antwort*, ed. Helmut F. Pfanner (Bonn: Bouvier, 1991), 177–86; Guy Stern, "The Exiles and the War of Minds," ibid., 311–24; Thomas Köbner und

in such an autonomous position as in the *Neue Zeitung*, which is why this paper proves to be such an apt object for historical investigation.

Despite the persistent problem of estimating the influence of information programs, there are indicators pointing to the paper's success. During the entire occupation period there existed no nationally distributed licensed German paper that competed with the *Neue Zeitung*. German papers' geographical reach remained confined to regional audiences. The only media offering themselves for comparison were the British, French, and Soviet official papers (designed for distribution in their respective zones) and the RIAS broadcasting station in Berlin. That in itself guaranteed the paper's appeal in the U.S. zone. Second, steadily rising circulation numbers and letters to the editor bore witness to the *Neue Zeitung*'s influence between 1945 and 1947, as does the decline in circulation after Wallenberg's dismissal. Third, the careers of the many employees who continued to uphold the journalistic techniques taught by Habe and Wallenberg in their subsequent jobs at German publications hint at the long-term impact of the paper. Finally, readers' favorable memories also testify to the lasting impact of the *Neue Zeitung* on its audience.

Historians need to investigate further the agencies of acculturation. While students of cultural imperialism have extensively analyzed intentions in the State Department, occupation scholars have studied the results of U.S. policy toward Europe. Yet, as Jürgen Habermas has stated, history is not exhausted by "what human actors mutually intend."[17] Nor is history what its players perceive. Between the two objects of study, one link is missing: the medium. As communication scholars, linguists, and social psychologists have argued for a long time, in the social discourse between a speaker and a recipient, "the medium" hides a third force, i.e., the agent of messages.[18] Agents do not just report but intentionally recreate, shape, and alter messages.

Therefore, in addition to describing intentions, which are rarely carried out exactly as planned, and studying effects, which are notoriously difficult to measure, one should focus on exactly what was done and who did it. As long as we are unclear on who the agents and what the tools were, the discussion surrounding cultural flows involving the United States will remain theoretical. We need to ask less whether or not the United States acted as a

Erwin Rotermund, *Rückkehr aus dem Exil: Emigranten aus dem Dritten Reich in Deutschland nach 1945. Essays zu Ehren von Ernst Loewy* (Marburg: Druckerei Wenzel, 1990).

17. Jürgen Habermas, *Zur Logik der Sozialwissenschaften: Materialien* (Frankfurt a.M.: Suhrkamp, 1970), 116.

18. See, for example, Hans Bühler, *Linguistik I: Lehr- und Übungsbuch zur Einführung in die Sprachwissenschaft*, 2d ed. (Tübingen: Max Niemeyer, 1971).

political and cultural model for Germany and more about whether and how transmission was implemented. The case study of the *Neue Zeitung* provides unique insights into precisely these issues.

The broader meaning of my findings—the importance of agents in the process of cultural transmission—emerges if one considers them in the context of current situations of cultural diplomacy in the Third World, Eastern Europe, and the Middle East. The significance of transmitters in the process of cultural foreign policy is a field that still remains largely neglected. Private as well as governmental organizations still concentrate primarily on programs and content rather than on agents when planning cultural ventures abroad. Few observers writing on overseas information and culture programs devote more than a couple of pages, if any, to the question of personnel.[19]

One wonders if the transmitters of U.S. values should never be American-born. Perhaps they should preferably be natives of the target country with fairly recent exposure to U.S. culture. People who have gone through a process of assimilation from one culture to another—as many of the émigrés did—are better equipped to bridge the gulf of understanding between them than are persons who stand on one side or the other.

One may speculate whether the end of the Allied presence in Germany will induce a profound change in the cultural relationship between Germany and the United States. On the official, political, and diplomatic levels, the ties between the countries are loosening. German newspapers have been paying less attention to U.S. political affairs during the past years because the country has huge economic and unity-related concerns. With the strengthening of the European Community, German leaders increasingly shift their attention from transatlantic to continental concerns. Simultaneously, American policy makers and journalists, inspired by both a growing tendency toward unilateralism and the attraction of the Pacific Rim, seem to be less interested in European political, cultural, and social affairs.[20] The recent closure of several Amerika Häuser manifests once again the United States' silent retirement from its former mission in Germany.

19. Green, *American Propaganda*, 168, 177; Manfred Strack, "Amerikanische Kulturbeziehungen zu (West-)Deutschland, 1945–55," *Zeitschrift für Kulturaustausch* 37 (1987): 283–300.

20. Günther Gillessen, "Wertewandel in der amerikanischen Aussenpolitik," *Frankfurter Allgemeine Zeitung*, 20 June 1995, 12; Jim Hoagland, "It Isn't Time for Eastward Expansion of NATO," *International Herald Tribune*, 21 June 1995, p. 8; Flora Lewis, "Atlantic Connections Begin to Fray," ibid., 23 June 1995; Jürgen Dormann, CEO, Hoechst AG, "Towards a Redefinition of the German-American Partnership," speech given at the 18th German-American Conference of the Atlantik-Brücke and the American Council on Germany, Berlin, 17 June 1995, reprinted in *Atlantik-Brücke e.V. Rundschreiben* No. 5, 1995.

At the same time, German-American relations move from the official level to the more informal, nongovernmental, and private level. The awareness of post–Cold War global economic interdependencies and environmental problems has revived the mutual interest of companies and individuals on both sides of the Atlantic.[21] While German interest in political relations with the United States may temporarily decline, German newspapers, market researchers, scientists, and consumers display an unlimited fascination with the United States. Mass tourism, video-phones, satellite television, Internet newsgroups, and electronic mail give participants boundless and inexpensive avenues to cultures and minds far away. Unrestrained by the political blinders of the Cold War, the new generation of German youth is perhaps the first to be able to develop an international consciousness along the lines that the editors of the *Neue Zeitung*—in contrast to their superiors—once had in mind.

21. Jürgen Rüttgers, Federal Minister for Education, Research, and Technology, "Globalism: A New Challenge for U.S.-German Partnership," speech given at the 18th German-American Conference of the Atlantik-Brücke and the American Council on Germany, Berlin, 16 June 1995, reprinted in *Atlantik-Brücke e.V., Rundschreiben* No. 4, 1995.

# BIBLIOGRAPHY

## PRIMARY SOURCES

### Manuscript Collections, Germany

*Berlin, Germany*
Landesarchiv Berlin
RG 260, Office of Military Government
Berlin Sector
RG 466, Office of the High Commissioner (U.S.)
Germany
State Department, Berlin Mission Files
Hans Habe collection
Letters
Ullstein Aktiengesellschaft, Archiv
*Neue Zeitung* collection

*Bonn, Germany*
Bundespresse- und Informationsamt
Archiv "Neue Zeitung" (Dienstarchiv, Redaktionsarchiv)
Stiftung Haus der Geschichte der Bundesrepublik Deutschland
Sammlung Max W. Kraus (92/09/007–105.14.14)
Friedrich Ebert Stiftung
Nachlaß Else Reventlow

*Koblenz, Germany*
Bundesarchiv Koblenz
RG 260, Office of the Military Government (U.S.) Germany
Information Control / Services Division
Presse- und Informationsamt der Bundesregierung, 1953–1955, B 145/873–B 145/1748
Dienstakten 085 Bd. II Nr. 33

*Marbach, Germany*
Schiller-Nationalmuseum, Deutsches Literaturarchiv
Sammlung Walter Kolbenhoff

Archiv Manfred George
Archiv Dolf Sternberger

*Munich, Germany*
Bayerisches Hauptstaatsarchiv
RG 260, Office of Military Government (U.S.) in Germany
RG 260, Office of Military Government in Bavaria
Education & Cultural Relations Division
Information Control Division / Information Services Division
Cultural Affairs: Information Control
German & Bavarian Public Opinion
Mission Organization
Historical Reports
Governor
Intelligence Division
Civil Affairs Division
Land Directors
Akten des Staatsministers Pressewesen, allgemein
Aktenabgabe 1976, Karton 37, vol. 4 (Koszyk)
Bibliotheksarchiv, Ludwig-Maximilians-Universität
*Die Neue Zeitung*, 1945–1955
Institut für Zeitgeschichte
RG 84, Office of the Political Adviser
RG 260, Office of Military Government (U.S.) in Germany
Civil Administration Division
Staff Conferences
Office of Public Affairs
Monthly Reports of the Military Governor, U.S. zone, 1945–1949, DK 101.006
Staff Meetings of the Directors of OMGUS
Information Control Division
Opinion Survey Branch
Political Affairs
Public Relations Office
Regional Government Coordinating Office
Military Government Gazette, Germany, Twelfth Army Group 1945
Military Government Handbook for Germany, Sept. 1944, I–III
Manpower Division, Visiting Expert Series
Supreme Headquarters Expeditionary Forces (SHAEF), DK 090
Amtsblatt des Kontrollrates in Deutschland, DK 004.002
Germany Basic Handbook, 090.007

Germany Zone Handbook, 090.008, No. 6 Hessen Region, Public Record Office WO 220/212 (IfZ copy)
No. 1 Berlin, PRO, WO 220/225
No. 6 Hessen Region, Public Record Office, WO 220/212 (IfZ copy)
No. 7 South West Germany, PRO, WO 220/213
No. 8 Bavaria, PRO, WO 220/209
RG 466 High Commission in Germany
Reports of the Historical Division, DK 157.028
Control Commission for Germany Berlin (British), DK 230
Sammlung Hans-Joachim Netzer, ED 352
Documents of the Prussian Department of the Interior, FB 223
Individual Manuscripts:
Bittorf, Susanne. "Die Insel in der Schellingstraße: Vor 30 Jahren wurde die Neue Zeitung eingestellt." Broadcasting program. Broadcasted in Bayerischer Rundfunk, 25 September 1983, 10.07 P.M.
Fragebogen zur Sicherung und Einschließung von Quellen zur Deutschen Emigration, 1933–1945, F 213, 1–4
Heintze, Heinz-Adolf Freiherr v. Folder "Zeugenschrifttum," ZS 3/45
Mierendorf, Martha. "German Jewish Club of 1933, Los Angeles," Süddeutscher Rundfunk, 10.1.1966, Ms 200/41
Radio Bremen, manuscripts, vol. 1: A—Mai Kommentare, Fg 06/1

*Private Manuscript Collections*
Peter Mendelssohn collection, courtesy Mrs. Anita Naef, Munich
Collection of ICD/OMGUS documents, courtesy Harold Hurwitz, Berlin
Collection of manuscripts, courtesy Ernst Cramer, Berlin

## Manuscript Collections, United States

*Abilene, Kansas*
Dwight D. Eisenhower Library
C. D. Jackson Papers
Dwight D. Eisenhower Papers

*Austin, Texas*
Harry Ransom Humanities Research Center, University of Texas at Austin
John Lehmann Collection

*Boston, Massachussetts*
Boston Mugar Memorial Library, Boston University
Hans Habe Collection

*Carlisle, Pennsylvania*
United States Army Military History Institute, Carlisle Barracks
Robert A. McClure Papers

*Cincinnati, Ohio*
American Jewish Archives
World Jewish Congress Collection

*Independence, Missouri*
Harry S. Truman Library
Harry S. Truman Papers
Dean Acheson Papers
Alvin J. Rockwell Papers
Abijah U. Fox Papers
Charles W. Thayer Papers
Oral History Interview with General Lucius D. Clay

*New York, New York*
New York Public Library, Manuscripts and Archives Division
Germany, 1945–1946, letters and reports to the editors of the *Neue Zeitung* (Saul Padover Collection)

*Stanford, California*
The Hoover Institute on War, Revolution and Peace
Robert Murphy Collection

*Suitland, Maryland*
Washington National Research Center
RG 84, U.S. Foreign Service Posts (Embassy)
Office of the U.S. Political Advisor for Germany, Berlin
Office of the U.S. Political Advisor for Germany, Frankfurt
West Berlin Consulate
Frankfurt Consulate General, 1946–1955
Munich Consulate General, 1946–1955
RG 260, Office of the Military Government (U.S.) in Germany
RG 466, Records of the High Commissioner for Germany
John McCloy
Berlin Element, Political Affairs Division
Office of the Land Commissioner for Bavaria
Intelligence Division
HICOG Publications

*Syracuse, New York*
The George Arents Research Library for Special Collections, Syracuse University
Dorothy Thompson Papers

*Washington, D.C.*
National Archives
RG 59, General Records of the Department of State
Decimal Files 1945–1949
Dec. File Name Index 1945–1949
Diplomatic Branch
Bureau of Intelligence & Research
Confidential U.S. State Department Central Files: Germany, 1950–1959, Internal Affairs & Foreign Affairs
General Records of Department of State
Decimal Files 1950–1954
Research and Analysis Branch
Research Reports of the Foreign Policy Studies Branch, Division of Historical Policy Research, 1944–1958
Records of the Assistant Secretary of State for Public Affairs, 1945–1950
Records of the Office of Public Opinion Studies, 1945–1975
RG 107, Records of the Office of the Secretary of War
Assistant Secretary of War John McCloy
Assistant Secretary of War Howard War Peterson
RG 165, Records of the War Department, General and Special Staffs
Civil Affairs Division, General Records
RG 226, Records of the Office of Strategic Services
Foreign Nationalities Branch Files, 1942, Entry 100, C0002
Personnel, School and Training Branch
Records of the OSS Washington Director's Office, Entry 190
Strategic Services Unit, Intelligence Unit Reports, postwar period
RG 331, Records of Allied Operational and Occupation Headquarters, World War II
Psychological Warfare Division, Supreme Headquarters Allied Expeditionary Forces
Twelfth Army Group

## Manuscript Collections, Great Britain

*Kew/Richmond, Great Britain*
Public Record Office
FO 1056, Foreign Office, Control Commission for Germany, Public Relations and Information Services, Group Files, 1945–1955
FO 371, Foreign Office, General Correspondence: Political, 1906–1957

## Interviews

Bahr, Egon. Bonn, Germany, 16 November 1992
Bönisch, Peter. Munich, Germany, 22 September 1992
Brandt, Wolfgang. Berlin, Germany, 26 September 1996
Cramer, Ernst. Berlin, Germany, 16 December 1991, 6 January 1993, 1 December 1994
Ebbinghaus, Carl Herrmann. Hinterzarten i.Br., Germany, 25 October 1992
Fischer, Eva. Berlin, Germany, 4 January 1993
Fleischer, Jack. Little Rock, Ark., 27 April 1993
Kellen, Konrad. Los Angeles, Calif., 27 July 1993
Kellermann, Henry. Bethesda, Md., 7 February 1993; Chevy Chase, Md., 16 May 1994
Kolbenhoff, Isolde. Telephone interview. Germering, Germany, 15 April 1997
Kolbenhoff, Walter. Germering, Germany, 22 February 1992
Konecky, William. New York, N.Y., 23 March 1993
Kraus, Max W. Washington, D.C., 6 and 13 July 1991; Chevy Chase, Md., 16 May 1994
Lehmann, Hans. Stockdorf, Germany, 17 October 1992
Lochner, Robert. Berlin, Germany, 10 April 1992
Löwenstein, Karl. New York, N.Y., 22 March 1993
Meitzner, Olaf. Munich, Germany, 28 August 1992
Netzer, Hans-Joachim. Munich, Germany, 13 December 1991
Rodes, Toby E. Telephone interview. Basel, Switzerland, 17 April 1994
Strohschneider, Gottfried. Munich, Germany, 14 February 1992
Stuart, Jack M. New York, N.Y., 12 July 1993
Ungewitter, Inge. Munich, Germany, 21 October 1992
Washburn, Lisa. Berlin, Germany, 26 September 1996
Wittler, Kurt. San Francisco, Calif., 22 July 1993
Wyden, Peter. Ridgefield, Conn., 20 March 1993
Wynder, Ernest L. New York, N.Y., 19 March 1993
Wust, Klaus. New York, 19 March 1993

## Letters to the Author

Asche, Klaus. Hamburg, Germany, 6 March 1993
Balleisen, Beate. Triftern, Germany, [7] August 1992
del Bondio-Reventlow, Beatrice. Munich, Germany, 21 February 1993
Davison, W. Phillips. Princeton, N.J., 17 January 1992, 2 December 1993, 15 March 1994, 11 November 1995, e-mail, 19 May 1998
Ebbinghaus, Carl-Hermann. Hinterzarten i.Br., Germany, 31 August 1992
Fleischer, Jack. Morrilton, Ark., 22/24 March 1993, 29 July 1993, 5 December 1993

Glaser, Hermann. Rosstal, Germany, 23 September 1992
Göbel, Joseph. Berlin, Germany, 5 September 1992
Gregoriades, Andrew. Geneva, Switzerland, 6 December 1992
Hensel, Georg. Darmstadt, Germany, 18 August 1992
Heym, Stefan. Berlin, Germany, 6 January 1993
Hoffmann, Dietrich. Göttingen, Germany, 19 September 1992
Joseph, Lou. Des Moines, Ill., 18 April 1995
Kellermann, Henry. Chevy Chase, Md., 16 May 1995, 10 July 1995
Koch, Alfred. Munich, Germany, 13 August 1992
Kolbenhoff, Walter. Germering, Germany, n.d. [1991–1992]
Knoller, Wilhelmine. Eicherloh, Germany, 31 August 1992
Kraus, Max W. Washington, D.C., 8 March 1993
Pfeifer, Hans-Wolfgang. Frankfurt a.M., Germany, 20 August 1992
Prölß, Willy. Nuremberg, Germany, 5 October 1992
Schneider, Wolf. Hamburg, Germany, 1 March 1993
Schörken, Rolf. Düsseldorf, Germany, 18 August 1992
Stuart, Jack M. New York, 24 March 1993
Thoma, Franz. Munich, Germany, 4 September 1992
Wiegand, Wilfried. Niedenau, Germany, 9 August 1992
Wittler, Kurt. Pasadena, Calif., 18 August 1993
Wynder, Ernst L. New York, 27 July 1993
Ziehen, Wolfgang. Gießen, Germany, 12 August 1992

## Newspapers

*Die Abendzeitung* (Nuremberg), 1949, 1984
*Allgemeine Zeitung* (Berlin), 1945–46
*Anniston Star* (Alabama), 1942
*Atlantik Brücke e.V. Rundschreiben* (Hamburg), 1995
*Berlin am Mittag*, 1947
*Berliner Zeitung*, 1948–49
*Daily Mail* (Paris edition), 1948
*Frankenpost* (Hof), 1949
*Frankfurter Allgemeine Zeitung* (Frankfurt a.M.), 1949, 1995
*Frankfurter Rundschau* (Frankfurt a.M.), 1949
*Hannoversche Allgemeine Zeitung* (Hannover), 1950
*The International Herald Tribune* (European Edition), 1995
*Main-Echo* (Aschaffenburg), 1949
*Der Morgen* (Berlin) 1949
*Die Neue Zeitung* (Munich)
*Neue Züricher Zeitung*, 1949
*Neues Deutschland* (Berlin), 1948–49

*The New Orleans*, 1942
*The News*, 1949
*New York Herald Tribune*, 1947–49
*The New York Times*, 1947–49, 1990–95
*The Oregonian* (Portland), 1942
*Rheinischer Merkur* (Bonn), 1995
*San Francisco News*, 1942
*Spokane Daily Chronicle*, 1941
*The Stars & Stripes*, 1949
*Süddeutsche Zeitung* (Munich), 1949–55
*Südost-Kurier* (Bad Reichenhall), 1946–1947
*Tägliche Rundschau* (Berlin), 1945–49
*Der Tagesspiegel* (Berlin), 1945–49
*taz* (Berlin), 1986
*Telegraf* (Berlin), 1947–49
*Vorwärts* (Berlin), 1949
*Washington Post*, 1984
*Die Welt* (Hamburg), 1962, 1972

## Periodicals and Weeklies

*Allgemeine unabhängige jüdische Wochenzeitung* (Düsseldorf), 1971, 1977
*Atlantic Monthly* (New York), 1943
*Aufbau* (New York), 1947–55
*Der Bund* (Bern), 1972
*Der Ruf: Unabhängige Blätter der jungen Generation* (Munich)
*Der Spiegel* (Hamburg), 1949–55
*Stern* (Hamburg), 1952
*Welt am Sonntag* (Hamburg), 1977, 1994
*Die Weltbühne* (Berlin), 1952
*Die Zeit* (Hamburg), 1994

## Visual and Audio Sources

Adler, Peter, and Rudolf Piechowiak, "Sie nannten sich die Psy-War-Boys: 'Krieg der Worte' gegen Hitler." Television broadcasting. Produced by Carsten-Krüger Film- und Fernsehproduktion. Zweites Deutsches Fernsehen, Germany, 1990.

Fischer, Alfred. Interview with Hans Wallenberg. Berlin, 7 June 1972. Audiocassette. Courtesy of Eva Fischer, Berlin.

Kästner, Erich. "Es gibt nichts Gutes, außer: Man tut es. Chansons und Prosa von Erich Kästner." Compact Disc. Recorded by Brückenhaus Audio Productions, Dresden, 1993.

Rollberg, Sabine. "Rückblick auf die Neue Zeitung." Television broadcasting. Westdeutscher Rundfunk, Germany, 1985.

Government Publications

*Foreign Relations of the United States 1948*. Vol. 2, *Germany and Austria*. Washington, D.C.: United States Government Printing Office, 1973.

Kellermann, Henry K. *Cultural Relations as an Instrument of U.S. Foreign Policy: The Educational Exchange Program between the United States and Germany, 1945–1954*. Washington, D.C.: Dept. of State Publication 8931, U.S. Government Printing Office, 1978.

McMahon, Arthur Whittier. *Memorandum on the Postwar International Information Program of the United States*. Washington, D.C.: Department of State Publication 2438, U.S. Government Printing Office, 1945.

Pilgert, Henry. *Women in West Germany*. N. p. [Bad Godesberg?]: Historical Division, Office of the Executive Secretary HICOG, 1952.

———. *The West German Educational System*. N. p. [Bad Godesberg?]: Historical Division, Office of the Executive Secretary HICOG, 1953.

———, and Helga Dobbert. *Press, Radio, and Film in West Germany, 1945–1953*. Bad Godesberg: Historical Division, Office of the Executive Secretary, Office of the U.S. High Commissioner for Germany, 1953.

Plischke, Elmer, and Henry P. Pilgert, *U.S. Information Programs in Berlin*. N. p. [Bad Godesberg?]: Historical Division, Office of the Executive Secretary HICOG, 1953.

U.S. Congress. House. Subcommittee of the Committee of Appropriations. *Hearings on Supplemental Appropriation Bill, 1954*. 83d Congress, 1st Session on H. R. 6200, 1953, pt. 1.

U.S. Department of State. *The Register of the U.S. Department of State*. No. 15. Washington, D.C.: Government Printing Office, 1950.

White, D. G. *U.S. Military Government in Germany: Radio Reorientation*. Karlsruhe: U.S. European Command, Historical Division, 1950.

## SECONDARY SOURCES

Adenauer, Konrad. *Erinnerungen, 1945–1953*. Stuttgart: Deutsche Verlags-Anstalt, 1965.

Aguilar, Manuela. *Cultural Diplomacy and Foreign Policy: German-American Relations, 1955–1968*. New York: Peter Lang, 1997.

Ambrose, Stephen E. *Eisenhower*. Vol. 1, *Soldier, General of the Army, President Elect, 1890–1952*. New York: Simon & Schuster, 1983.

Andersch, Alfred. *Die Kirschen der Freiheit*. Stuttgart: Reclam, 1967.

———. "Der Seesack." In *Literaturmagazin 7: Nachkriegsliteratur,* ed. Nicolaus Born and Jürgen Manthey, 116–33. Reinbek b. Hamburg: Rowohlt, 1977.

Anderson, George L., ed. *Issues and Conflict: Studies in Twentieth Century American Diplomacy.* Lawrence: University of Kansas Press, 1959.

Arnold, Matthew. *Culture and Anarchy: An Essay in Political and Social Criticism.* London: Smith, Elder, 1869.

Backer, John H. *The Decision to Divide Germany: American Foreign Policy in Transition.* Durham, N.C.: Duke University Press, 1978.

———. *Winds of History: The German Years of Lucius DuBignon Clay.* New York: Van Nostrand Reinhold, 1983.

Baerwald, Friedrich. "Zur politischen Tätigkeit deutscher Emigranten im Council for a Democratic Germany." *Vierteljahreshefte für Zeitgeschichte* 28 (1980): 372–83.

Bahr, Egon. *Zu meiner Zeit.* Munich: Blessing, 1996.

Balfour, Michael. "Reforming the German Press, 1945–49." *Journal of European Studies* 3 (1973): 268–75.

Bausch, Ulrich M. *Die Kulturpolitik der US-amerikanischen Information Control Division in Württemberg-Baden von 1945 bis 1949: Zwischen militärischem Funktionalismus und schwäbischem Obrigkeitsdenken.* Stuttgart: Klett-Cotta, 1992.

Benz, Wolfgang, ed. *Die Bundesrepublik Deutschland: Geschichte in drei Bänden.* 3 vols. Frankfurt: Fischer Taschenbuch Verlag, 1983.

———. *Potsdam 1945. Besatzungsherrschaft und Neuaufbau im Vier-Zonen-Deutschland.* Munich: Deutscher Taschenbuch Verlag, 1986; 2d ed., 1992.

Benz, Wolfgang, and Marion Neiss. *Deutsch-jüdisches Exil: Das Ende der Assimilation? Identitätsproblem deutscher Juden in der Emigration.* Berlin: Metropol Verlag, 1994.

Bigsby, C. W. E. "Europe, America, and the Cultural Debate." In *Superculture: American Popular Culture and Europe*, ed. C. W. E. Bigsby, 1–27. Bowling Green, Ohio: Bowling Green University Popular Press, 1975.

Bischof, Günter. "The Politics of Anti-Communism in the Executive Branch During the Early Cold War: Truman, Eisenhower, and McCarthy(ism)." In *Anticommunism and McCarthyism in the United States, 1954: Essays on the Politics and Culture of the Cold War*, ed. by André Kaenel, 53–78. Paris: Edition Messene, 1995.

Bischof, Günter, and Stephen Ambrose, eds. *Eisenhower and the German POWs: Facts Against Falsehood.* Baton Rouge: Louisiana State University Press, 1992.

Bittorf, Susanne. "Die *Neue Zeitung* im Spiegel Münchener Gesellschaft und Kultur: Eine Fallstudie zur amerikanischen Umerziehungs- und Demokratisierungspolitik in Deutschland, 1945–1949." Master's thesis, Ludwig-Maximilians-Universität, Munich, 1982.

Blanchard, Margaret. *Exporting the First Amendment: The Press-Government Crusade of 1945–1952.* New York: Longmann, 1986.

Boehling, Rebecca. *A Question of Priorities: Democratic Reform and Economic Recovery in Postwar Germany*. Providence, R.I.: Berghahn Books, 1996.

Bollenbeck, Georg. *Bildung und Kultur: Glanz und Elend eines deutschen Deutungsmusters*. Frankfurt: Insel Verlag, 1994.

Borchers, Hans, and Klaus W. Vowe. *Die zarte Pflanze Demokratie: Amerikanische Re-education in Deutschland im Spiegel ausgewählter politischer und literarischer Zeitschriften, 1945–1949*. Tübingen: Narr, 1979.

Bosch, William J. *Judgment on Nuremberg: American Attitudes Toward the Major German War-Crime Trials*. Chapel Hill: University of North Carolina Press, 1970.

Brecht, Arnold. "Re-establishing German Government." *Annals* 267 (1950): 28–42.

Bredella, Lothar, ed. *Mediating a Foreign Culture: The United States and Germany*. Tübingen: Narr, 1991.

Breit, Peter. "Culture and Authority: American and German Transactions." In *The American Impact on Postwar Germany*, ed. Reiner Pommerin, 125–148. Providence, R.I.: Berghahn Books, 1995.

Breitenkamp, Edward. *The U.S. Information Control Division and Its Effects on German Publishers and Writers, 1945–1949*. Grand Forks, N. Dak.: University Station, 1953.

Breitman, Richard, and Alan M. Kraut, *American Refugee Policy and European Jewry, 1933–1945*. Bloomington, Ind.: Indiana University Press, 1987.

Brickner, Richard. "Is Germany Incurable?" *Atlantic Monthly* 171 (1943): 84–93.

Brooke, Stephen. "Atlantic Crossing? American Views of Capitalism and British Socialist Thought, 1932–1962." *Twentieth Century British History* 2 (1991): 107–36.

Bühler, Hans. *Linguistik I: Lehr und Übungsbuch zur Einführung in die Sprachwissenschaft*. 2d ed. Tübingen: Max Niemeyer, 1971.

Bungenstab, Karl-Ernst. *Umerziehung zur Demokratie? Re-Edukation-Politik im Bildungswesen der U.S. Zone, 1945–49*. Düsseldorf: Bertelsmann Universitätsverlag, 1970.

Burkhardt, Wolfgang. "Die Feuilleton- und Kunstbeilage der *Neuen Zeitung*: Ein Beitrag zur Geschichte der Nachkriegspresse in Deutschland." Master's thesis, Freie Universität Berlin, 1969.

Chay, Jongsuk, ed. *Culture and International Relations*. New York: Praeger, 1990.

Chotiner, Barbara Ann, and John W. Atwell. "Soviet Occupation Policy toward Germany, 1945–1949." In *U.S. Occupation in Europe after World War II: Papers and Reminiscences from the April 23–24, 1976, Conference Held at the George C. Marshall Research Foundation, Lexington, Virginia*, ed. Hans A. Schmitt, 45–63. Lawrence: Regents Press of Kansas, 1978.

Claude, Inis L., Jr. "American Values and Multinational Institutions." In *Institutions for Projecting American Values Abroad*, ed. Kenneth W. Thompson, 9–1 to 9–9. Lanham, Md.: University Press of America, 1983.

Clay, Lucius D. *Decision in Germany.* Garden City, N.Y.: Doubleday, 1950.

———. "Proconsuls of a People, by Another People, for Both People." *Americans as Proconsuls: United States Military Government in Germany and Japan, 1944–1952,* ed. by Robert D. Wolfe, 103–13. Carbondale: Southern Illinois University Press, 1984.

Cook, Blanche Wiesen. "First Comes the Lie: C. D. Jackson and Political Warfare." *Radical History Review* 31 (1984): 42–71.

Cooper, Laura E., and Cooper B. Lee. "The Pendulum of Cultural Imperialism: Popular Music Interchanges Between the United States and Britain, 1943–1967." *Journal of Popular Culture* 27 (Winter 1993): 61–78.

Cowley, Malcolm. *Exile's Return: A Literary Odyssey of the 1920s.* London: Penguin Books, 1976.

Crossmann, Richard. "Psychological Warfare." *The Journal of the Royal United Service Institution* 587 (August 1952): 329.

Daugherty, William E. *A Psychological Warfare Casebook.* 4th ed. Baltimore: Johns Hopkins University Press, 1968.

Dinnerstein, Leonard. *Uneasy at Home: Antisemitism and the American Jewish Experience.* New York: Columbia University Press, 1987.

Dobkowski, Michael N. *The Tarnished Dream: The Basis of American Anti-Semitism.* Westport, Conn.: Greenwood Press, 1979.

Duignan, Peter. *The Rebirth of the West: The Americanization of the Democratic World.* Lanham, Md.: Rowman & Littlefield, 1996.

Dultz, Wilhelm. "Unpolitische Demokratie." *Einheit: Theoretische Zeitschrift des wissenschaftlichen Sozialismus* 2, no. 8 (August 1947): 798–800.

Eisenberg, Carolyn. "U.S. Policy in Post-War Germany: The Conservative Restoration." *Science & Sociology* 46 (Spring 1982): 24–38.

Eisenhower, Dwight D. *The Papers of Dwight David Eisenhower.* Ed. Alfred D. Chandler, Jr., and Louis Galambos. Baltimore: Johns Hopkins University Press, 1978.

Elson, Robert T. *The World of Time, Inc.: The Intimate History of a Publishing Enterprise.* New York: Atheneum, 1973.

Enderle, Luiselotte. *Erich Kästner.* Munich: Rowohlt, 1966.

Farago, Ladislas. *War of Wits: The Anatomy of Espionage and Intelligence.* New York: Funk & Wagnalls, 1954.

Fehrenbach, Heide. *Cinema in Democratizing Germany: Reconstructing National Identity after Hitler.* Chapel Hill: University of North Carolina Press, 1995.

Fiebig-von Hase, and Ursula Lehmkuhl, ed. *Enemy Images in American History.* Providence, R.I.: Berghahn Books, 1997.

Fischer, Heinz-Dietrich. *Parteien und Presse in Deutschland seit 1945.* Mainz: Schünemann Universitätsverlag, 1971.

———. *Reeducations- und Pressepolitik unter britischem Besatzungsstatus: Die Zo-*

*nenzeitung* Die Welt, *1946–1950. Konzeption, Artikulation, und Rezeption.* Düsseldorf: Droste, 1978.

Ford, Emmet B. "Diplomacy and the Transmission of Values." In *Institutions for Projecting American Values Abroad,* ed. by Kenneth W. Thompson, 11-1 to 11-8. Lanham, Md.: University Press of America, 1983.

Frei, Norbert. *Amerikanische Lizenzpolitik und deutsche Pressetradition: Die Geschichte der Nachkriegszeitung* Südost-Kurier. Munich: Oldenbourg. 1986.

———. "Die Presse." In *Die Bundesrepublik Deutschland: Geschichte in drei Bänden,* ed. Wolfgang Benz, 3: 275–318. Frankfurt: Fischer Taschenbuch Verlag, 1983.

Frei, Norbert, and Johannes Schmitz. *Journalismus im Dritten Reich.* Munich: Becksche Reihe, 1989.

Frevert, Ute. *Frauengeschichte: Zwischen Bürgerlicher Verbesserung und Neuer Weiblichkeit.* Frankfurt: Suhrkamp Verlag, 1986.

Freyburg, W. Joachim, and Hans Wallenberg, eds. *Hundert Jahre Ullstein, 1877–1977.* Berlin: Ullstein, 1977.

Frohner, Gesine. "Die *Allgemeine Zeitung:* Portrait einer Zeitung für die Berliner Bevölkerung." Master's thesis, Freie Universität Berlin, 1966.

Füssl, Karl-Heinz. *Die Umerziehung der Deutschen: Jugend und Schule unter den Siegermächten des Zweiten Weltkriegs, 1945–1955.* Paderborn: Schöningh, 1994.

Gans, Herbert J. *Popular Culture and High Culture: An Analysis and Evaluation of Taste.* New York: Basic Books, 1974.

Garaty, John A., ed. *Dictionary of American Biography.* Supplement six. New York: Scribner's, 1980.

Gassert, Philipp. *Amerika im Dritten Reich: Ideologie, Propaganda, und Volksmeinung.* Stuttgart: Franz Steiner Verlag, 1997.

Gehring, Hansjörg. *Amerikanische Literaturpolitik in Deutschland, 1945–1953: Ein Aspekt des Reeducationsprogramms.* Stuttgart: Deutsche Verlags-Anstalt, 1976.

Gelberg, Karl-Ulrich, ed. *Kriegsende und Neuanfang in Augsburg 1945: Erinnerungen und Berichte.* Munich: Oldenbourg Verlag, 1996.

Gerhart, Eugen C. *America's Advocate: Robert H. Jackson.* Indianapolis, Ind.: Bobbs-Merril, 1958.

Gerhardt, Gunther. *Das Krisenmanagement der Vereinigten Staaten während der Berliner Blockade, 1948/1949: Intentionen, Strategien und Wirkungen.* Berlin: Duncker & Humblot, 1984.

Gienow, Jessica C. E. "Cultural Transmission and the U.S. Occupation in Germany: The *Neue Zeitung*, 1945–55." Ph.D. dissertation, University of Virginia, Charlottesville, 1995.

———. "Wer jetzt Luftschlösser baut, gehört übers Knie gelegt." *Frankfurter Allgemeine Zeitung* 242 (18 October 1995): 45.

Gienow-Hecht, Jessica C. E. "When Spengler Saw Jefferson: The U.S. Army Newspaper *Neue Zeitung* and the Image of America in Postwar Germany, 1945–1947." In *Faces in the Mirror: American and European Reciprocal National Invention,* ed. Stephen Fender, 89–109. Keele, U.K.: Keele University Press, 1996.

———. "Trial by Fire: Newspaper Coverage of the Nuremberg Trial, 1945–46." In *Studies in Periodical and Newspaper History 1995 Annual,* ed. Michael Harris and Tom O'Malley, 167–83. Westport, Conn.: Greenwood Press, 1997.

———. "Anti-Communism and Other Enemy Images in the U.S. Occupation of Germany, 1947–48." In *Enemy Images in American History,* ed. Ragnhild Fiebig-von Hase and Ursula Lehmkuhl, 281–300. Providence, R.I.: Berghahn Books, 1997.

———. "U.S. Cultural Policy towards the Federal Republic of Germany, 1949–1968." In *The United States and Germany in the Era of the Cold War,* ed. Detlef Junker. Cambridge, Mass.: Cambridge University Press, forthcoming.

———. "Art Is Democracy and Democracy Is Art: Culture, Propaganda, and the *Neue Zeitung* in Germany, 1944–1947," *Diplomatic History,* 23 (Winter 1999): 21–43.

Gimbel, John. *The American Occupation of Germany: Politics and the Military, 1945–1949.* Stanford, Calif.: Stanford University Press, 1968.

Gossel, Daniel A. *Die Hamburger Presse nach dem Zweiten Weltkrieg: Neuanfang unter britischer Besatzungsherrschaft.* Hamburg: Verlag Verein für Hamburgische Geschichte, 1993.

Graml, Hermann. "Die Außenpolitik." In *Die Bundesrepublik Deutschland,* ed. Wolfgang Benz, 1:331–77. Frankfurt: Fischer Taschenbuch, 1983.

Grazia, Victoria de. "Mass Culture and Sovereignty: The American Challenge to European Cinemas, 1920–1960," *Journal of Modern History* 61, no. 1 (March 1989): 53–87.

Grebing, Helga. "Die Parteien." In *Die Bundesrepublik Deutschland,* ed. by Wolfgang Benz, 1: 126–91. Frankfurt: Fischer Taschenbuch Verlag, 1983.

Green, Fitzhugh. *American Propaganda Abroad.* New York: Hippocrene Books, 1988.

Griffith, Robert. *The Politics of Fear: Joseph R. McCarthy and the Senate.* Lexington, Ky.: University Press of Kentucky, 1970.

Gross, Franz B. "Freedom of the Press and Military Government in Western Germany: The Origins and Developments of the New German Press, 1945–49." Ph.D. dissertation, Harvard University, 1952.

Grothe, Peter. *To Win the Minds of Men: The Story of the Communist Propaganda War in East Germany.* Palo Alto, Calif.: Pacific Books, 1958.

Gulgowski, Paul W. *The American Military Government of United States Occupied Zones of Post World War II Germany in Relation to Policies Expressed by Its Civilian Governmental Authorities at Home, During the Course of 1944/45 Through 1949.* Frankfurt: Haag + Herchen Verlag, 1983.

Gurevich, Pavel. *Dialogue of Culture or Cultural Expansion?* Moscow: Progress Publishers, 1990.

Habe, Hans. *A Thousand Shall Fall.* New York: Harcourt, Brace, 1941.

———. *Our Love Affair with Germany.* New York: Putnam's, 1953.

———. *Ich stelle mich.* Vienna: Verlag Kurt Desch, 1955.

———. *Off Limits: A Novel of Occupied Germany.* London: Harrap, 1956.

———. *Im Jahre Null: Ein Beitrag zur Geschichte der deutschen Presse.* Munich: Verlag Kurt Desch, 1966.

Habermas, Jürgen. *Zur Logik der Sozialwissenschaften: Materialien.* Frankfurt: Suhrkamp, 1970.

Hagemann, Walter. *Publizistik im Dritten Reich: Ein Beitrag zur Methodik der Massenführung.* Hamburg: Hansischer Gildenverlag, 1948.

Hale, Oron J. *The Captive Press in the Third Reich.* Princeton, N.J.: Princeton University Press, 1964.

Harenberg, Karl-Heinz. "*Die Welt:* Eine deutsche oder eine britische Zeitung?" Ph.D. dissertation, Universität Hamburg, 1976.

Hay, Gerhard. "Literarische Positionen im München der Nachkriegszeit." In *Trümmerzeit in München: Kultur und Gesellschaft einer deutschen Großstadt im Aufbruch, 1945–1949,* ed. by Friedrich Prinz, 209–219. Munich: C. H. Beck, 1984.

Heald, Morrell, and Lawrence S. Kaplan. *Culture and Diplomacy: The American Experience.* Westport, Conn.: Greenwood Press, 1977.

Heideking, Jürgen, and Christof Mauch, eds. *Geheimdienstkrieg gegen Deutschland: Subversion, Propaganda und politische Planungen des amerikanischen Geheimdienstes im Zweiten Weltkrieg.* Göttingen: Vandenhoeck & Ruprecht, 1993.

Heinemann, Manfred, ed. *Umerziehung und Wiederaufbau: Die Bildungspolitik der Besatzungsmächte in Deutschland und Österreich.* Stuttgart: Klett-Cotta, 1981.

Hein-Kremer, Maritta. *Die amerikanische Kulturoffensive: Gründung und Entwicklung der amerikanischen Information Center in Westdeutschland und West-Berlin, 1945–1955.* Cologne: Böhlau, 1996.

Henke, Klaus-Dietmar, and Hans Woller. *Politische Säuberung in Europa: Die Abrechnung mit Faschismus und Kollaboration nach dem Zweiten Weltkrieg.* Munich: Deutscher Taschenbuchverlag, 1991.

Herbet, Dominique. *Die Neue Zeitung: Un journal américaine pour la population allemande, 1945–1949.* Villeneuve-d'Aseq: Presses universitaires du Septentrion, 1997.

Hermand, Jost. *Die Kultur der Bundesrepublik Deutschland, 1965–85.* Munich: Nymphenburger Verlagsbuchhandlung, 1986.

Herzfeld, Hans. *Berlin in der Weltpolitik, 1945–1970.* Berlin: Walter de Gruyter, 1973.

Herzstein, Robert E. *Roosevelt and Hitler: Prelude To War.* New York: Paragon House, 1989.

Heym, Stefan. *The Crusaders.* Boston: Little, Brown, 1948.

———. *Reden an den Feind.* Ed. Peter Mallwitz. Munich: Bertelsmann, 1986.

———. *Nachruf.* Munich: Bertelsmann Verlag, 1988.

———. "Schreiben Sie Was, Wann, Wo und Warum!" In *Das Undenkbare denken: Festschrift für Egon Bahr zum siebzigsten Geburtstag*, ed. Dieter S. Lutz, 65–67. Baden-Baden: Nomos Verlagsgesellschaft, 1992.

Hobbing, Enno. *How to Act and Talk Like A College Graduate in Eleven Days.* Bethesda, Md.: Stone Trail Press, 1986.

Hobsbawm, Eric J. "Kultur als Ghetto." In *"Kultur-Zerstörung"? Zehnte Römerberggespräche in Frankfurt a. M.*, ed. Hilmar Hoffmann, 60–69. Königstein/Ts.: Athenäum, 1983.

Hogan, Michael J. *The Marshall Plan: America, Britain, and the Reconstruction of Western Europe, 1947–1952.* Cambridge: Cambridge University Press, 1987.

Hunt, Michael H. *Ideology and U.S. Foreign Policy.* New Haven: Yale University Press, 1987.

———. *American Foreign Policy and American Values.* Chicago: Peacock, 1988.

Huntington, Samuel. *American Politics: The Promise of Disharmony.* Cambridge, Mass.: Belknap Press, 1981.

Hurwitz, Harold J. *Die Stunde Null der deutschen Presse: Die amerikanische Pressepolitik in Deutschland, 1945–1949.* Cologne: Verlag Wissenschaft und Politik, 1972.

———. "Antikommunismus und amerikanische Demokratisierungsvorhaben in Deutschland." *Aus Politik und Zeitgeschichte* 29 (1978): 29–46.

———. *Die Eintracht der Siegermächte und die Orientierungsnot der Deutschen, 1945–1946.* Cologne: Verlag für Wissenschaft und Politik, 1984.

———. *Demokratie und Antikommunismus in Berlin nach 1945.* Vol. 2, *Die Anfänge des Widerstands.* Cologne: Verlag Wissenschaft und Politik, 1990.

Huster, Ernst-Ulrich, et al., eds. *Determinanten der westdeutschen Restauration, 1945–1949.* Frankfurt: Suhrkamp, 1972.

Hutchinson, Peter. *Stefan Heym: The Perpetual Dissident.* Cambridge: Cambridge University Press, 1992.

*Internationales Biographisches Archiv/Munzinger Archiv.* Ravensburg: Archiv für publizistische Arbeit, Munzinger Archiv, 1949ff.

Iriye, Akira. "Culture and Power: International Relations and Intercultural Relations." *Diplomatic History* 10 (Spring 1979): 115–28.

———. *Power and Culture: The Japanese-American War, 1941–1945.* Cambridge, Mass.: Harvard University Press, 1981.

Jacoby, Wade. "The Politics of Institutional Transfer: Two Postwar Reconstructions in Germany, 1945–1995." Ph.D. dissertation, Massachusetts Institute of Technology, Cambridge, 1996.

Jäger, Georg. *Schule und literarische Kultur.* Stuttgart: J. B. Metzlersche Verlagsbuchhandlung, 1981.

Jaher, Frederic Cople. *A Scapegoat in the New Wilderness: The Origins and Rise of Anti-Semitism in America.* Cambridge, Mass.: Harvard University Press, 1994.

Joseph, Franz M., and Raymond Aron, eds. *As Others See Us: The United States Through Foreign Eyes.* Princeton, N.J.: Princeton University Press, 1959.

Junker, Detlev. "Hitler's Perception of Franklin D. Roosevelt and the United States of America." In *FDR and His Contemporaries: Foreign Perceptions of an American President,* ed. Cornelis A. van Minnen and John F. Sears, 145–56. New York: St. Martin's Press, 1992.

Kaenel, André, ed. *Anticommunism and McCarthyism in the United States, 1954: Essays on the Politics and Culture of the Cold War.* Paris: Edition Messene, 1995.

Kästner, Erich. *Der tägliche Kram: Chansons und Prosa, 1945–1948.* Zurich: Atrium, 1949.

———. *Notabene 45: Ein Tagebuch von Erich Kästner.* Berlin: Cecilia Dressler Verlag, 1961.

———. *Mein liebes, gutes Muttchen, Du! Briefe und Postkarten aus 30 Jahren.* Hamburg: Albrecht Knaus, 1981.

Kater, Michael. "Forbidden Fruit? Jazz in the Third Reich." *American Historical Review* 94, no. 1 (February 1989): 11–43.

Katz, Barry. *Foreign Intelligence: Research and Analysis in the Office of Strategic Services, 1942–1945.* Cambridge, Mass.: Harvard University Press, 1989.

Kellermann, Henry. "Von Re-education zu Re-orientation: Das amerikanische Reorientierungsprogramm im Nachkriegsdeutschland." In *Umerziehung und Wiederaufbau: Die Bildungspolitik der Besatzungsmächte in Deutschland und Österreich,* ed. Manfred Heinemann, 86–102. Frankfurt: Klett-Cotta, 1981.

Kim, Kyong-Kun. "Die *Neue Zeitung* im Dienste der Reeducation für die deutsche Bevölkerung, 1945–1946." Ph.D. dissertation, Ludwig-Maximilians-Universität, Munich, 1974.

Köbner, Thomas, und Erwin Rotermund, eds. *Rückkehr aus dem Exil: Emigranten aus dem Dritten Reich in Deutschland nach 1945. Essays zu Ehren von Ernst Loewy.* Marburg: Druckerei Wenzel, 1990.

Kolbenhoff, Walter. *Von unserm Fleisch und Blut.* Munich: Nymphenburger Verlag, 1947.

———. *Heimkehr in die Fremde.* Munich: Nymphenburger Verlag, 1949. Reprint, Frankfurt: Suhrkamp Verlag, 1988.

———. *Schellingstraße 48: Erfahrungen mit Deutschland.* Frankfurt: Fischer Taschenbuch Verlag, 1984.

Kontje, Todd Curtis. *The German Bildungsroman: History of a National Genre.* Columbia, S.C.: Camden House, 1993.

Kordon, Klaus. *Die Zeit ist kaputt: Die Lebensgeschichte des Erich Kästner.* Weinheim: Beltz & Gelberg Verlag, 1995.

Kostuch, Gerhart, and Franz Kröger. *Germany Seen Through British and American Eyes.* Frankfurt: Moritz Diesterweg, 1969.

Koszyk, Kurt. *Kontinuität oder Neubeginn? Massenkommunikation in Deutschland, 1945–1949.* Ed. Forschungsschwerpunkt Massenmedien und Kommunikation. Siegen: Universität-Gesamthochschule Siegen, 1981.

———. *Pressepolitik für Deutsche, 1945–1949: Geschichte der deutschen Presse.* Berlin: Colloquium Verlag, 1986.

Kraske, Gary E. *Missionaries of the Book: The American Library Profession and the Origins of Cultural Diplomacy.* London: Greenwood Press, 1985.

Kraus, Max W. *They All Come to Geneva and Other Tales of a Public Diplomat.* Cabin John, Md.: Seven Locks Press, 1988.

Krauss, Marita. *Nachkriegskultur in München: Münchener städtische Kulturpolitik, 1945–1954.* Munich: Oldenbourg, 1985.

Krieger, Wolfgang. *General Lucius D. Clay und die amerikanische Deutschlandpolitik, 1945–1949.* Stuttgart: Klett-Cotta, 1987.

Kroes, Rob. *If You've Seen One, You've Seen the Mall: European and American Mass Culture.* Urbana: University of Illinois Press, 1996.

———, Robert W. Rydell, and Doeko F. J. Bosscher, eds. *Cultural Transmissions and Receptions: American Mass Culture in Europe.* Amsterdam: VU University Press, 1993.

Krohn, Claus-Dieter, Erwin Rotermund, Lutz Winckler, and Wulf Koepke, eds. *Exil und Remigration.* Munich: edition text + kritik, 1991.

Kuisel, Richard F. *Seducing the French: The Dilemma of Americanization.* Berkeley: University of California Press, 1993.

Kuklick, Bruce. *American Policy and the Division of Germany: The Clash with Russia over Reparations.* Ithaca, N.Y.: Cornell University Press, 1972.

Kurz, Jan. *"Swinging Democracy": Jugendprotest im 3. Reich.* Münster: Lit Verlag, 1995.

Lange-Quassowski, Jutta B. "Amerikanische Westintegrationspolitik, Reeducation, and deutsche Schulpolitik." In *Umerziehung und Wiederaufbau: Die Bildungspolitik der Besatzungsmächte in Deutschland und Österreich,* ed. Manfred Heinemann, 53–67. Frankfurt: Klett-Cotta, 1981.

———. *Neuordnung oder Restauration: Das Demokratiekonzept der amerikanischen Besatzungsmacht und die politische Sozialisation der Westdeutschen. Wirtschaftsordnung—Schulstruktur—Politische Ordnung?* Opladen: Leske Verlag + Buderich, 1979.

Lederer, William J., and Eugene Burdick. *The Ugly American.* New York: Norton, 1958.

Leffler, Melvyn P. *A Preponderance of Power: National Security, the Truman Administration, and the Cold War.* Stanford, Calif.: Stanford University Press, 1992.

———. *The Specter of Communism: The United States and the Origins of the Cold War, 1917–1953.* New York: Hill & Wang, 1994.

Lerner, Daniel. *Psychological Warfare Against Nazi-Germany: The Sykewar Campaign, D-Day to VE-Day.* 2d ed. Cambridge, Mass.: M.I.T. Press, 1971.

———, ed. *Propaganda in War and Crisis: Materials for American Policy.* New York: George W. Stewart, 1951.

Levin, Lawrence W. *Highbrow/Lowbrow: The Emergence of Cultural Hierarchy in America.* Cambridge, Mass.: Harvard University Press, 1988.

Lewis, Rand C. *A Nazi Legacy: Right-Wing Extremism in Postwar Germany.* New York: Praeger, 1991.

Lewison, Robert. "Education for What?" In *This Is Germany,* ed. Arthur Settel, 89–115. New York: Sloane, 1950.

Liedtke, Rüdiger. *Die verschenkte Presse: Die Geschichte der Lizensierung von Zeitungen nach 1945.* Berlin: Verlag für Ausbildung und Studien in der Elefanten Press, 1982.

Litchfield, Edward, et al., eds. *Governing Postwar Germany.* Ithaca, N.Y.: Cornell University Press, 1953.

Loth, Wilfried. *Stalins ungeliebtes Kind: Warum Moskau die DDR nicht wollte.* Berlin: Rowohlt Berlin, 1994.

Luft, Friedrich. *Die Stimme der Kritik: Gespräch mit Hans-Christoph Knebusch in der Reihe "Zeugen des Jahrhunderts."* Göttingen: Lamuv Verlag, 1991.

Lundestad, Geir. *The American "Empire" and Other Studies of U.S. Foreign Policy in a Comparative Perspective.* Oxford: Oxford University Press/Oslo: Norwegian University Press, 1990.

Lutz, Dieter S. *Das Undenkbare denken: Festschrift für Egon Bahr zum siebzigsten Geburtstag.* Baden-Baden: Nomos Verlagsgesellschaft, 1992.

Maase, Kaspar. *Bravo America: Erkundigungen zur Jugendkultur der Bundesrepublik in den fünfziger Jahren.* Hamburg: Junius Verlag, 1992.

McAuliffe, Mary Sperlin. *Crisis on the Left: Cold War Politics and American Liberals, 1947–1954.* Amherst: University of Massachusetts Press, 1978.

McClellan, Woodford. *Russia: The Soviet Period and After.* 3d ed. Englewood Cliffs, N.J.: Prentice Hall, 1994.

Maier, Charles S. *In Search of Stability: Explorations in Historical Political Economy.* New Rochelle, N.Y.: Cambridge University Press, 1987.

———, and Günther Bischof, eds. *The Marshall Plan and Germany: West German Development within the Framework of the European Recovery Program.* New York: Berg, 1991.

Matz, Elisabeth. *Die Zeitungen der US-Armee für die deutsche Bevölkerung, 1944–1946.* Münster: Verlag Fahle, 1969.

May, Elaine Tyler. *Homeward Bound: American Families During the Cold War Era.* New York: Basic Books, 1988.

May, Lary, ed. *Recasting America: Culture and Politics in the Age of Cold War.* Chicago: University of Chicago Press, 1989.

Menck, Clara. "The Problem of Reorientation." In *The Struggle for Democracy in Germany,* ed. Gabriel A. Almond, 281–307. Chapel Hill: University of North Carolina Press, 1949.

Merritt, Anna J., and Richard L. Merritt. *Public Opinion in Occupied Germany: The OMGUS Surveys, 1945–1949*. Urbana: University of Illinois Press, 1970.

Merritt, Richard L. *Democracy Imposed: U.S. Occupation Policy and the German Public, 1945–1949*. New Haven: Yale University Press, 1995.

Messer, Robert L. *The End of an Alliance: James F. Byrnes, Roosevelt, Truman, and the Origins of the Cold War*. Chapel Hill: University of North Carolina Press, 1982.

Mettler, Barbara. *Demokratisierung und Kalter Krieg: Zur amerikanischen Informations- und Rundfunkpolitik in Westdeutschland, 1945–1949*. Berlin: Verlag Volker Spiess, 1975.

Milward, Alan S. *The Reconstruction of Western Europe, 1945–51*. London: Methuen, 1984.

Minnen, Cornelis A. van, and John F. Sears. *FDR and His Contemporaries: Foreign Perceptions of an American President*. New York: St. Martin's Press, 1992.

Moeller, Robert G. *Protecting Motherhood: Women and the Family in the Politics of Postwar West Germany*. Berkeley: University of California Press, 1993.

Molnar, Thomas. *The Emerging American Culture*. New Brunswick: Transaction Publishers, 1994.

Montgomery, John D. *Forced To Be Free: The Artificial Revolution in Germany and Japan*. Chicago: University of Chicago, 1957.

Mosberg, Helmuth. *Reeducation: Umerziehung und Lizenzpresse im Nachkriegsdeutschland*. Munich: Universitas, 1991.

Mosse, George L. *German Jews Beyond Judaism*. Bloomington: Indiana University Press, 1985.

———. "The End Is Not Yet: A Personal Memoir of the German-Jewish Legacy in America." In *The German-Jewish Legacy in America, 1938–1988: From Bildung to the Bill of Rights*, ed. Abraham J. Peck, 11–15. Detroit: Wayne State University Press, 1989.

Müller, Guido, ed. *Deutschland und der Westen: Festschrift für Klaus Schwabe zum 65. Geburtstag*. Stuttgart: Franz Steiner Verlag, 1998.

Müller, Hans Dieter. *Der Springer-Konzern*. Munich: Piper, 1968.

Müller, Winfried. *Schulpolitik in Bayern im Spannungsfeld von Kultusbürokratie und Besatzungsmacht, 1945–1949*. Munich: Oldenbourg, 1995.

Murphy, Robert. *Diplomat Among Warriors*. Garden City, N.Y.: Doubleday, 1964.

Naimark, Norman M. "The Soviet Gulag in Eastern Germany, 1945–50." In *The Soviet Empire Reconsidered: Essays in Honor of Adam B. Ulam*, ed. Sanford R. Lieberman, David E. Powell, Carol Saivetz, and Sarah M. Terry, 69–92. Boulder, Colo.: Westview Press, 1994.

———. *The Russians in Germany: A History of the Soviet Zone of Occupation, 1945–1949*. Cambridge, Mass.: Belknap Press, 1995.

Nelson, Kenneth-Raymond. "United States Occupation Policy and the Establishment of a Democratic Newspaper Press in Bavaria, 1945–1949." Ph.D. dissertation, University of Virginia, Charlottesville, 1966.

Netzer, Hans-Joachim. "Die *Neue Zeitung*." *Gazette: Internationale Zeitschrift für Zeitungswissenschaft* 2, no. 1 (Leiden), 1956.

Niethammer, Lutz. *Entnazifizierung in Bayern: Säuberung und Rehabilitierung unter amerikanischer Besatzung*. Frankfurt: Fischer, 1972.

Ninkovich, Frank. "The Currents of Cultural Diplomacy: Art and the State Department." *Diplomatic History* 1 (summer 1977): 215–37.

———. *The Diplomacy of Ideas: U.S. Foreign Policy and Cultural Relations, 1938–1950*. Cambridge: Cambridge University Press, 1981.

Nolan, Mary. *Visions of Modernity: American Business and the Modernization of Germany*. New York: Oxford University Press, 1994.

Norman, Albert. *Our German Policy: Propaganda and Culture*. New York: Vantage Press, 1951.

Oshinsky, David M. *A Conspiracy So Immense: The World of Joe McCarthy*. New York: Free Press, 1983.

Paddock, Alfred H. *U.S. Army Special Warfare: Its Origins: Psychological and Unconventional Warfare*. Washington, D.C.: National Defense University, 1982.

Paley, William S. *As It Happened: A Memoir*. Garden City, N.Y.: Doubleday, 1979.

Paper, Lewis J. *Empire: William S. Paley and the Making of CBS*. New York: St. Martin's Press, 1987.

Pauley, Bruce F. *Hahnenschwanz und Hakenkreuz: Der Steirische Heimatschutz und der österreichische Nationalsozialismus, 1918–1934*. Trans. Peter Aschner. Vienna: Europaverlag, 1972.

———. *Hitler and the Forgotten Nazis: A History of Austrian National Socialism*. Chapel Hill: University of North Carolina Press, 1981.

———. *Eine Geschichte des österreichischen Antisemitismus: Von der Ausgrenzung zur Auslöschung*. Trans. Helga Zoglmann. Vienna: Kremayr & Scheriau, 1993.

Peck, Abraham J., ed. *The German-Jewish Legacy in America, 1938–1988: From Bildung to the Bill of Rights*. Detroit: Wayne State University Press, 1989.

Pells, Richard. "American Culture Abroad: The European Experience Since 1945." In *Cultural Transmissions and Receptions: American Mass Culture in Europe*, ed. Rob Kroes, Robert W. Rydell, and Doeko F. J. Bosscher, 67–83. Amsterdam: VU University Press, 1993.

———. *Not Like Us: How Europeans Have Loved, Hated, and Transformed American Culture Since World War II*. New York: Basic Books, 1997.

Peterson, Edward. *The Many Faces of Defeat: The German People's Experience in 1945*. New York: Peter Lang, 1990.

Petras, James. "Cultural Imperialism in the Late 20th Century." *Journal of Contemporary Asia* 23 (1993): 139–48.

Pfanner, Helmut F. *Der Zweite Weltkrieg und die Exilanten: Eine literarische Antwort*. Bonn: Bouvier, 1991.

Pike, David. *The Politics of Culture in Soviet-Occupied Germany, 1945–1949*. Stanford, Calif.: Stanford University Press, 1992.

Pittenger, Benjamin Floyd. *Indoctrination for American Democracy*. New York: Macmillan, 1941.

Poiger, Uta G. "Rock'n Roll, Kalter Krieg, und deutsche Identität." In *Amerikanisierung und Sowjetisierung in Deutschland, 1945–1970*, ed. Konrad H. Jarausch and Hannes Siegrist, 275–89. Frankfurt: Campus, 1996.

Pronay, Nicholas, and Keith Wison, eds. *The Political Re-education of Germany and Her Allies After World War II*. London: Croom Helm, 1985.

Radkau, Joachim. *Die deutsche Emigration in den USA: Ihr Einfluß auf die amerikanische Europapolitik, 1933–1945*. Düsseldorf: Bertelsmann, 1971.

Raue, Günter. *Im Dienste der Wahrheit: Ein Beitrag zur Pressepolitik der sowjetischen Besatzungsmacht, 1945–1949*. Leipzig: Karl-Marx-Universität, 1966.

Rauhut, Franz. "Die Herkunft der Worte und Begriffe 'Kultur,' 'Civilisation,' und 'Bildung.' " *Germanisch-Romanische Monatsschrift* 3 (April 1953): 81–91.

Reinhardt, Stephan. *Alfred Andersch: Eine Biographie*. Zurich: Diogenes Verlag, 1990.

Roebling, Irmgard, und Wolfram Mauser, eds. *Mutter und Mütterlichkeit: Wandel und Wirksamkeit einer Phantasie in der deutschen Literatur. Festschrift für Verena Ehrich Haefeli*. Würzburg: Königshausen & Neumann, 1996.

Rolin, Roger, ed. *The Americanization of the Global Village: Essays in Comparative Popular Culture*. Bowling Green, Ohio: Bowling Green State University Popular Press, 1989.

Rollberg, Sabine. "Von der Wiederauferstehung des deutschen Geistes: Eine Analyse des Feuilletons der *Neuen Zeitung*, 1945–1949." Ph.D. dissertation, Albert-Ludwig-Universität, Freiburg, 1981.

Roloff, Gerhard. *Exil und Exilliteratur in der deutschen Presse, 1945–1949: Ein Beitrag zur Rezeptionsgeschichte*. Worms: Heintz, 1976.

Rosenberg, Emily S. *Spreading the American Dream: American Economic and Cultural Expansion, 1890–1945*. New York: Hill & Wang, 1982.

Roth, Maren. "Zur Problematik der Reeducation in Bayern (mit Methoden der Oral History): Politischer Anspruch und Schulrealität. Das Beispiel des Theresien-Gymnasiums in München." Master's thesis, Ludwig-Maximilians-Universitat, Munich, 1996.

Ruhl, Klaus-Jörg. *Die Besatzer und die Deutschen: Amerikanische Zone, 1945–1948*. Düsseldorf: Droste, 1980.

Rupieper, Hermann-Josef. "Bringing Democracy to the Frauleins: Frauen als Zielgruppe der amerikanischen Demokratisierungspolitik in Deutschland, 1945–1952." *Geschichte und Gesellschaft* 17 (1991): 61–91.

———. *Die Wurzeln der westdeutschen Nachkriegsdemokratie: Der amerikanische Beitrag, 1945–1952*. Opladen: Westdeutscher Verlag, 1993.

———. " 'To Solidify the Bond of Friendship between our Nation and Germany': Die amerikanische Katholische Kirche in Nachkriegsdeutschland." In *Deutschland und der Westen: Festschrift für Klaus Schwabe zum 65. Geburtstag,* ed. Guido Müller, 220–26. Stuttgart: Franz Steiner Verlag, 1998.

Saldern, Adelheid von. "Überfremdungsängste: Gegen die Amerikanisierung der deutschen Kultur in den zwanziger Jahren." In *Amerikanisierung: Traum und Alptraum im Deutschland des 20. Jahrhunderts,* ed. Alf Lüdtke, Inge Marßolek, and Adelheid von Saldern, 213–44. Stuttgart: Franz Steiner Verlag, 1996.

Salentin, Ursula. *Hildegard Hamm-Brücher: Der Lebensweg einer eigenwilligen Demokratin.* Freiburg i. Br.: Herderbücherei, 1987.

Santis, Hugh De. *The Diplomacy of Silence: The American Foreign Service, the Soviet Union, and the Cold War, 1933–1947.* Chicago: University of Chicago Press, 1980.

Schäfer, Hans Dieter. *Das gespaltene Bewußtsein: Deutsche Kultur und Lebenswirklichkeit, 1933–1945.* 3d ed. Munich: Carl Hanser Verlag, 1983.

Schildt, Axel. *Moderne Zeiten: Freizeit, Massenmedien und "Zeitgeist" in der Bundesrepublik der 50er Jahre.* Hamburg: Christians, 1995.

Schiller, Herbert I. *Mass Communications and American Empire.* New York: Augustus M. Kelley, 1969.

———. *The Mind Managers.* Boston: Beacon Press, 1973.

———. *Communication and Cultural Domination.* White Plains, N.Y.: International Arts and Sciences Press, 1976.

———. *Culture Inc.: The Corporate Takeover of Public Expression.* New York: Oxford University Press, 1989.

Schlesinger, Stephen C., and Stephen Kinzer. *Bitter Fruit: The Untold Story of the American Coup in Guatemala.* Garden City, N.Y.: Doubleday, 1982.

Schmidt, Eberhard. *Die verhinderte Neuordnung, 1945–1952: Zur Auseinandersetzung um die Demokratisierung der Wirtschaft in den westlichen Besatzungszonen und in der Bundesrepublik Deutschland.* Frankfurt: Europäische Verlagsanstalt, 1970.

Schmidt, Maruta, and Gabi Dietz, eds. *Frauen unterm Hakenkreuz.* Berlin: Elefanten Press, 1983.

Schmitt, Hans A., ed. *U.S. Occupation in Europe after World War II: Papers and Reminiscences from the April 23–24, 1976, Conference Held At the George C. Marshall Research Foundation, Lexington, Virginia.* Lawrence: The Regents Press of Kansas, 1978.

Schmitz, Johannes. "DANA/DENA: Nachrichtenagentur in der amerikanisch besetzten Zone Deutschlands, 1945–1949." Master's thesis (Diplomarbeit), Ludwig-Maximilians-Universität, Munich, 1984.

Scholtz, Harald. *Erziehung und Unterricht unterm Hakenkreuz.* Göttingen: Vandenhoeck & Ruprecht, 1985.

Schwabe, Klaus. "German Policy Responses to the Marshall Plan." In *The Marshall Plan and Germany: West German Development within the Framework of the European Recovery Program,* ed. Charles Maier and Günther Bischof, 225–81. New York: Berg, 1991.

Schwartz, Thomas A. *America's Germany: John J. McCloy and the Federal Republic of Germany.* Cambridge, Mass.: Harvard University Press, 1991.

Schwarz, Hans-Peter. *Vom Reich zur Bundesrepublik: Deutschland im Widerstreit der außenpolitischen Konzeptionen in den Jahren der Besatzungsherrschaft, 1945–1949.* Neuwied: Luchterhand, 1966.

Selle, Gert. *Kultur der Sinne und ästhetische Erziehung: Alltag, Sozialisation, Kunstunterricht in Deutschland vom Kaiserreich zur Bundesrepublik.* Cologne: Dumont, 1981.

Settel, Arthur, ed. *This Is Germany.* New York: William Sloane, 1950.

Shlaim, Avi. *The United States and the Berlin Blockade, 1948–1949: A Study in Crisis Decision-Making.* Berkeley: University of California Press, 1983.

Smith, Bradley F. *Reaching Judgment at Nuremberg.* New York: Basic Books, 1977.

———. *The Shadow Warriors: O.S.S. and the Origins of the C.I.A.* New York: Basic Books, 1983.

Smith, Jean Edward. "The View from USFET: General Clay's and Washington's Interpretation of Soviet Intentions in Germany, 1945–48." In *U.S. Occupation in Europe after World War II: Papers and Reminiscences from the April 23–24, 1976, Conference Held At the George C. Marshall Research Foundation, Lexington, Virginia,* ed. Hans A. Schmitt, 64–85. Lawrence: Regents Press of Kansas, 1978.

———. *Lucius D. Clay: An American Biography.* New York: Holt, 1990.

Smith, Sally Bedell. *In All His Glory: The Life of William S. Paley, the Legendary Tycoon and His Brilliant Circle.* New York: Simon & Schuster, 1990.

Söllner, Alfons, ed. *Zur Archäologie der Demokratie in Deutschland.* 2 vols. Frankfurt: Europäische Verlagsanstalt, 1982.

Sorensen, Thomas C. *The Word War: The Story of American Propaganda.* New York: Harper & Row, 1968.

Sorkin, David J. *The Transformation of German Jewry, 1789–1840.* New York: Oxford University Press, 1987.

Steiner, Arthur. *Jeder lernt Englisch: Der populäre Sprachkurs der* Neuen Zeitung. Munich: Die Neue Zeitung, 1946.

Steininger, Rolf. *The German Question: The Stalin Note of 1952 and the Problem of Reunification.* New York: Columbia University Press, 1990.

Stern, Guy. "The Exiles and the War of Minds." In *Der Zweite Weltkrieg und die Exilanten: Eine literarische Antwort,* ed. Helmut F. Pfanner, 311–24. Bonn: Bouvier Verlag, 1991.

Storey, John. *An Introductory Guide to Cultural Theory and Popular Culture.* New York: Harvester/Wheatsheaf, 1993.

Strack, Manfred. "Amerikanische Kulturbeziehungen zu (West-)Deutschland, 1945–1955." *Zeitschrift für Kulturaustausch* 37 (1987): 283–300.

Strauss, Herbert A., and Werner Röder. *International Biographical Dictionary of Central European Emigrés, 1933–1945.* 2 vols. Munich: K. G. Saur, 1980–83.

Stuckenschmidt, Hans Heinz. *Zum Hören geboren: Ein Leben mit der Musik unserer Zeit.* Munich: Piper, 1979.

Swanberg, W. A. *Luce and His Empire.* New York: Scribner's, 1972.

Takahashi, Yuji. "The Resistance of the Asian Masses and Their Culture." *Perspectives of New Music* 30 (Summer 1992): 90–100.

Tent, James F. *Mission on the Rhine: Reeducation and Denazification in American-Occupied Germany.* Chicago: University of Chicago Press, 1982.

———. *The Free University of Berlin: A Political History.* Bloomington: Indiana University Press, 1988.

Thompson, Dorothy, and Rose Wilder Lane. *Dorothy Thompson and Rose Wilder Lane: Forty Years of Friendship: Letters, 1921–1960.* Ed. William Holtz. Columbia: University of Missouri Press, 1991.

Thompson, Kenneth W., ed. *Moral Dimensions of American Foreign Policy: Ethics in Foreign Policy Service.* New Brunswick, N.J.: Transaction Books, 1984.

———. *Institutions for Projecting American Values Abroad.* Lanham, Md.: University Press of America, 1983.

Thomson, James C., Jr., Peter W. Stanley, and John Curtis Perry. *Sentimental Imperialists: The American Experience in East Asia.* New York: Harper & Row, 1981.

Tjulpanov, Sergej. *Deutschland nach dem Kriege, 1945–1949: Erinnerungen eines Offiziers der Sowjetarmee.* Trans. and ed. Stefan Doernberg. 2d ed. Berlin: Dietz Verlag, 1987.

Tomlinson, John. *Cultural Imperialism: A Critical Introduction.* Baltimore: Johns Hopkins University Press, 1991.

Trampe, Gustav. *Die Stunde Null: Erinnerungen an Kriegsende und Neuanfang.* Stuttgart: Deutsche Verlags-Anstalt, 1995.

Tusa, Ann, and John Tusa. *The Nuremberg Trial.* Reprint. New York: Atheneum, 1984.

Vaillant, Jérôme. *Der Ruf: Unabhängige Blätter der jungen Generation, 1945–1949.* Munich: K. G. Saur, 1978.

Vollnhals, Clemens. *Evangelische Kirche und Entnazifizierung: Die Last der deutschen Vergangenheit.* Munich: Oldenbourg, 1989.

Wagnleitner, Reinhold. "The Irony of American Culture Abroad: Austria and the Cold War." In *Recasting America: Culture and Politics in the Age of the Cold War,* ed. Lary May, 285–301. Chicago: University of Chicago Press, 1989.

———. *Coca-Colanization and the Cold War: The Cultural Mission of the United States in Austria After the Second World War.* Trans. Diana M. Wolf. Chapel Hill: University of North Carolina Press, 1994.

Walker, R. B. J., "The Developing Role of Cultural Diplomacy in Asia." In *Issues and Conflicts: Studies in Twentieth-Century American Diplomacy*, ed. George L. Anderson, 43–62. Lawrence: University of Kansas Press, 1959.

Warburg, James P. *Germany: Bridge or Battleground.* London: Heinemann, 1947.

Wegwitz, Bettina. "Erich Kästner als Redakteur: Journalist der Nachkriegszeit für die *Neue Zeitung* und den *Pinguin.*" Master's thesis, Ludwig-Maximilians-Universität, Munich, 1989.

Wehner, Jens. "Zur politischen Kultur im Nachkriegsdeutschland: Die *Neue Zeitung* in den Jahren 1945–1949 (unter besonderer Berücksichtigung des Feuilletons unter der Leitung Erich Kästners)." Staatsexamensarbeit für das Lehramt an Gymnasien, n. p., 1981.

———. *Kulturpolitik und Volksfront: Ein Beitrag zur Geschichte der Sowjetischen Besatzungszone Deutschlands, 1945–1949.* Frankfurt: Peter Lang, 1992.

*Who's Who In America.* Vol. 1. Chicago: Marquis, 1968.

Whitton, John Boardman, ed. *Propaganda and the Cold War: A Princeton University Symposium.* Washington, D.C.: Public Affairs Press, 1963.

Williams, Raymond. *Culture and Society, 1780–1950.* New York: Columbia University Press, 1958.

Willett, Ralph. *The Americanization of Germany, 1945–1949.* London, New York: Routledge, 1989.

Winckler, Lutz. "Mythen der Exilforschung." In *Exilforschung: Ein Internationales Jahrbuch.* Vol. 13, *Kulturtransfer im Exil*, ed. Claus-Dieter Krohn, Erwin Rotermund, Lutz Winckler, and Wulf Koepke, 68–81. Munich: edition text + kritik, 1995.

Winkie, Joy Darlene. "A Study of the United States Information and Propaganda Activities in the Federal Republic of Germany." Master's thesis, University of Minnesota, Minneapolis, 1958.

Wistrich, Robert S. *Antisemitism: The Longest Hatred.* New York: Pantheon Books, 1991.

Wolfe, Robert D. *Americans as Proconsuls: United States Military Government in Germany and Japan, 1944–1952.* Carbondale: Southern Illinois University Press, 1984.

Wuermeling, Henric L. *Die weiße Liste: Umbruch der politischen Kultur in Deutschland 1945.* Frankfurt: Ullstein, 1981.

Wyden, Peter. *Day One: Before Hiroshima and After.* New York: Simon & Schuster, 1989.

———. *Wall: The Untold Story of Divided Berlin.* New York: Simon & Schuster, 1989.

———. *Stella.* New York: Simon & Schuster, 1992.

———. "Auf Egon Bahr warf man keine Tintenfässer" In *Das Undenkbare denken: Festschrift für Egon Bahr zum siebzigsten Geburtstag,* ed. Dieter S. Lutz, Baden-Baden: Nomos Verlagsgesellschaft, 1992.

Zachau, Reinhard K. "Hans Habe als Herausgeber der *Neuen Zeitung.*" In *Deutsch-jüdisches Exil: Das Ende der Assimilation? Identitätsproblem deutscher Juden in der Emigration,* ed. Wolfgang Benz and Marion Neiss, 151–64. Berlin: Metropol Verlag, 1994.

———. " 'Gute Europäer in Amerikas Uniform': Hans Habe und Stefan Heym in der Psychological Warfare." In *Der Zweite Weltkrieg und die Exilanten: Eine literarische Antwort,* ed. Helmut F. Pfanner, 177–86. Bonn: Bouvier Verlag, 1991.

Zink, Harold. *The United States in Germany, 1944–1955.* Princeton, N.J.: Van Nostrand, 1957.

# INDEX